PRAISE FOR ODDITIES
That is Mostly Untrue

"If I had to choose between reading Oddities and passing a tangerine-sized kidney stone through my urethra, I guess I'd read the book. Wait, can I change my answer?"
— *Conan O'Brien*

"I don't like the profanity. Can I fix you some soup?"
— *The Author's Grandma*

"It has pages with words on them."
— *Vanity Fair*

"You can read it on the shitter."
— *Guy at Panera Bread with a Scorpion Neck Tattoo*

"Oddities is hilarious and heartbreaking—it gave me all the feels. Um, is that good enough? Okay, Cool! You can Venmo me the cizzash."
— *Jenni, Hostess at PF Chang's*

"The divine wisdom of Oddities unblocked my sacral chakra and opened my third eye. There *may* have been some peyote involved."
— *Lady Who Sells Dream Catchers at the Renaissance Faire*

"It's heavy enough—you could easily crush a person's skull with it. Do you hear the aardvarks singing? I like trashcans."
— *Murderous Hobo Waiting for the Bus*

"Leave me alone I will dog walk you."
— *Cardi B*

Also by Rodger Cambria

Flan With the Wind: A Guide to Mexican Custard

Everybody Sharts

Silent Punning: A Brief History of Mime

Ferretworld

*Lick it Up: The Collected Poetry of
Gene Simmons and KISS*

1001 Uses For Twine

*Don't Be a Dick & Other Life Lessons
to Teach Your Kids*

*Judith Light is the Damn Boss:
An Unauthorized Biography*

oddities.

Rodger Cambria

MONKEYBOY

*Melbourne * Redondo Beach * San Francisco*

PUBLISHED BY MONKEYBOY PRESS
November 1, 2019

Some of the stories that follow began their lives else-
where in different forms: "The Swagman Cometh,"
"A Little Bit Country," "After the Glitter Fades," and
"Smoke Gets in Your Eyes," *Spin* magazine; "The
Highwayman" and "The Girl From the North Coun-
try," *Harp* magazine; "You Can Still Rock in Amer-
ica" and "All the Young Dudes," *Blurt* magazine;
"With a Song in Their Hearts," *Penthouse* magazine.

Cover Design by Chris Tokunaga

M O N K E Y B O Y
*Melbourne * Redondo Beach * San Francisco*

For all the misfit toys

Contents

A Note From the Author

Hello, friend.

This book's journey, from its gestation in the dark recesses of my brain to its final resting place on your coffee table, has been long and unorthodox. It was written in smoky tour bus lounges, backstage dressing rooms, airports, dive bars, casinos, county fairs, truck stops, and hotel rooms from Poughkeepsie to Prague because I've spent the last fifteen years living a strange double-life as both a writer and a rock and roll roadie. One day I'd be at home working on a story about over-the-top marriage proposals for a glossy women's magazine, and the next day I'd be on tour with Ted Nugent. And I don't know what's weirder: getting paid to write about archaic matrimony rituals for an audience largely comprised of pre-menopausal women, or being on tour with a 67-year-old man in a snakeskin vest who's singing "Wang Dang Sweet Poontang" at a rib fest in Toledo.

Though Oddities was conceived under challenging circumstances, my research and reporting methods were sound. The journalism in this book is, to the best of my abilities, completely accurate. The bits about my personal life, however, are based entirely on my memories, and memories often betray us. Though some of the names in these pages have been changed for privacy reasons and certain timelines have been manipulated or condensed, the spirit and integrity of these stories remains intact. So put on your coziest drawstring pants, settle into a comfy chair, and enjoy the book.

Introduction

When I was growing up, my mom was a free-spirited hippie-cum-New Age massage therapist with an alternative lifestyle and an eclectic social circle. She had friends who were gay and who were straight, who were broke and who were millionaires, who were white and who were brown, who were artists and who were investment bankers. She had friends who were Christians, Jews, and Hindus, and she had druid friends who worshipped pagan gods while dancing nude by the light of the moon.

In 1987, my mom became friends with a woman named DJ who operated a brothel out of her lavish home near San Francisco. DJ lived in the house with her lawyer boyfriend, their gay male roommate, and three gorgeous young women who worked for her as escorts. But this was no seedy roadside rub 'n' tug operation selling $20 hand jobs to long-haul truck drivers: a date with one of DJ's girls cost upwards of $1000 and took place on the premises of her sprawling hilltop estate, a veritable pleasure palace complete with theme rooms, sexy costumes, and a professional videographer for those who wanted to document their naughty escapades. And not just anyone could play with DJ's girls: they serviced an exclusive, referral-only client list that included prominent community leaders, wealthy businessmen, and at least one local sheriff. It was like that movie *The Best Little Whorehouse in Texas*, but with less Dom DeLuise and more Quaaludes. *"Y'all come back now, y'hear?"* And like the close-knit relationships between brothel proprietor Dolly Parton and her employees in that 1982 film, DJ and her staff became a kind of surrogate family: they lived together, they worked together, they cooked meals together, and they vacationed together. And yes, they even spent their holidays together, something I got to experience in 1988 when I came home from college over winter break.

I hadn't met DJ, but I'd heard stories from my mom about the sexy business she ran from her home and the legendary erotic parties she would host. So when DJ invited us over for Christmas Eve, I didn't know what to expect. Would there be flagrant nudity? Dry-humping under the mistletoe? Would the evening dovetail into a holiday-themed cocaine orgy? As a shy, sexually insecure college sophomore with body image issues, this specter of public hedonism was terrifying. And if those scenarios weren't awkward enough, let's not forget THAT I WOULD BE THERE WITH MY MOM.

As we pulled up to DJ's house, we were greeted by a dazzling display of twinkling holiday lights, an inflatable snowman in the yard, and a festive, handmade wreath on the door. Inside, there was a roaring fire in the fireplace, eggnog with paprika sprinkles, and Doris Day crooning "Winter Wonderland" on the stereo. In the living room stood a large Christmas tree, decorated not with toys or traditional ornaments, but with small plastic penises and hand-rolled marijuana joints hanging from tiny hooks. Throughout the evening, guests would pluck Christmas joints from the tree and light them up. Later, when we gathered around the long cedar table for a fine meal of glazed ham, everyone clasped hands and said grace before eating. It was, by all accounts, a warm and loving holiday scene, like one of those Norman Rockwell illustrations on the cover of the *Saturday Evening Post*. Except, you know, with prostitutes and a Christmas tree covered in tiny cocks and Schedule 1 narcotics.

The truth is, most of the people at that table didn't have anywhere else to go for the holidays. DJ's parents hadn't spoken to her since her brief foray into the adult film business some years earlier, and David, her gay friend and housemate, along with two of the young women who worked for her as escorts, had become estranged from their own biological families. Had it not been for DJ opening her home to them, they'd be eating alone on Christmas Eve. And that's just sad.

~

Groucho Marx famously said, "I would never want to belong to a club that would have someone like me as a member." While this quip from the cigar-chomping vaudevillian may have been sincere, the opposite is true for most people. In fact, many of us spend our lives searching for like-minded individuals who share our interests and our beliefs. It's why we join bowling leagues and book clubs and knitting circles; it's why we go on theme cruises and road trips to fan conventions. For most of us, it's not enough to simply walk through this world alone like Caine in *Kung Fu*. We want people to know us. To know that we're here. To know that we exist. And here's something my mom always told me: belonging to a community and having the ability to connect with other human beings in a deep and profound way are the key ingredients for a happy life. I'd add comfortable shoes and a regular bowel movement to the recipe, but that's just me.

This collection of stories is about the search for community and acceptance in a world that is increasingly isolating. It's about those who exist on the fringes of society, the shadow people, the marginalized and the misunderstood. It's about old rock groupies and drunk rednecks, sword swallowers and sideshow carnies. It's about space Nazis and porn star karaoke singers, Celine Dion roadies and time traveling monks. It's about a group of lovely and generous prostitutes sharing a Christmas ham with a 20-year-old college kid and his mom. But mostly, it's about a collective desire to belong, to be loved, and maybe—just maybe—to be part of something that's bigger than ourselves. Because we've all been lonely weirdos at some point in our lives. And no one wants to eat ham alone.

"There's a quality of legend about freaks. Like a person in a fairy tale who stops you and demands that you answer a riddle. Most people go through life dreading they'll have a traumatic experience. Freaks were born with their trauma. They've already passed their test in life. They're aristocrats."

—**Diane Arbus**

The Swagman Cometh

It's a snowy December morning at the Palace Theater in Albany, New York and our entire road crew is buzzing. "Lib broke her ankle last night," our production manager stammers. "She can't do the show and the rest of the tour might be cancelled." The tour in question is *Peppa Pig's Big Splash*, a musical production for kids based on the popular Nickelodeon cartoon series, and Lib is the perky, twenty-something actor who plays the titular character in the stage show. But Lib doesn't wear a pig costume when she performs as Peppa—rather, she voices and operates an enormous Peppa Pig puppet. In fact, every actor in *Peppa Pig's Big Splash* operates one of these sculpted foam creatures, *because it's a fucking puppet show.*

At noon, we receive word that tonight's show will go on and the remainder of the tour will continue as scheduled. Like most theater productions, there is an understudy on *Peppa Pig* who is ready to step into the lead role. She's a serious actor who is excited to get her shot in the spotlight, almost too excited, at times recalling the conniving Ann Baxter in *All About Eve*. Except with less Bette Davis and more singing hogs.

As a longtime roadie in the live entertainment business, I thought I'd done it all: I've toured with hundreds of chart-topping pop, metal, country, and hip-hop artists. I've toured with Hollywood actors who fancy themselves musicians, like Billy Bob Thornton and Jason Schwartzman of *Rushmore*. I've worked with comedians like Dave Chappelle and Jeff Foxworthy. I've worked with the Harlem Globetrotters, professional surfers, monster trucks, and WWE Wrestling. I've worked with Meat Loaf and Ke$ha, for fuck's sake. But in all my years of touring, I've never done anything like *Peppa Pig's Big Splash*. And therein lies my existential dilemma: I am 47-years-old, and I am a puppet roadie.

There are moments on this tour, usually late at night, when I'll find myself alone on a darkened stage with Peppa and all the other creepy dead-eyed puppets laying in crumpled piles, waiting to be packed away in their road cases. And it almost feels as though they're watching me. Judging me. Because if there's anything that will make a grown man pause and take stock of his life, it's the cold sting of lifeless puppet eyes burrowing into his soul. After all, I grew up wanting to be a writer, not a roadie on some snot-nosed kiddie tour with a dancing potato and a goddamn cartoon pig. So here, deep in the bowels of a rundown theater in a dying rustbelt town fifty miles from nowhere, I find myself asking the big questions:

How did I end up here? And where the fuck am I going?

When I was a kid, my mom and I were globetrotting vagabonds, always on the go, never staying in one place too long. Though we existed in a perpetual state of change, the one constant in our lives was music. No matter where we went, no matter how far away or exotic the land, music connected us, grounded us, and made every new place feel like home. In Madrid, we listened to my mom's Linda Ronstadt and Chuck Mangione records. In Lisbon, it was Christopher Cross and Air Supply. And in Bakersfield, we played the Doobie Brothers' *Minute by Minute* until the grooves wore out and the neighbors banged on the wall. Every memory from my childhood is like a mini movie with its own soundtrack of smooth seventies jams. If I close my eyes, I can still see my mom twirling in the living room to Fleetwood Mac's *Mirage* or Steely Dan's *Gaucho* with a joint in one hand and a glass of cheap merlot in the other. "Music is *magic*," she always said. "It can transport you—it can take you anywhere."

In first grade, our teacher asked us what we wanted to be when we grew up and had us share our answers with the class. Darrell Spinosa, a gangly kid known for his ability to flatulate "Do-Re-Mi" from *The Sound of Music*, said he wanted to be an astronaut. I remember thinking, "Darrell farts show tunes. Like NASA is gonna send *him* into space." Most of my classmates had more earthbound career aspirations, and there were a predictable number of baseball players, ballerinas, and veterinarians in our midst. But I was an odd kid and had a different vision of my future. So when it was my turn in front of the class, I said, "I want to be a clown." I didn't mean a *clown*-clown, like in the circus. I meant someone who makes people laugh. Specifically, I wanted to write stories that would make people laugh. But like many creative professions, there was no clearly defined path showing me how to get there. Or at least, none that I had the wherewithal or maturity to identify. So I took the steps that I thought made sense: I became editor of my high school newspaper and wrote a weekly column, I got a part-time job in college reviewing movies for the paper at a local military base, and I graduated with degrees in English Literature and Film Studies, which, in retrospect, have the same amount of real-world practicality as a double major in origami and interpretive dance. In 1994, I moved to Los Angeles with one terrible screenplay I'd written and six hundred dollars to my name.

Hollywood, here I come!

When I first arrived in Southern California, I shared a roach-infested apartment in the Valley with two aspiring actors. Though we were all just starting out, my room-mates quickly landed bit parts on TV shows like *Chicago Hope* and *Law & Order*, roles that they attacked with the focus and intensity of a young Sir John Gielgud at the Royal Shakespeare Company, delivering memorable per-formances as "Cop #2," "Grumpy Waitress," and "Corpse in River." For the better part of that first year, my room-mate Bryan made a good living playing either serial killers or victims of serial killers, or as he'd describe these roles in a fake British accent, "the wielder of the axe or the tree that falls."

I did not have such luck.

Almost immediately, I found myself asking the ques-tion that all aspiring writers and artists ask themselves at some point: How am I going to pay my goddamn rent? There are two kinds of broke when you're young and short on money: there's *Pabst broke*, which is when you buy a six-pack of shitty beer at the minimart and drink it *before* you go out to the bar so you can get buzzed on the cheap.

Then there's *ass-broke*, which is when you get in line with all the homeless junkies at the blood bank in Van Nuys to sell your plasma.

I was both.

Desperate for work—and tired of catching beard lice from the hobos at the blood clinic—I registered with a West Hollywood temp agency that placed its clients in jobs within the entertainment industry, or at least on its outer fringes. On your first day, they made you take a typing test, and all your future work assignments would be based on this score. A good result, say 85 words per minute, would land you cushy, high-profile assignments like answering phones at the William Morris Agency or being a 2nd assistant to a big-time producer at Paramount. But on *my* test, I only typed a paltry twelve words a minute. The test administrator, a gum-chomping woman with peach-colored hair and penciled in eyebrows who had been giving these exams for more than forty years, said she'd never seen a score this low from someone who wasn't severely retarded, legally blind, or suffering from massive head trauma.

"I once saw a quadriplegic type eighteen words a minute using a mouth stick," she said, coughing a bit of phlegm into a napkin. "But your score is worse. It defies explanation."

As a result, I got all the meathead assignments: jobs that either required physical labor, like moving a celebrity's furniture onto the lawn so the carpet in the house could be cleaned, or "runner" jobs, where I'd spend all day driving to studios, agencies, and production companies around town, picking up and dropping off scripts, contracts, and other showbizzy items. I found it baffling that the agency deemed me unqualified to answer a telephone in a producer's office because of a low typing score, but had no qualms about putting me behind the wheel of a three-ton diesel-powered weapon made of chrome and steel and turning me loose on the streets of Hollywood.

One of my early assignments sent me to the office of fitness guru and motivational speaker Susan Powter, whose platinum flattop hairstyle and "Stop the insanity!" catchphrase propelled her to stardom in the nineties. She was moving her office to a new location across town, and I, along with several other terrible typists from the agency, were hired to load her furniture onto a truck. During Powter's popular live show, she would bring several large blocks of animal fat shrink-wrapped in clear plastic onto the stage to illustrate how much extra weight an obese person carries around. "This is what fifty pounds of fat looks like," she'd tell the horrified audience. These props were stored in her office when she wasn't performing, and I was tasked with carrying them, one by one, down six flights of stairs to the moving truck below. On my third trip down, I accidentally bumped one of the fat blocks into the corner of a coffee table, puncturing its outer plastic wrap, and causing white lipidinous goo to ooze all over my hands and shirt. When I pushed my floppy bangs out of my eyes so I wouldn't trip and fall down the stairs, the goo got in my hair. When I wiped the perspiration from my cheek, the goo got on my face. *On my face.*

As I clutched that leaking lard block to my chest, sweaty, out of breath, and smeared in gelatinous animal fat, I thought to myself, "It can't get any worse than this."

It got worse than that.

A few weeks later, the agency got me a full-time job as

a runner for a celebrity business management company in Encino. Every day, I would drive out to the homes of its high-profile clients like Rod Stewart, Stevie Nicks, Kenny G, or Pauly Shore and bring them documents to be signed or checks to be endorsed. During this period, I worked incredibly long hours, I wasn't writing at all, and I felt like a complete failure. Also, my ankles began to swell because I was subsisting entirely on Top Ramen and Sunny Delight.

The management company was buzzing because it had just signed second-year NBA star Shaquille O'Neal, arguably their most important client in terms of his basketball salary and mammoth endorsement deals with Reebok, Pepsi, and Taco Bell. One afternoon, the president of the company, Lester Knispel, told me that Shaq had requested $5000 in cash and wanted it delivered to the set of *Kazaam*, the movie he was currently filming in which he portrayed "a rappin' genie with an attitude" who gets conjured from a magic boom box. Knispel took the money from a large vault, put it in a sealed envelope, and handed it to me.

"Hurry," he said. "Shaq is waiting."

I drove across town to the studio lot and was escorted onto the movie set.

"Mr. O'Neal is in his dressing room," the security guard said, pointing to a small room at the end of a long hallway behind the sound stage. I knocked on the door, and a booming baritone voice told me to come in. To my surprise, Shaq was wearing his full genie costume, complete with oversized turban, sparkly gold vest, puffy harem pants, and pointy shoes. It's impossible to fully grasp the physical enormity of Shaquille O'Neal until you've seen him up close. He's a massive, imposing presence, and if this were a fairy tale you'd half expect him to live in a magical land at the top of a beanstalk.

"I have your money, Mr. O'Neal," I said extending the envelope.

Shaq snatched it from my hand, tore it open, and waved the stack of neatly rubber-banded hundred dollar bills in my face.

"Five grand, *right*? It's all here, *right*?" he said with a scowl.

"I didn't count it myself," I said. "But I assume it's all there."

"It *better* all be here," he said menacingly.

"Well if you're concerned, maybe *you* should count it," I replied. "Just to be safe."

This angered Shaq.

"I don't wanna count it," he growled. "But if it *is* short, I'll tell Lester to fire you, and he will. Now get the hell out of here."

And with that, he dismissed me with a wave of his enormous palm frond hand. Maybe Shaq was just having a bad day. Maybe he hated his job—wearing that ridiculous costume in a truly awful movie—as much as I hated mine. But then again, he got paid seven *million* dollars to appear in *Kazaam*, whereas I got paid seven *regular* dollars an hour to be an errand boy for cranky celebrities.

As I left that evil giant's dressing room, I knew I'd hit a low point in my young professional life. Like, subterranean low. Because feeling morally defeated and creatively unfulfilled is one thing. But being berated by a seven-foot tall man in a sequined genie outfit is something else entirely.

A few months after the Shaq incident, I was at home

between temp assignments and down to my last few dollars when the phone rang.

"It's for you," my roommate yelled.

"Who is it?" I asked.

"It's the Doobie Brothers."

Of course, it wasn't *actually* the Doobie Brothers on the phone, because that would be weird. It was their merchandise company, and they were offering me a job on the band's upcoming tour. It paid a decent weekly salary plus $30 per diem. If you aren't up on your dead languages, per diem is Latin for "lap dance" since the money usually ended up under the garter of a Puerto Rican stripper named Chardonnay. The band would also cover all my transportation and lodging expenses, provide catered meals on show days, and let me ride on the tour bus with the crew.

And just like that, I became a rock and roll roadie.

My transition to their world, however, was not exactly seamless, because I didn't fit the typical roadie profile. I certainly didn't look like a roadie. In those days, most crew guys had shaggy beards, mustaches, and long hair, while I was clean-cut and sported a close-cropped style that owed more to *Gomer Pyle, U.S.M.C.* than the majestic flowing locks of dark metal overlord Ronnie James Dios. Also, many crew guys were covered in elaborate tattoos that commemorated loved ones or honored special events in their lives. I met this one old roadie named Detox whose tattoo of a one-legged prostitute hopping down a neon-lit street was a reminder of a drunken night in Bangkok. Though I don't have any permanent body ink myself, I *did* get a temporary tattoo of Garfield the cat eating a lasagna when I was thirteen.

Our music preferences were also wildly different. Most roadies grew up listening to cool heavy metal bands, and if you ask any crew guy about the first record he ever bought, he'll invariably say it was Iron Maiden's *Number of the Beast, Led Zeppelin IV,* or Judas Priest's *Hell Bent for Leather.* In stark contrast, the first three records I purchased were Olivia Newton-John's *Physical,* The Go-Gos' *Beauty and the Beat,* and the *Flashdance* movie soundtrack. To say that I did not rock would be a colossal understatement.

Also, most roadies, while highly intelligent and dedicated to their craft, did not go to college in those days. And the ones who did certainly didn't study *Feminist Theory & Criticism of Contemporary Cinema* or *Queer Imagery in 19th Century Literature.* But I *rocked* that shit, Camille Paglia-style. I eventually found my footing with these scruffy headbanging wanderers, parlaying my two-month tour with the Doobies into fourteen years with more than a hundred different artists, from Bruce Springsteen, Jay Z, Aerosmith, and KISS, to Celine Dion, Elvis Costello, Carrie Underwood, and GWAR.

When people learn that I've worked as a rock and roll roadie, they usually wrinkle up their noses as though they've just smelled something foul and give me a look that says, "Oh, you're one of *them?*" That's because most people think rock roadies are the inbred brother-cousins of circus carnies, another misunderstood profession with a dubious reputation. In fact, the prevailing opinion of roadies is that we're all drug addicts, sociopaths, and sexual deviants who will attempt to violate your wife and daughter at a Josh Groban concert.

This is mostly untrue.

The circus analogy, however, is not without merit: carnies and roadies both live nomadic existences, traveling from town to town, setting up the show each morning and tearing it down each night. We sleep odd hours, eat unhealthy foods, and often work with clowns. *Hello, Justin Bieber!* And both professions attract individuals who, for a variety of reasons, want to live beyond the constraints of traditional society. To most people, the unconventional lifestyle of the rock roadie is an exotic curiosity at best, and the principle domain of dirtbags, degenerates, and felons at worst. But when you strip away all the sensational aspects of being a roadie—the constant travel, the loose women, and the abundance of recreational substances—it's really just a job like any other.

Except when it's not.

The first day of a rock tour is a lot like the first day of school. The crew, generally ten to twelve guys, gathers on the bus, swapping handshakes, quietly scrutinizing each other, and trying to discern three things: who is the lazy guy, who is the asshole (anyone who refers to himself as a "technician" is immediately suspect), and who can score the drugs. Many of the guys will know each other from previous gigs *("Hey man, didn't you run monitors on Depeche Mode?")*, but for me, each new tour is usually a gathering of strangers. To try and fit in with the group, I use the same tactics I used as a child whenever we moved to a new town: I adopted their fashion style—typically a black Slayer T-shirt paired with ratty, knee-length cargo shorts—and I tried to impress them with my toys. As I've gotten older, my Hungry Hungry Hippos, Slip 'N Slide, and Rock 'Em Sock 'Em Robots have given way to a dizzying collection of DVDs, X-Box games, and Ukrainian cheerleader porn.

While certain rules apply to every tour, like always lock the bus and *never* shit in its toilet, each specific crew has its own way of doing things. When I arrived at the first show on the Elvis Costello tour, the production manager, a pale, cocaine-inhaling Irishman named Milo, handed me an all-access laminate, a copy of the tour itinerary, and a key to the bus. He introduced me to the crew—Opie, Eightball, Chunk, Taliban Dan, and the others—then rattled off the crew rules in a monotonous drone, much like a flight attendant giving an in-flight safety demonstration. "No smoking and no drugs in the front lounge of the bus," he said in his thick brogue accent. "However, you may smoke, snort, or shoot anything in the back lounge." He cleared his throat and continued. "And don't give your laminate to any sluts. If you need bitch passes, come find me in the production office."

Many rock roadies have colorful nicknames like Spider, Chaka, Boxcar, or Wingnut—and there's a story behind each one. But according to the roadie code, you can't make up your own nickname; someone has to give it to you. This tradition of assigning nicknames to your peers is not exclusive to the culture of rock roadies: it's common among firefighters, military personnel, circus carnies, wildcat oil drillers, and fraternity brothers. Though these may seem like wildly disparate groups, they all have something in common: they not only work together, but they also live together in cramped quarters, often under difficult or stressful conditions. Calling each other by nicknames is a way to denote intimacy—to say, "Yes, you are part of my tribe."

There is a definite and immutable hierarchy among road crews which goes like this: production manager, front-of-house mixer, monitor tech, instrument techs, lighting director, rigger, bus and truck drivers, and at the very bottom, me. I was the tour merchandiser, responsible for the sale of band T-shirts, ball caps, and other overpriced souvenirs. On a typical day, while the other roadies were pushing cases, flying speakers, laying cable, and rigging lights—all potentially dangerous activities—I was busy folding T-shirts and arranging the sizes into neat little piles. It's like working at the Gap, with the added incentive of illegal narcotics and genital herpes.

Although rock merchandising does not involve the physical risks associated with other crew jobs, it is not without challenges. One of the more frustrating aspects is navigating the bureaucratic quagmire of International Customs—specifically, bringing merchandise from the United States into Canada to sell at Canadian concert dates. In 1998, I landed a job on the Celine Dion tour at the peak of her *Titanic* success. One of our merchandise items was a small stuffed frog wearing a tiny Celine T-shirt, because Celine Dion loves frogs. People send her toy frogs from all over the world, and before each concert she has them playfully arranged in her dressing room. Celine's fans loved the plush amphibians too, and they were a huge seller. As a result, I found myself declaring a payload of 9,000 toy frogs to a humorless Canadian customs official who informed me that the frogs themselves could enter Canada, but the tiny t-shirts they were wearing could not—something about trade sanctions with the country that manufactured them. So there, at the Canadian border, in the middle of the night, during a blinding snowstorm, I carefully undressed 9,000 frogs.

Upon my arrival at the arena in Ottawa, one of Celine's

assistants strode up to me, a deadly serious look on her face. She was holding a small shirtless frog and waving it for effect.

"These frogs are naked!" she said tersely. "What happened to their shirts?"

I told her about the customs incident.

She studied the toy for a moment, examining it from all angles, then looked me in the eye: "Maybe you can find them some tiny pants. Because we can't sell naked frogs. *Celine won't have it.*" Trying to find a decent margarita in Ottawa is difficult. Trying to find 9,000 pairs of tiny frog pants on a snowy Sunday evening is enough to burst a vein in your head.

Other times, the challenges of being a rock merchandiser come from a band's improbable migration to the moral high ground. When I was on the road with the Doobie Brothers, I found a stash of t-shirts from a prior tour mixed in with the current product line and decided to sell them at our shows. These shirts featured an old-timey illustration of dogs playing poker in a saloon while toking on burrito-sized Cheech & Chong joints.

When the wife of one of the founding band members saw the old shirts at the next show, she demanded that we stop selling them.

"The band doesn't want to sell any products with images or references to marijuana smoking," she said.

I reminded her that the band had approved the artwork, and that these shirts were a big seller several years earlier.

"Well the guys don't smoke weed any more," she told me. "And they no longer want to endorse that behavior."

"But the name of the band is the *Doobie* Brothers, right?"

I replied. "Simply having their name on a marquee is a tacit acknowledgement of their participation in the drug culture."

But arguing with the wife of a band member is always a losing proposition. See *Ono, Yoko*.

Most bands, however, will sell anything with their name on it as long as they get paid. KISS, for example, has licensed its name to more than 3000 products, including Kondoms, Koffins, and Koffee. "I don't care if you sell *KISS* crack," frontman Gene Simmons once told his Vice President of Licensing, "as long as you spell *crack* with a K."

Life as a roadie moves at a grueling pace. Most bands play four or five shows a week while on tour, and when a road crew does get a day off, it's rarely in a desirable city like New York or Miami. Instead, a break usually comes in a place like Rapid City, South Dakota, or Hattiesburg, Mississippi. And many road crews have their own day-off rituals. The Cowboy Junkies crew, for example, liked to do drugs and visit the local zoo. We watched the penguins on acid in San Francisco, the monkeys on Valium in the Bronx, and the lemurs in Denver after smoking something called a "Boulder Salad" —a colorful blend of Northern California sensimilla and Indian hashish. They Might Be Giants' crew liked to get stoned and race go-carts at Malibu Grand Prix parks all across the country. This was fun until, after smoking some wicked Thai stick in Oklahoma, I drove my car off the racetrack, across a miniature golf course, and nearly killed a guy in a Teletubby costume at a children's birthday party.

A typical rock tour runs anywhere from three to twelve weeks. The biggest bands play stadiums and arenas, mid-level artists hit the amphitheaters or "sheds," while smaller groups play theaters and clubs. And then there's the dreaded fairground circuit. As a general rule, if the audience is standing on horse hay, if the smell of pig shit is heavy in the air, and if corn dogs are sold from a trailer shaped like a sausage, the band's best days are probably behind them.

Many roadies are on tour up to 300 days a year, leap-frogging from the end of one tour to the beginning of another. At times, the transition from one band to the next can be jarring, like going from Lionel Richie to Megadeth, or Barry Manilow to Wu Tang Clan. Years ago, I left the easy-listening Dan Fogelberg tour and went directly to the grotesque circus of GWAR, which is the kind of head-trip that can only be duplicated by mainlining a cocktail of Old Milwaukee and Crystal Meth directly into your cerebellum. Please don't try this at home because it will melt your brain. Literally.

Fogelberg's crew had a no-smoking and no-drug policy on the bus, which was a refreshing change of pace from the debauchery of most tours. Instead of getting high and watching *Spongebob Squarepants*, we would watch *Antiques Roadshow* and swap amusing stories about our cats. On a particularly raucous evening, we might bust open a case of Zima and play Boggle.

The day after the Fogelberg tour ended, I was on a plane to join GWAR for a handful of shows. GWAR, for the uninitiated, is a band that dresses in enormous foam rubber monster costumes and performs theatrical decapitations, mutilations, and bloodlettings onstage while playing songs like "Slaughterama" and "Sex Cow." For me, the only way to cope with the surreal disparity of these bands was to cloud my mind with hallucinogenic drugs. Because a head full of mescaline narrows the enormous gap between Fogelberg and GWAR considerably. To the roadie, pot smoking exists in the pantheon of daily rituals, and bong hits have taken their place alongside morning coffee, checking e-mail, and flossing. Back in 1994, They Might Be Giants crewmembers were epic potheads. On one particular morning, Dingo, the Giants' grizzled drum tech, brewed a pot of coffee using stagnant bongwater just to see if it would get us high.

It didn't.

As we discovered, the toxic combination of bongwater and espresso beans rapidly induces violent diarrhea. The beverage, appropriately dubbed "crappucino," earned a place on the long list of failed roadie drug experiments, narrowly edging out the Percodan smoothie for top honors.

Whenever I talk to people about my days as a rock and roll roadie, they always want to know about groupies: *Do groupies exist? Will they really do anything to get backstage?* Groupies do exist, but sadly, most do not look like Kate Hudson in *Almost Famous*. And the ones who do don't generally go for roadies. The exception, of course, is legendary groupie Sweet Connie, a true egalitarian who is always willing to show the road crew some love. In most cases, though, a roadie is likely to be propositioned near the loading dock by a leathery woman who will trade sexual favors for a backstage pass, a seedy transaction I've dubbed *quid pro blow*. Though getting sucked off behind a garbage dumpster by a total stranger in Lycra hot pants is not without its charms, these casual liaisons rarely end well.

My first encounter with a groupie took place during my rookie year of touring in the early nineties. I met her at a show in Michigan, and while some of the logistical details have gone fuzzy with the passage of time, the following remains crystal clear: her name was Bonnie, she was in her mid-30s with badly bleached hair, and she wore skintight jeans with a leopard print crop top and white stiletto pumps. Bonnie was something of a legend in those parts, and they called her "The Battle Creek Freak." We chatted and exchanged flirty smiles during sound check, but I assumed that was the end of it. After the show, she sauntered up to me, leaned in close enough that I could smell the menthol lights on her fetid, wine-cooler breath, and whispered in my ear, "Do you want to go out to my van?"

I was in my early twenties, and though I wasn't technically a virgin—I'd had several boozy, fumbling liaisons with generous coeds back in college—the lurid fornication suggested here was clearly on a whole other level. Bonnie took my hand and led me outside to a metallic green van with a giant screaming eagle painted on its side. She swung open the door, revealing a tattered mattress in the back covered with a single dirty sheet. We climbed inside and pulled the door closed behind us. There was no pretense of romance: she immediately kissed me, then wiggled out of her top and turned around so I could unhook her bra. I quickly noticed two things: a jagged eight-inch scar behind one of her kidneys—probably the remnants of a drunken knife fight—and a large grinning tattoo of Burt Reynolds just above her right shoulder blade. But here's the ass-kicker: when she twisted her torso, the loose skin around Burt's eye folded in such a way that he appeared to be winking.

The Battle Creek Freak proceeded to violate me in ways that are still illegal in several Southeastern states. Although I eventually lost consciousness, I do recall the sting of a Malaysian flogging cane and the hum of a large vibrating egg. When I came to, in the back of a green van on a warm summer night, I was no longer a boy: I was a man. A man who was about to visit the free clinic with a scorching case of Chlamydia.

Most roadies have a love/hate relationship with the musicians who employ them—I remember the Doobie Brothers' crew half-jokingly referring to the band as "the enemy." This attitude comes from the fact that musicians, especially the younger ones, often take the production crew's hard work for granted. On a lot of tours, the pop band du jour will arrive three minutes before the show starts and immediately complain about the audio system, concerns which could have been addressed earlier if they'd bothered to show up for sound check. Then the band plays a few songs, takes all the credit for putting on a great show, and invariably leaves with the hottest women. The roadies, meanwhile, have been at the venue for 16 hours, eating greasy, tasteless catering, while risking life and limb to make the future subject of VH1's *Where Are They Now* look and sound better than anything they are actually capable of. And invariably, the roadie leaves not with a beautiful woman, but with ten other tired roadies who may or may not have had the opportunity to bathe. Most bands that have remained successful over time, however, treat their roadies with the utmost dignity and respect. They understand that the longevity of their careers is in part due to the efforts of their production crew, who make them look and sound, night after night, like they superstars they are.

Most bands.

There are, however, those artists who have the reputation of being difficult. A semi truck driver told me he quit the Prince tour because he was instructed to never make eye contact with His Purpleness. If you're Steven Tyler's monitor guy on an Aerosmith tour, you might as well start sending out resumes now because you'll likely be out of a job soon. I've heard Tyler changes monitor techs like most people change underpants. And while it may be true that "Girls Just Wanna Have Fun," Cyndi Lauper's roadies want to throw themselves off a tall building. I toured with Cyndi and she's a handful. Ask anyone.

My first brush with a difficult artist came early in my touring career. I can't share her name for legal reasons, but this scarlet-haired piano playing chanteuse had a string of hits when she broke through in the early nineties. Though I only worked on her tour for a brief time, I witnessed numerous examples of bad behavior. One memorable incident happened before a show in Cedar Rapids, Iowa.

I was in the theater lobby when I heard the screams. Instinctively, I followed the shrill bellow as it pulled me through the auditorium, across the stage, and down the rickety iron staircase to a dank subterranean catacomb of offices and dressing rooms. The screams grew louder, and as I turned the corner past catering, I saw something that was both frightening and exhilarating: a bona-fide rock star tantrum. The Artist was in the hallway outside her dressing room, and she was pelting the runner, a pimply teenager who worked for the promoter, with bruschetta and lime wedges from a small hors d'oeuvres platter. As the teen cowered, she thrust a small cube of pepper jack cheese into his face, and shook it menacingly.

"How big is this cheese?" she demanded.

"I don't know," the teen stammered. "This is my first day."

The Artist snatched a ruler from her dressing room table and proceeded to measure the cube of cheese, carefully, on all sides. "This cheese is one inch by one inch," she announced in a commanding voice. "And what does the rider say?"

The runner glanced at the contract in his trembling hand. "It's supposed to be cut into half-inch cubes."

She stood, hands on hips, wild-eyed and enraged. "How am I supposed to eat this?" she wailed. "This cheese is too big. It's ruined." She stormed into her dressing room, slamming the door behind her.

The teen looked at me, with fear in his eyes. "Do you think she'll have me fired?"

I placed my hand on his heaving shoulder. "She'll probably have you killed."

* * *

When our first grade teacher asked us what we wanted to be when we grew up, there were future baseball players and ballerinas and even an abnormally flatulent astronaut in our group—but there were no rock and roll roadies. That's because no one sets out to become a rock roadie, even roadies themselves: most crew guys are aspiring musicians trying to support themselves while they pursue their own rock and roll dreams. Likewise, when I first took the roadie job, it was a way to pay my rent while I tried to start my writing career, with the added benefits of free liquor, traveling the world on someone else's dime, and meeting pretty women, many of whom would perform shocking and shameful acts for a free Mötley Crüe t-shirt or a Kid Rock beer cozy. In other words, it was a party that came with a paycheck. Admittedly, I didn't do much writing during my first few years on the road. But after a half-decade of monster bong loads on dirty tour buses, dropping acid and going to strip clubs, and general rock and roll debauchery—including the time I shat myself on a white couch at a Hollywood party—I had something of an epiphany while working on the KISS *Psycho Circus* tour.

It was a warm October night and the band, in full character make-up, was shredding through its encores as I wandered out front to catch the end of the show. The Dodger Stadium audience was cheering and waving their cigarette lighters in the dark as drummer Peter Criss, seated on a stool under a single spotlight at the center of the stage, belted out the last few strains of the rock ballad "Beth." When the song ended, Criss rose to his feet, looked out into the vast crowd, and said with a complete lack of irony, "To all of you in the KISS Army, we salute you," as he raised his fist in the air. It was one of those great rock and roll moments, full of theater and bombast, that had so intoxicated me over the years. But on this particular balmy evening, the moment lingered a bit longer than usual. Long enough to remind me that, rock star or not, Peter Criss was really just a grown man dressed in a cat suit.

There is a long history of melodrama within the KISS

band—in 1980, Peter Criss quit or was fired, depending on whom you ask, and he didn't perform with them again until 1995. At that point, he was no longer an official member of the group but rather a hired employee of the KISS Corporation. He was just a guy, like the rest of us, trying to do the one thing that he loved. And that's when it hit me: working in the rock and roll tour business could be *my* path to becoming a writer, if I didn't blow it by getting loaded all the time and acting like a degenerate. Being a roadie gave me a flexible schedule, a livable wage, and provided a wellspring of strange and colorful experiences that fueled my creative fire. After that fateful night on the KISS tour, I shifted my focus from screenplays to magazine writing and sold my first story to a national publication. From that point forward, my writing career was off and not exactly running, but certainly walking at a brisk pace. But most importantly, I made enough money writing to pay my goddamn rent.

* * *

It's after midnight and eerily quiet in this rundown theater where, hours earlier, *Peppa Pig's Big Splash* delighted an audience of ebullient nine-year-olds with its maddeningly infectious song and dance. While the show's cast and crew are at a nearby pub celebrating the understudy's successful debut, I once again find myself alone on a darkened stage staring into the joyless dead eyes of a grotesque unblinking hog puppet, its unholy porcine gaze piercing my soul like a laser. Normally this would depress me, but tonight is different. With the last *Peppa Pig* show in sight and middle age rumbling towards me like a freight train,

I realize that the time has come for me to leave the rock and roll business behind. I've been touring for more than twenty years and it's been a hell of a ride, but I'm ready to move on and see what's next. Like my mom used to say, I'm ready to go wherever the music takes me.

When I do walk away from the roadie world, there will be plenty of things I *won't* miss about it: the lousy food, the moldy, disgusting showers in backstage dressing rooms, riding smelly tour buses to shitty county fair gigs, North Dakota, and listening to Celine Dion sing "My Heart Will Go On" EVERY FUCKING NIGHT for three months straight. But the roadie lifestyle is exhilarating in its own gloriously weird way. And the thrill of being in a new city every day, the camaraderie of the crew, and if you're on tour with a good band, hearing amazing live music every night, is something that gets under your skin and stays there forever, like genital herpes or "the Gimp" scene in *Pulp Fiction*. Over the years, certain moments have left me truly awed: Stevie Nicks joining Tom Petty & the Heartbreakers on stage for an inspired "Stop Dragging My Heart Around" at the Greek Theater in Berkeley, James Taylor performing "Fire and Rain" during a violent thunderstorm at Red Rocks Amphitheater in Colorado, Elvis Costello delivering a blistering rendition of "What's So Funny About Peace, Love, and Understanding" at the Ryman Auditorium in Nashville, and Bruce Springsteen doing an impassioned, balls-out "Born to Run" for 80,000 fans at Giant's Stadium in New Jersey, to name just a few. And there are some moments that can only be described, to borrow a line from ELO, as *strange magic*. Like when a paunchy, middle-aged percussionist named Peter Criss, wearing ill-fitting Spandex pants and ridiculous platform moon boots, whose singing voice is barely a rasp after decades of hard living and whose drum playing, even on his best day which was probably in 1974, is merely adequate, whose jowls are sagging and whose wrinkled face is painted up like a deranged feline clown, reaches deep into his bourbon-pickled soul and brings forth a miracle as he improbably whips a crowd of 50,000 into a joyous, frenzied mass using only his waning charisma and sheer force of will. For me, it's these sublimely surreal moments that can make being a rock roadie seem like it's the only job on earth worth having. I don't know what the future holds, but if REO Speedwagon should call my name five years down the line, I can't promise that I won't come running.

With a Song in Their Hearts

In 1983 when I was a chubby, awkward high school fresh-man, I started calling a local telephone party line known as *Dial-A-Spazz*, a free service where random teenagers could talk to each other on the phone in an anonymous group setting. Though I was an unpopular kid who strug-gled with low self-esteem, the anonymity of *Dial-A-Spazz* allowed me to assume an entirely different persona. When I called the line, I became "Jack," a wily, smooth-talking jokester who existed on the smart-ass spectrum some-where between *Meatballs*-era Bill Murray and Han Solo. As Jack, I was brash, funny, outgoing, and confident. And the girls on the line liked me. Or at least, they liked that version of me.

Ten years later when I was in college, I discovered karaoke. Though it was a different medium than *Dial-A-Spazz*, it had a similar transformative effect on me: when I stepped onto a karaoke stage, I became a different person. And usually, that person was Neil Diamond. I'm not a great singer, or even a good singer, but after six gin and tonics I could belt the hell out of "Cracklin' Rosie." And when I strutted across the stage, people liked me. Or at least they liked that liquored-up, hip-swaying version of me. And so began my two-decade preoccupation with karaoke, culminating in a strange writing assignment that would take me across the Atlantic Ocean to Finland.

I'm a nervous flier, especially on long flights over vast bodies of water, so I usually ply myself with booze and anxiety pills at the first hint of turbulence—and we just hit some *serious* white-knuckle chop over Reykjavik that gave me palpitations. So when I arrive in Helsinki on this cool September morning, I'm already irritable, jet-lagged, and halfway twisted on Lorazepam and Tanqueray. I catch a taxi to the harbor and board the M/S *Galaxy*, a luxury liner offering daily cruises across the Baltic Sea to Estonia.

After dropping my bags in the windowless cabin that will be my home for the next three days, I make my way downstairs to the Starlight Show Lounge. At this point, the Lorazepam has fully kicked in, adding a foggy, surreal effect to the proceedings. As if on cue, I'm immediately approached by a large Irish man dressed in a green velvet leprechaun suit. We begin chatting, and when he learns that I'm on assignment for a well-known erotic men's magazine, he insists on buying me a drink. This is a scene that will repeat itself numerous times over the next three days, though not all my benefactors will be dressed as magical elves. The bartender pours us shots of Salmiakki Koskenkorva, a foul Finnish liqueur that tastes like burnt hair and copy machine toner. The enormous leprechaun raises his glass and toasts, "E'res to ya, mate!"

At the front of the large theater, the stage goes dark except for a lone spotlight, and a hush comes over the crowd. It's just before midnight when a fleshy, egg-shaped man with a towering pompadour and white satin jumpsuit takes the stage and launches into the Elvis Presley classic "Burning Love." His name is Jouni Viirtala, but I will come to know him as the Elvis of Finland. His wide, spongy hips undulate to the rockabilly beat, his voice a soaring vibrato of passion and repressed sexual angst:

Lord Almighty, I feel my temperature rising
Higher higher, it's burning through to my soul
Girl, you gonna set me on fire
My brain is flaming, I don't know which way to go.

While this may sound like a Vegas-themed peyote trip, what I'm actually witnessing is a standout performance from the 2006 Karaoke World Championships, or KWC. Over the next two days, 44 participants from 20 countries will vie for the hefty prize package and the coveted championship title. Now in its fourth year, the KWC has become the world's premier venue for competitive karaoke. Admittedly, there seems to be a world championship for every bizarre pastime these days, from rock-paper-scissors and air guitar to pillow fighting and kickball. These events, however, are mostly pop-culture shtick designed to boost tourism and are not taken seriously by the media or the participants. But competitive karaoke is a different beast. For one thing, it requires actual talent (sorry, air guitar shredders). It can also be a springboard to a legitimate recording career. Mary J. Blige, then an unknown singer from Yonkers, landed her first record deal when executives heard her karaoke cover of Anita Baker's "Caught Up in the Rapture of You." Taylor Swift peddled tapes of her amateur karaoke performances to record labels in Nashville long before she was a platinum-selling artist and six-time Grammy winner. And Tommy DeCarlo, a credit manager at Home Depot in Charlotte, North Carolina, became the new lead singer of the iconic rock band Boston when founder Tom Scholtz saw videos of his karaoke performances on MySpace. "This is the first generation of pop stars to grow up with karaoke," says Kurt Slep, CEO of Sound Choice, a leader in the karaoke industry since 1985. "In fact, most successful performers today have used karaoke to hone their craft at some point in the early stages of their careers. It's helped create a whole generation of professional singers."

But most significantly, karaoke has become a global industry generating an estimated ten billion dollars in annual revenue. No longer relegated to seedy hotel lounges, bowling alley bars, or happy hours at T.G.I. Friday's, karaoke has emerged as a bona fide cultural phenomenon that crosses all social, political, religious, and ethnic lines. In Japan, 280,000 bars are outfitted with karaoke systems and 64 million people, nearly half the population, performs karaoke on a regular basis. There are thousands of karaoke bars in the US, and hundreds of thousands more across the world. And it doesn't stop there: the Karaoke Channel is delivering monster ratings on digital cable and satellite TV, and sing-along tracks are available for your cell phone, computer, DVD player, and iPod. Next year, CBS will launch a karaoke-themed reality show, and a number of British churches have installed the Hymnal Plus, a karaoke system that allows parishioners to sing along with their favorite gospel tunes, including a disco version of "Amazing Grace." There are karaoke taxicabs in Bangkok, naked karaoke parties in Tampa, and "pornaoke" events across the UK, where participants provide the dialogue and sound effects to vintage porno movie clips. Even our educational and medical communities are utilizing karaoke. The KinderCare chain uses karaoke machines in its classrooms as learning tools for children, and hospitals use karaoke-based music therapy programs to help Alzheimer patients revive lost memories and to help stroke victims who may have lost their ability to speak. Like it or not, karaoke has ensconced itself in all facets of our culture, burrowing its way into our collective psyches. And it's not going away any time soon.

The M/S *Galaxy*, home of the 2006 Karaoke World Championships, is a full-service cruise ship making daily runs from Helsinki to the medieval walled city of Tallinn in Estonia. For this particular voyage, karaoke systems have been installed in every nightclub, lounge and casino, allowing passengers to sing almost anywhere on the boat. There are even karaoke machines on the poolside deck, which seems like a novel idea until I witness an excessively hairy, psoriatic man in a Speedo performing "Little Red Corvette" from the confines of his chaise lounge. Additionally, the KWC performances are broadcast on TV monitors in all the restaurants and gift shops, and the audio from the event is piped into the bathrooms, elevators, and even into the passenger cabins. As one elderly woman lamented, "I am on the boat for vacation. But the karaoke is everywhere. You cannot escape it."

It's around 2 AM on this first night of the competition and the Starlight Lounge is jumping. Japan's Takahiro Masuda just ripped through a pitch-perfect version of Led Zeppelin's "Rock and Roll," and now Ari Koivunen, a 19-year-old heavy metal wunderkind from Finland, is powering his way through the Scorpions "Still Loving You."

Borrowing from the successful *American Idol* format, the contest features a series of performance and elimination rounds with the top five men and women advancing to the finals. The competitors choose their own songs to perform and are judged on voice quality, stage presence, and entertainment value by a multinational jury panel. At the end of the second day, an overall male and female winner will be announced during a lavish awards ceremony.

These competitors, however, are not the casual karaoke singers you might find in the bar at a local Applebee's, getting drunk with their buddies and warbling their way through Garth Brook's "Friends in Low Places" once or twice a year. These are the people who perform karaoke several nights a week, the ones who take voice lessons, who stitch their own glittery costumes and work out dance routines in their basements. They take karaoke seriously, which is obvious in their pre-performance rituals. Helena Virt of Estonia sips hot tea before she takes the stage to soothe her throat, and Nicole Steinsdörfer of Germany meditates while listening to her song selection on headphones. To them, karaoke is not a hobby: it's a lifestyle and a potential career path. Though they are extremely talented individuals and gracious competitors, I have to believe that anyone who would fly to the other side of the world for a karaoke contest must be deranged on some level.

The singing competition has all the rabid nationalism of the World Cup Finals, with legions of boisterous fans draped in the flags of their countries. Estonia has the largest contingent with more than twenty supporters. They wear matching shirts, hand-decorated with the names of the Estonian performers written in sparkle dust and puffy paint. A fresh-faced, genial group, they could be easily mistaken for camp counselors or members of the high school glee club. The Irish fans, however, are not of the sparkle dust ilk. Numbering at least fifteen including the leprechaun, they are a loud, wild, drunken mob. Though they occasionally heckle other fans, it is all in the good-natured spirit of the event.

I cannot say the same about the Russians. Though only three of them made the journey to support their national team, they are a dark and menacing presence. These hairy, barrel-chested brutes, adorned with Cyrillic neck tattoos and excessive man-jewelry, are seated at a cocktail table next to me. One of them, a stocky man in his fifties, wears an all-white tracksuit with the words *Soviet Union* emblazoned on the back in fiery, Communist red. I'm certain they are Russian mafia or ex-KGB, dispatched from Moscow to assure victory for their karaoke comrades. The group is so intimidating that I find myself compelled to cheer for the Russian competitors regardless of their performance quality. When Svetlana Erukhimova finishes a tepid, burlesque rendition of "Feelings" in which she sounds like Natasha from *Rocky and Bullwinkle*, I applaud with the thunderous fervor of a madman, beating my hands together until my palms are red and swollen and tender. "Bravo!" I scream, but the only thought in my head is, *Please don't kill me.*

The first round of competition ends sometime after 3 AM, and like many of the audience members, I migrate upstairs to the Zenith Disco because it is the only place on the ship still open and serving alcohol. And after eight hours of non-stop karaoke, a couple of prescription sedatives and a stiff drink are in order. The disco, a term I hadn't heard since 1982, has all the hallmarks of a small dance club, with one glaring exception: instead of a DJ spinning records, the music is provided by karaoke. Scandinavian death metal karaoke, to be precise. The song catalogue reads like the entries in a serial killer's diary, with cheery titles like "Excuse Me While I Kill Myself," "Unleash Hell," and "Descending Curtain of Death." After an hour of these gloomy songs, the Elvis of Finland takes the microphone and launches into a blistering version of AC/DC's "Highway to Hell," one of the happier tunes in the library. Though he shows impressive range for a big man in a satin pantsuit, the song clearly loses some its rock and roll punch when following the likes of "Triple Corpse Hammerblow" and "The Suicider."

Unfortunately, many of these songs are performed in their native languages, so I'm not able to grasp the poetry and nuance of the lyrics. While I'm waiting at the bar, a pretty young woman cozies up to me and introduces herself. She tells me her name is Katya and that she's 22, from the Ukraine by way of Estonia. I tell her that I'm an American journalist on assignment and she scoots a bit closer, hanging on my every word. I turned 38 just a few days earlier, and frankly, it's been a long time since I've had a conversation with a 22 year-old that didn't involve the phrases "Mocha Frappuccino" or "lap dance." On stage behind us, a man screams his way through though a hyper-aggressive death metal song in Finnish. I tell Katya I'm writing a story on karaoke and ask if she'll translate the lyrics for me. She closes her eyes and listens to the performance for a moment, then leans in close to whisper in my ear. I feel her hot breath on my neck. In broken English, she says, "The song is about, how you say, the devils? And they eat the flesh."

I nod. Flesh-eating devils.

Then she looks into my eyes and says with a sly, dazzling smile, "I make nice blowjob for you, yes? Two-hundred fifty Euro." When they said this was a full-service cruise, they weren't kidding. I've made some bad decisions in my life, but having sex with a Ukrainian prostitute on an Estonian booze cruise at 5 AM would probably take top honors. I thank Katya for her offer but gracefully decline and head back to my cabin for the night.

While there's no disputing karaoke's impact on global culture, there are many theories to explain its enduring popularity. Anthropologists chalk it up to a revival of public singing, an age-old tradition that is hard-wired into our DNA. "People have certain innate desires," says Kurt Slep of Sound Choice. "Sex is one. Eating is another. And singing. Human beings have been singing since the dawn of time." In fact, a new study by Professor Iegor Reznikoff, a specialist in ancient music at the Paris West University Nanterre La Défense, suggests that Paleolithic humans were singing between 10,000 and 40,000 years ago as a means of communication, navigation, and ritual. The evidence also suggests that this ancient singing may have been accompanied by music, as whistles and flutes carved from bone have been found at numerous Paleolithic sites. *Crooning cavemen? Bone flutes?* Clearly, what Reznikoff is describing is the birth of musical theater. Perhaps it's the prevalence of prescription drugs in my system, but as I drift off to sleep, visions of an all-Neanderthal production of *Mama Mia* dance in my head. Once you get past all the matted body hair and grunting, it's really quite fabulous.

Some see karaoke as a self-help tool akin to a support group, providing the performers with the encouragement and adulation lacking in their everyday lives. "When you go to the stage, even if you're a really bad singer, everyone cheers for you and you feel good," says Heidi Hujanen, Director of International Affairs for the KWC. And I think there's some truth to this. After all, the only time most of us will ever experience cheers from a live audience is when we're belting out "Love Shack" from a rickety karaoke stage in the cocktail lounge of an unexceptional airport Sheraton. *Tin roof, rusted!*

For others, karaoke provides a much-needed sense of community in a society that feels increasingly isolating. We live in an age where people spend more time at home watching television than socializing with others, where suburban sprawl has made town squares, neighborhood parks, and other public gathering spaces a thing of the past, where participation in civic and religious organizations has steadily declined for decades, and where cyber relationships on the Internet have become a substitute for real human interactions. In fact, many of our popular forms of entertainment, such as going to a movie, a concert, or a stage play, are passive activities that only reinforce our status as anonymous audience members. When we sit in a dark theater and watch a show, even though hundreds or even thousands of people may surround us, it is typically a solitary experience and we remain essentially alone in the crowd. Karaoke, however, can bring people together in a meaningful way. The very act of going out to a karaoke bar fosters a certain intimacy among the participants. Hiroshi Ogawa, a Professor of Sociology at Japan's Kansai University, suggests that karaoke creates a cozy space enclosed by its "virtual music wall," and that sharing this space and performing in front of others reinforces a group consciousness. Johan Fornäs, author and Director of the Advanced Cultural Studies Institute of Sweden, notes that when people go to a karaoke bar they enter into a social contract with the other patrons where everyone is expected to take turns singing. By assuming the dual role of both audience member and performer in karaoke, we willingly expose ourselves to the other participants, leaving us open and vulnerable to each other as the final shreds of our anonymity are stripped away.

Beyond forging camaraderie among boozed-up strangers, karaoke reinforces existing communities and helps different groups maintain their cultural identities. This is particularly evident in immigrant communities, such as New York's Chinatown where Hong Kong transplants sing karaoke versions of old Cantonese operas in an effort to remain connected to their cultural traditions. In Los Angeles, Vietnamese immigrants recall a glamorous colonial past by singing the tangos outlawed by Vietnam's Communist government in the 1970s. Even the gay community uses karaoke to maintain its cultural identity and to connect to an idealized vision of its past. Rob Drew, author of *Karaoke Nights: An Ethnographic Rhapsody* and Professor of Communication at Saginaw Valley State University, suggests that drag queens "nostalgically conjure a pre-AIDS, gay milieu through lip-synced renditions of old recordings by Shirley Bassey and Tallulah Bankhead."

Many sociologists, however, attribute karaoke's success to something more reflective of modern society: our obsession with celebrity. In 1968, Andy Warhol predicted that everyone would become famous for fifteen minutes. It appears he was right. Reality shows like *Survivor, The Apprentice,* and *American Idol* have spawned an entire sub-genre of celebrities who are just like you and me, only more attractive and with larger breasts. But it's not just the beautiful people getting their fifteen minutes: shows like *The Biggest Loser*, *Beauty and the Geek*, and *The Littlest Groom* are making stars out of the flabby, the pencil-protected, and the vertically-challenged. The perception, then, is that everyone can become famous. And perception, goes the old saw, is reality. In his book *Intimate Strangers: The Culture of Celebrity in America*, Richard Schickel writes, "If we do not somehow manage to insert ourselves into this reality, we run the danger of being, in our own eyes, unpersons." This says a great deal about the value we place on celebrity, and how it has come to define us as human beings. Or put in karaoke terms, *I sing, therefore I am*. And it's not just academic sorts who think this. Earlier in the day, I overheard a singing contestant tell an interviewer, "If you aren't somebody, you're nobody." Karaoke fills this void, allowing us to become celebrities for a few moments while we're on stage. "Everyone wants to be a rock star," says Kristin O, a sassy karaoke host from Michigan. "Everybody wants a taste of fame. And karaoke gives them that opportunity."

Though karaoke has many incarnations, perhaps none is more revealing than Porn Star Karaoke, or PSK. Every Tuesday night, leaders of the adult film industry gather at a Los Angeles bar called Sardo's and perform karaoke for a small circle of friends, insiders, and fans. Before I left for Helsinki, I attended PSK with adult film producer Oliver Bone and a bevy of porn actresses including Monica Mayhem, star of *Hole Sweet Hole*, *Ass Jumpers*, and *Fast Times at Deep Crack High 3*. Curiously, Porn Star Karaoke is not the sordid affair one might expect. There is no nudity, no vulgarity, and sadly, the evening does not dovetail into a fantastic orgy. The porn stars are there to sing. Monica Mayhem, a native of Brisbane, Australia who's been singing since she was six-years old, performed stellar renditions of No Doubt's "I'm Just a Girl" and Rage Against the Machine's "Killing in the Name."

"Singing is a release," says Mayhem. "It's a way for us to show off our other talents. It's a way to escape." Though her day job may include filming an anal gangbang scene or getting fisted by a lazy-eyed pirate dwarf, by night she can sing anthems of strength and rebellion, asserting herself in ways that may otherwise escape her daily routine. When she belts out the lyrics, "Oh, I've had it up to here" and "Fuck you, I won't do what you tell me," she seems to be making a personal statement.

Whereas the attainment of celebrity is about shedding anonymity and differentiating oneself from the masses, porn stars do karaoke for the exact opposite reason: they do it to rejoin the masses. For three and a half minutes, the length of a Lionel Richie song, a porn star can step out of his or her skin and become an average suburban middle class American. To me, this momentary transcendence is the heart of karaoke's appeal. And it happens every night, in karaoke bars around the world. When people sing against type—the shy, mousy accountant who sings a sexy Madonna song or the porn starlet who sings an anthem of girl power—they transcend themselves if only for a moment. In my younger days when I'd sing Neil Diamond's "Cherry, Cherry" or David Lee Roth's "Just a Gigolo" at the Silver Cloud karaoke bar in San Francisco, I would transform into a daring lothario, a bold and flirtatious cocksman with all the swagger of, well, someone else. And that was the point. But when the music would stop, I'd revert back to my nebbish self: a pudgy insecure lad with wrinkle-resistant Dockers and a nine-dollar haircut.

The second day of competition begins at 11 AM, and the boat is rocking. Not rocking in the figurative sense, the way you might say Bon Jovi rocks (which they totally do), but actually rocking in a violent back and forth motion. A massive storm had formed in the pre-dawn hours, turning the glassy Baltic Sea into a swirling black cauldron. At this point, the ship is pitching so severely that the performers are having trouble maintaining their balance on the stage. I should probably mention that I suffer from motion sickness in all its regurgitative forms: I get seasick, airsick, carsick, and on one regrettable trip to the Grand Canyon, donkeysick. As the storm's intensity grows, I feel myself getting queasy as the bile begins to rise in my esophagus. Frantically, I thumb through my Estonian travel dictionary for the phrase, *"I'm feeling nauseated. May I please have a vomit sack?"* Luckily I remember that Lorazepam—the pills I take to manage my flying anxiety—is sometimes prescribed to chemotherapy patients because it has a side effect of reducing nausea. I fish the bottle out of my camera bag and pop three of the little white pills, washing them down with a cruel Estonian vodka. As I would learn the hard way, which is really the only way to learn anything, this particular medication has the exact opposite of its intended effect when combined with copious amounts of grain alcohol and a lack of sleep: instead of soothing my frayed nerves, it makes me jittery and paranoid. Thankfully it did alleviate my nausea, because there's nothing more demoralizing than vomiting into a messy public toilet while listening to the karaoke version of Whitney Houston's "I Will Always Love You" for the third time in a soul-crushing span of twenty-two minutes.

In the afternoon, the top 15 men and women semifinalists are announced and surprisingly, all four Russian competitors make the cut. Perhaps it's the narcotic-induced paranoia or just the cynicism that comes with middle age, but I immediately suspect foul play. Of the four Russians advancing, only Veronica Konnova, a true talent and a clear frontrunner among the women, deserves a spot in the semifinals. The other three Russian performers are average at best, and their advancing raises some serious questions. Could this be a sign of jury tampering? It wouldn't be unprecedented. At the 1999 Figure Skating World Championships, two Russian and Ukrainian judges were suspended for collusion, and during the 2002 Olympic figure skating finals, the Russian team was stripped of its Gold Medals when they were accused of strong-arming a French judge. If it can happen in ice skating, why not karaoke? My suspicions are bolstered when a series of mysterious technical "glitches" begin plaguing the top performers. As Malaysia's Tham Hui Chye hits the chorus of "Dancing Queen," the audio suddenly drops out and she is forced to start again. Michelle Lynch of Ireland, one of the strongest performers in the competition, flees the stage when her Bonnie Tyler song stalls and then skips forward. I'm now convinced this is the handiwork of the Russians, but I had better watch my step. In the last year, there have been several high-profile cases of passengers "disappearing" on cruise ships, and I don't want to meet a similar fate. And really, the last thing I'd want is Nancy Grace harassing my parents, co-workers, and grade school classmates should I suddenly go missing. Greta Van Susteren, maybe. But not Nancy Grace. Not ever.

When the top five men and women finalists are announced and the only Russian to advance is Veronica Konnova, I realize that my judgment has been clouded by the unfortunate combination of drug-fueled delusions and geopolitical bigotry. It's worth noting here that, as a Cold War kid who grew up in the 1970s and 1980s, my ignorant, hackneyed views of Russia were largely informed by the villains of early James Bond movies, Ivan Drago from *Rocky IV*, and the classic Soviet invasion film *Red Dawn*, starring a pre-*Dirty Dancing* Patrick Swayze. In other words, I am an idiot.

It's now 4 AM, and I've been listening to karaoke continuously for 34 hours. The storm has finally moved beyond us, and my Lorazepam-induced neurosis has subsided. During a brief break in the action, I hit the bathroom to splash some cold water on my face. When I look in the mirror, I barely recognize the person staring back at me. I'm completely strung out, my cheeks puffy from the booze and fatigue. My bloodshot pupils are fully dilated and I've been wearing the same rumpled, stinking clothes since I arrived in Finland. I've got three days of spotty beard growth on my face, and my right eye twitches uncontrollably like I'm some kind a maniacal hobo. Though I've made many errors in judgment, it appears I was right about one thing: anyone who would fly halfway around the world for a karaoke contest must be deranged. I just didn't expect that person to be me.

The judges have submitted their final votes, and the

winners of the 2006 Karaoke World Championship are about to be announced. The contestants nervously await the decision, some pacing, others praying, their faces all strained with anticipation and exhaustion. Mark Wilson of Australia and Tham Hui Chye of Malaysia take first place for the men and women respectively. Veronica Konnova places third, and the disappointment visibly wells in her eyes. The stocky Russian man in the white tracksuit embraces her, plants a gentle kiss on her forehead and whispers something reassuring in her ear. In the end, the Russians were not gangsters or thugs, but rather, doting spouses and supportive friends just like you or me. For the grand finale, all the competitors, sponsors and event organizers join hands on the stage and sing, "We Are the World." It is a saccharine-sweet moment, free from all irony, cynicism and ill will. "Karaoke epitomizes not just a way of making music but a way of life," says author and professor Rob Drew. "It casts a model for how we can live every moment of every day, its Utopian ideals cobbled together from impossible dreams."

The sun is coming up as I leave the Starlight Show Lounge, and I can actually feel myself smiling. Maybe the world needs a bit of saccharine every now and again to remind us of a simpler time, when we were still young and full of hope. Of course, saccharin causes cancer in laboratory animals, but that's a discussion for another day.

The Cruel Kind

My mom used to say I was big-boned, but really I was just fat. And being a fat kid wasn't easy. In elementary school, my perfectly trim, perfectly perfect blue-eyed classmates called me names like lard-ass, fatso, and blubber-butt. By third grade, everyone called me Stubby—a demoralizing portmanteau of *short* and *tubby*. And while my svelte contemporaries shopped for stylish corduroy pants with flared bottoms and groovy velour sweater vests, I wore oversized t-shirts and Husky jeans bought at Sears because they were the only ones that fit. It was humiliating.

But that wasn't the worst of it.

If there was ever a human pyramid to be built, my substantial girth relegated me to the bottom row. "You're an essential part of the structure," my PE teacher would say. "You're the building block, the foundation."

Basically, I was furniture with an overbite.

In gym class where the curriculum required every student to climb a scratchy rope from floor to ceiling, most kids shimmied their way to the top without a hitch. I, on the other hand, would get four feet off the ground before my fleshy buttocks succumbed to the forces of gravity, causing me to slide back down to the bottom, my hands and inner thighs swollen red from the friction.

I hated that rope.

And because I wasn't fast or physically adroit, I was always the last one picked when teams were divvied up for schoolyard games. "We don't want him," the team captain would say. "We've already got two girls and a kid with scoliosis."

Then there was dodgeball, perhaps the cruelest of all school-sanctioned activities. This medieval bloodsport, often mandatory in physical education classes, involves children flinging recreational equipment at each other's heads. The inherently violent game, fueled by the raging hormones of fifth graders, revealed the true savagery and bloodlust of the pre-pubescent set. In the dodgeball jungle, it was hunt or be hunted, kill or be killed. Every recess became the *Hunger Games*, every gym class *Lord of the Flies*. And like Piggy, my literary doppelganger, being a fat kid just made me a bigger, slower target. Day after day, week after week, I'd get pelted in the face with that remorseless rubber ball. And when the game would reach its inevitable barbarous conclusion, I'd stagger to my next class in a daze, muttering incoherently to myself, *Okay grandma. I'll take out the garbage*, like a punch-drunk boxer suffering the effects of a brutal TKO. And this was back in the 1970s, before every American kid was dough-faced and pre-diabetic. At least today, if you're a chubby kid, you're probably not the only one. But me? I was *the* fat kid.

But that wasn't the worst of it.

Compounding the issue, my mom and I moved around a lot when I was young. We fancied ourselves suburban gypsies, nomads of the tract housing development. And when we moved, it wasn't across town or to a neighboring county. It was to a different time zone, a different coast, maybe even a different continent. By the time I got to eleventh grade, I'd already attended eleven different schools in multiple states and a foreign country. So I wasn't just *the* fat kid, I was *the new* fat kid. And this was nearly every year for my entire school-age life. As a result, I developed a chameleon-like ability to adapt to my environment and fit in with my peers at each new stop: I wore a smart European-style beret when I lived in Spain in second grade. I cultivated an impressive, flowing mullet when I moved to Florida in sixth grade. And then there was the towering Flock of Seagulls haircut with the button-up paisley shirts, pegged jeans, and penny loafers—think Ducky from *Pretty in Pink*—that I would wear at the first of two high schools I attended in Northern California. This ability to transform myself based on the local cultures and styles was my way of saying, *I may be new here, but I'm not so different from you. May I sit at your lunch table and drink my juice box?*

Moving to a new school every year did have certain advantages. If I found myself in a bad situation—getting harassed by a bully or being spurned by a girl I fancied—I knew that I'd be long gone before the semester ended. If there was a teacher I did not like, or if I was assigned to read a soul-crushingly dull 1000-page novel from the 19th century highlighting the flaws of the British judicial system (I'm looking at you, *Bleak House*), I knew that I could skip it altogether since I was leaving town before the book report was due. When my mom and I got to the next place, and there was always a next place, I'd be able to start over with a clean slate.

Naturally, there's a downside to this kind of transitory

existence: any relationship I formed in school had the shelf life of Cool Whip. Although I desperately wanted to make friends, to be part of a community, I also knew there was a good chance I'd be leaving and not coming back. So I made friends and got involved in school activities, but I also learned how to shut down my emotions for when the inevitable uprooting took place. Often I wouldn't even tell my classmates I was leaving. That way, there'd be no goodbye parties, no tearful send-offs. One day I'd be at school, and the next day I was just... gone.

When I was in 7th grade, my mom and I moved to a town called Tiburon, a posh Northern California suburb perched at the edge of the San Francisco Bay. Tiburon—Spanish for "trust fund"—and Belvedere, its adjacent unincorporated island neighbor, were two of the wealthiest small cities in America. Collectively, these sister hamlets were the domain of hedge fund managers, world-renowned surgeons, corporate attorneys, and Hollywood screenwriter Joe Eszterhas, the genius who gave us *Showgirls*. It was the kind of place that had a private yacht club *with a waiting list* because there were too many boats and not enough slips, where a Gucci tennis skirt paired with Chanel sneakers was the go-to errand-running outfit of every stay-at-home millionaire mom, and where sleek Ferraris and purring Jaguars roamed its quaint, cobblestone streets like jackals on the Serengeti. It was a land of old money and lavish estates, where well-heeled families of dignified lineage imported leggy Scandinavian au pairs to care for their immaculately styled Von Trapp-esque children. These were privileged people.

My mom and I, however, were not.

We lived in a Section 8 apartment complex for low-income families, the only such property in town and a curious sight as it was nestled between multi-million dollar homes, which I'm sure our affluent neighbors just *loved*. My mom drove a beat-up 1978 Honda Civic hatchback and did whatever she could to make ends meet, from cleaning houses and cutting hair, to running the household of a wealthy family, not unlike Alice on *The Brady Bunch*. To help with the bills, we rented out the extra bedroom in our apartment to a variety of characters over the years. There was Paul, who worked at the gas station in town and gave me stacks of his old *Hustler*, *Chic*, and *Oui* porno magazines. There was Jeff, a good-looking massage therapist, who had a lot of his special lady-friends sleep over. There was John, who worked for the transit authority and built my 8th grade science project for me. And there was a shifty guy named Kenny whose job, as far as I could tell, was making balloon animals and smoking a lot of weed. Money was always tight, but my mom worked hard to provide for us. Still, with our government subsidized housing, my proletariat wardrobe, our rusted, sputtering automobile, and our odd rotation of pornography-wielding roommates, I was something of an oddity among my wealthy peers. Because this time around I wasn't *just* the new fat kid.

I was *the poor* new fat kid.

But that wasn't the worst of it.

When we first arrived in Tiburon, during that horrific sociological experiment known as "middle school," I found myself in the awkward early throes of puberty, and I had all the telltale symptoms.

There was acne.

There was body odor.

There were unwanted erections at inappropriate times. But most disconcertingly, there was *hair*. Not on my genitals, mind you, like all the other boys who proudly displayed their burgeoning pubes in the locker room like so many Benetton-clad peacocks fanning their plumes. No, I would remain pubeless for another year, my barren childlike groin a deforested wasteland, my testicles smooth and shiny like flesh-colored snow globes. Instead, my first wisps of adolescent hair sprouted on my lip. So I wasn't just the poor new fat kid in town. Because I *totally* could have handled that.

I was the poor new fat kid *with a mustache*.

Perhaps if I'd been able to cultivate a thick, lustrous soup strainer like Burt Reynolds, Tom Selleck, or the guy from Hall & Oates, I would have appeared strong and virile. Perhaps. But *my* peach-fuzzed faux stache was closer in style and follicle density to "Rhythm of the Night" singer El DeBarge or Pedro from *Napoleon Dynamite*, not exactly icons of masculinity. To be fair, this was some twenty-three years before *Napoleon Dynamite* opened in movie theaters, so I'd like to think I was ahead of the curve on that one. I was the Early Pedro. *Pedrolopithecus Americanus*.

As the only kid in the 7th grade with facial hair, I endured a constant barrage of mustache jokes—real gems like, "I loved you in *Smoky and the Bandit*" and "Hey Cheech, can you score me some weed?" I'm not sure why I didn't just shave it off right away, as it would have saved me a lot of grief. Maybe it was because I only saw my dad twice a month and was too embarrassed to ask for his help. Or maybe it was because the mustache deflected attention away from my doughy face and ample ass, giving my peers a different, less hurtful target for their jibes.

Mustache jokes, I could deal with. Fat jokes, not so much. It wasn't until a blonde, ski-tanned athletic kid in my class asked if I enjoyed fighting in *The Octagon*, a thinly veiled reference to Chuck Norris and his epic cookie duster, that I took my mom's pink BIC Lady razor and finally shaved it off.

Problem solved, right?

Wrong.

Because even without the mustache fuzz, I was still the same lonely fat kid trying to fit in.

The Germans have a wonderful word called *kummerspeck* that loosely means "the excess weight one gains from emotional overeating" but literally translates as *grief bacon*. This, in a toffee-coated nutshell, sums up my childhood relationship with food. Instead of feeling sad about leaving everything behind in the middle of the school year for the umpteenth time or frightened at the prospect of starting over again in a new place, I would eat. And boy, I could really put it away. I'd gorge myself stupid on a confectionary cavalcade of Pop-Tarts, donuts, Charleston Chews and Zagnut Bars, and it seemed to make me feel better. Or at least, less bad. After years of therapy—and when I say therapy, I mean watching *Oprah*—I realized I'd been using food to self-medicate ever since I was old enough to peel the cellophane wrapper off a box of Goobers. Steak-umm® hoagie sandwiches had become my emotional anesthesia, tubes of Pillsbury chocolate chip cookie dough my Prozac. The way I dealt with sadness, alas, was to bury it under a thick layer of empty calories and transfats until everything went numb.

* * *

Albert Einstein famously wrote, "The distinction between past, present, and future is only a stubbornly persistent illusion." His theories of relativity suggest that time, inseparable from the fabric of space, is an unpartitioned contiguous reality, where the past, present, and future exist simultaneously. Our yesterdays become indistinguishable from our todays and tomorrows; our history, then, inescapable and ever-present. Which means some of us are totally fucked.

And so:

The year is 2011, and I am 43 years old. Each afternoon, a group of salty fishermen and geriatric surf bums gather around a wooden bench outside my neighborhood Starbucks, regaling each other with exotic, rum-soaked tales from their youthful days in the South Pacific, each story more outlandish than the previous, each invariably culminating in a fistfight with a monkey and a fortnight spent in a Tongan jail. They tell bawdy jokes, they argue about politics and women, they talk about their prostates: "Doc says mine is the size of a cantaloupe. That's why it takes me 45 minutes to piss."

They are boisterous, colorful characters, and in the dying afternoon light they might easily be mistaken for background players on a Coen Brothers movie set. They are the kind of people that make you more interesting simply by being in their presence. And I know that if I could spend just a few minutes with them, I too would be punching monkeys and wrestling marlin from the sea with my bare hands.

"You're stalking them like a lunatic," my wife chides every time we pass them going for coffee. "Just go over there and talk to them." But it's a tight-knit group, and entrée doesn't come easily. You must bide your time until they summon you, like a stand-up comic on the old *Tonight Show* hoping Johnny Carson waves you over to the couch after your set.

I've walked past this motley, grizzled crew nearly every afternoon since I moved to Redondo Beach, observing them, picking up bits of their conversations, secretly longing to join in their laughter and participate in their manly camaraderie: *A cantaloupe you say? Well my prostate is the size of a chickpea, and my urine flows like the mighty Thames!* Each day I see them huddled around that bench, and each day I wonder if this is the day they invite me over.

This has been going on for three years.

So when I pulled in front of Starbucks this afternoon I wasn't expecting *this* to be the day I'd finally breach their inner circle. As I climbed out of my car, I heard a craggy, sandpaper voice calling behind me.

"Hey you. Yeah—*you*."

When I turned around, I was greeted by a leathery fisherman straight from Central Casting, a man who looked like an older version of Robert Shaw in *Jaws*, complete with navy pea coat, wool turtleneck sweater, and tattered Greek fisherman's cap. It was 82 degrees outside.

"Say, what kind of car is that?" he asked, motioning to my vehicle with a knobby, gnarled thumb.

"This? It's a 1999 Jeep Cherokee."

"You like it?"

"It always starts when I turn the key," I reply. "So yeah, I like it."

The old fisherman rose from the bench and hobbled over to my car, running his hand along the dusty frame. "I like the square lines on this beauty. *Classic.*" He turned to the other men gathered around the bench. "*This* is a car that makes sense. Durable. Reliable. It's exactly what I need." He used his hand to shield the sun from his eyes and peered through the window, surveying the interior. "See that? No frills, no gimmicks. I don't need Blueteeth, whatever the hell that is. And I don't need no GPS. If I get lost, that's *if*, I'll use a goddamn paper map." He turned back to me. "You've got taste, kid," he said, flashing a yellowed, decaying jack-o-lantern grin. "Come over and talk to us on your way out."

I continued into Starbucks, elated. Sure, I'd cleared the first hurdle—getting the invitation from the group—but if I wanted to successfully join their ranks, I would have to employ the same integrative tactics I used as a child when we landed in a new place. I immediately started making a mental list of things I will do to fit in with this colorful new group:

> *(1) Grow an unruly beard.*
> *(2) Start smoking a pipe. Corncob?*
> *(3) Wear overalls. Everywhere.*
> *(4) Start spitting in public.*
> *(5) Get a hat, like The Captain wears in The Captain*
>   *& Tennille.*

Inside the cafe, I ordered a Pumpkin Spice latte and grabbed a banana from the basket on the counter. I exited the store and sheepishly approached the bench.

This was my moment.

A shaggy, sixtyish man in flip-flops, board shorts, and a frayed "Got Weed?" t-shirt, eerily resembling the Dude in *The Big Lebowski*, welcomed me with a cautious smile.

"What's your name, chief?"

Before I could respond, the old fisherman I'd met earlier cut me off, pointing at the banana in my hand. "You buy that inside?"

I told him yes.

"What'd you pay for it?" he asked.

"A dollar, I think." And this is where it all went terribly wrong.

"A dollar? For one goddamn banana?" he growled. "You can get two *pounds* of bananas for a dollar at the market."

"I just wanted a banana," I pleaded. "It was convenient."

The old fisherman stepped towards me, his hot gusty breath stinking of bourbon and cheese. "Those corporate cocksuckers think they can charge whatever they want, and you and the other sheep just go along with it? I mean, who spends a dollar for a banana? That's just stupid. STUPID!" He turned to the bench, his face red with anger. "This whole goddamn world is going to hell."

Just like that, I was back on the outside looking in. An oddity among the oddities. And this, really, is the central theme of my life. Well *that*, and trying to squeeze my fleshy buttocks into pants with a 34-inch waist. It was as though I'd slipped through some kind of existential wormhole, watching as time seemed to fold in on itself, middle school bleeding into middle age, the past indistinguishable from the present. *Fucking Einstein.*

But that wasn't the worst of it.

The old fisherman turned back to me, sniffing at the steam rising from my coffee cup, his face contorted in disgust. "What the hell is that—*pumpkin*?"

I wanted to smash him in the head with my delicious seasonal beverage. I wasn't upset that he was mocking me. After all, a grown man drinking a frothy melon latte deserves a certain amount of ribbing. What got me was the utter contempt that dripped from his words. It was a tone I'd come to know, echoed by different voices throughout my youth.

"Okay. Well. It was nice talking to you," I said as I turned and walked away. Behind me, I could hear them all laughing. But it wasn't the fun kind of laughter. It was the cruel kind.

I got in my car and drove down to the beach to drink my coffee. Even with a cardboard sleeve, the cup was almost too hot to hold in my hand. I stared out at the ocean and took a long gulp of the scalding brew. It burned my tongue and blistered the inside of my mouth, scorching my esophagus all the way down to the pit of my stomach, but I didn't mind. I was just glad to feel anything at all.

Gypsies, Tramps, and Thieves

"DON'T SIT ON THAT—THERE'S SNAKES IN THERE!" are not words I expected to have directed towards me, ever. Even backstage at a carnival sideshow. Even from the toothless mouth of a hulking, shirtless, Buddha-bellied sword swallower in a Scottish kilt. So I freeze mid-squat, my ample denimed ass hovering inches above the industrial-sized Igloo cooler filled not with beer or ice as I'd expected, but large carnivorous reptiles, including a ten-foot long boa constrictor named Meatball. Later, an old carny will advise me to never handle a snake of this size while I'm naked because it might mistake my testicles for field mice. This really raises more questions than it answers, namely, *Are there a lot of naked snake handlers?* And more concerning, *Do my balls really look like furry woodland rodents?*

But I did not come to the World of Wonders Sideshow, currently in residence at the Volusia County Fair in central Florida, to talk about my figs. I'm here to meet John "Red" Lawrence Stuart, the aforementioned sword swallower, who's been in the carny business for more than 45 years. Red, whose nickname references both his flowing crimson locks and his self-described "flaming" sexual orientation, isn't like most 62 year-olds: besides eating swords—and he holds several world records for this dangerous feat—he also swallows car axels, coat hangers, neon tubes, bayonets, and early in his career, live snakes, as detailed by Mark Hartzman in his book *American Sideshow*: "He learned to swallow an endangered Eastern Indigo snake, just like a sword. The snake slithered down his throat headfirst, its jaws trapped shut by his esophagus." Additionally, Red performs as a human pincushion and blockhead, hammering steel nails into his skull, needles into his face, and screwdrivers up his nose all in the name of family entertainment. His coworkers include a creepy contortionist clown, a half-man born without legs who walks on his hands, and a fire-breathing dwarf. For most people, this is the stuff of nightmares. But for Red and his sideshow cohorts, it's just another day at the world's weirdest office.

I've always been fascinated by the strange, nomadic nature of circus life, partly due to my own peregrinations as a child, but mostly because of my time as a rock and roll roadie, a profession that shares much of its DNA with the carnival business. Aside from the obvious similarities—the constant travel, the repetitive physicality of setting up a show each day and tearing it down each night, and the public's misguided opinion of the people who hold those jobs—the two professions have something else in common: cultures deeply rooted in mythology.

Since the earliest days of rock and roll, outlandish myths and bizarre urban legends have surrounded some of its most famous practitioners, like delta blues pioneer Robert Johnson selling his soul to the devil in exchange for his extraordinary musical talent, Keith Richards getting his druggy, toxic blood drained and replaced with clean blood in a mysterious Swiss clinic, Marilyn Manson shitting in a cat litter box in his dressing room, or members of Led Zeppelin fucking a groupie with a live mud shark.

In the carnival sideshow, the entire foundation of the business is built on mythology. To create the most shocking and exotic exhibits, sideshow managers routinely fabricated their performers' personal biographies and the nature of their afflictions. With the right backstory and marketing, a girl with a scaly skin condition from Ohio becomes *the Cobra Woman of Tangiers*. Other times, performers are presented as missing links from dark and mysterious jungles like the notorious *Wild Men of Borneo* exhibit, or they are imbued with high-ranking or royal status and given titles such as "General," "Princess," and "Count," like famous dwarf performers General Tom Thumb and Commodore Nutt. Out on the midway, barkers and bally talkers regale passersby with fantastic descriptions of dog-faced girls, lobster men, and giant Cyclops babies who could be viewed in the main tent for just a few shiny coins. Ward Hall is the 84-year old owner of the World of Wonders sideshow and is celebrating his 70th year in the business. "I'm a professional liar," he said in an interview from 2008. "Do you believe you are going to see a real two-headed woman here? Because it is my job to convince these people that they are going to see these things. And I've always been good at it. I could take a Volkswagen and make you believe it is a Rolls Royce."

Red greets me on the carnival midway outside the World of Wonders tent, and though this is the second day I'll spend watching him ply his gruesome trade, his appearance is still jarring. He's a physically imposing man: with his leathery torso and forearms awash in faded tattoos, his shock of wild red hair, and his frayed tartan kilt, he looks more like a deranged extra from the movie *Braveheart* than an AARP cardholder. "Come on," he says as we shake hands. "We can talk backstage." I follow him through a slit in the tent that leads to a small dressing room where he plops onto a rickety folding chair, its hinges threatening to buckle under his heft. This area, also functioning as a repair shop and performers' lounge, is really just a cramped spot behind the stage sectioned-off from the crowd with a tarp. There's no floor, just mud and matted grass. In one corner, a folding table is cluttered with half-eaten jars of peanut butter, baby wipes, empty Mountain Dew cans, and a small vanity mirror perched atop a dusty Reagan-era boom box. Red lights up a cigarette and takes a drag. "You mind?"

I actually do mind, but when a large man with a sword asks you that question, especially when you've already almost sat on his expensive snake, you smile and say, "Go right ahead."

Though Red lacks a formal education, he is clearly intelligent in a near-savant kind of way, casually tossing off Buddhist mantras, bits of obscure Civil War history, and quantum physics theories like he's reading items off a grocery list. Right now he's explaining how the earth's magnetic poles work, then he quickly pivots into how to navigate by the stars, a skill he learned piloting boats on the Delaware River as a teen.

I fish my tape recorder out of my bag and set it on the table in front of him. "Okay, Red. You ready to tell your story?" He nods, takes a deep pull off his cigarette, and starts talking.

Red's childhood, full of heartbreak, abandonment, and poverty, coupled with the innate oddness of his adult life spent as a carnival sideshow performer, reads like *Oliver Twist* filtered through the darkly surreal lens of David Lynch. He was born in 1951 on an Army base near New Brunswick, New Jersey to an unwed fifteen year old with a wild streak and a taste for gin. In the winter of 1955, when Red was just four years old, his mother left him at a Baptist orphanage in southwest Philadelphia with only the clothes on his back. "I spent my first night there in the girl's dorm," says Red. "They thought I was a female because I had long red hair. And when they realized I wasn't, they cut it all off." But for Red, the indignities were only beginning. "When I first got to the orphanage it was during Christmas. My mom came to see me, but she didn't have any money to get me any gifts. So the people who ran the orphanage made each kid give me one of their Christmas presents." He chuckles, adding, "So right off the bat the other kids hated me." Red would only see his mother one other time, four years later. "When she came to visit in 1959, she gave me her wedding band and engagement ring, and she gave me a silver half dollar with my birth year on it. And she said she was gonna come back and get me. Of course, she never came back." Red clears his throat and adds flatly, "Regretfully, my mother would rather chase men and get drunk than take care of her kid."

As a ward of the state, Red would spend the next ten years in and out of various foster homes, group homes, and government institutions. "I was in one orphanage for about two months when it failed a state inspection and was deemed unsafe for children. They actually condemned the building while I was living there," says Red.

"So they shipped me off to the Elwyn Institute, simply because they had an empty bed. It was a home for the mentally retarded."

Red takes a long drag off his cigarette. "Man, I was just lost," he says, exhaling a plume of smoke. "I was living in the retarded home and I'd become a junior counselor. They had a buddy system where they paired you up with another kid, and my buddy was a narcoleptic. I was also in the Boy Scouts, and to get my Canoeing Merit Badge, the two of us had to take a 21-foot canoe down Ridley Creek for two miles and paddle back up. Well, my buddy went into one of his narcoleptic fits and passed out. It took me four and a half hours to ride that canoe all the way back."

In the fall of 1966, at the age of 15, Red was allowed to leave his group home in Pennsylvania on the condition that he found work. So he hitchhiked to New Orleans where he promptly landed a job setting up carnival rides at a fair during Mardi Gras. "That's where I met a gypsy named Toni Del Rio who ran the sideshow. She was a half and half—a hermaphrodite. She said, 'Red, how'd you like to learn to swallow swords, eat fire, and drive nails into your head?' And I said 'Sure, why not?'"

The first act she taught Red was human blockhead: pounding nails, screwdrivers, tent pegs, chopsticks, and other objects into your sinus cavity through your nostrils. Red recounts this initial lesson with a genuine warmth and fondness, the way you might describe a childhood memory of your favorite Christmas or the first time you met your spouse: "She took a steel barn nail, raised the tip of my nose, and pushed it all the way up there as far as it would go. My nose bled, my eyes ran like crazy, and I felt like I wanted to sneeze. But it didn't hurt," says Red.

"That was a four-inch long nail. She told me to keep it in there, and after about fifteen minutes she pulled it out and told me to blow my nose. After dinner, she told me to put it back in myself. Through trial and error, I figured out where my sinus track was. And using meditation, or mind control if you wish to call it that, you can make it so your body doesn't react to it any more."

By Holy Thursday, less than forty days later, under the tutelage of a hermaphroditic gypsy, Red had learned every major torture act, including sword swallowing, glass eating, blockhead, pincushion, eating fire, bed of nails, and climbing a ladder of swords. But Toni Del Rio was more than his instructor. "She was a mother figure, a father figure, a teacher, and a guru, all rolled into one," says Red. "Late at night after the carnival midway would close, we'd meet up and talk about esoteric teachings and Hinduism and witchcraft. Now, my IQ is 156 so I'm usually one of the smartest people in the room, but I had *zero* common sense. As far as life experience goes, I was a total idiot. Toni Del Rio taught me about surviving in the world."

Red checks his email while I scan through my notes. "You mentioned eating glass," I say. "How does *that* work?"

"You just eat it, like it's goddamn nachos. And it passes right on through you," he says. "But I don't eat glass no more, because I don't have any teeth."

"And why do you wear the kilt?" I ask him. "Is your family from Scotland?"

Red smoothes the wrinkles from his lap and adjusts his leather sporran. "My full name is John Lawrence Stuart XXVIII," he says. "I'm a descendent of the Royal House of Stuart."

"Come again?"

"I'm from the royal lineage of Mary Stuart, better known as Mary, Queen of Scots," he says. "On my father's side."

"So, you're royalty? And you eat glass?"

"Correction. I *ate* glass." Red glances at his watch. "We'll have to finish this later," he says, taking a couple of quick drags off his cigarette before carefully stubbing it out and dropping it into an empty Mountain Dew can. "It's time to go to work." He turns and hobbles up the small aluminum stepladder that leads to the stage. When he gets to the top, he looks back at me, flashing a sly toothless grin before stepping through the curtain and disappearing to the other side. I immediately grab my phone and update my Facebook status: *Hangin' backstage with sideshow carnies—EPIC!!*

As a writer, when I go to work, it usually involves sitting in cushy chair in a café where they play Norah Jones on an endless loop while I type words into my laptop. Maybe I'll even have a scone. But Red and his fellow performers—these guys *work*. And it's sweaty, hard, painful work that's rarely accompanied by shitty smooth jazz or exotic breakfast pastries.

The World of Wonders is a classic ten-in-one sideshow offering ten acts—sword swallowing, knife throwing, bed of nails, fire eating, and others—under one tent for a single admission price. It's what they call a *grind show*, which means they start performing when the fair opens, sometimes as early as 9 AM, and they don't stop until it closes, which can be as late as midnight. The entire show, that is, the time it takes all ten acts to perform, lasts about 45 minutes; the moment it finishes, it resets and starts over from the beginning. This grueling schedule requires Red to pound nails into his skull and stab needles into his face anywhere from fifteen to twenty times a day, seven days a week, for the duration of the fair. In fact, everyone in the sideshow must perform his or her act that many times in a given day.

"And if you're in multiple acts, which most of us are," says Tessa Fontaine, who eats fire and charms snakes in the World of Wonders production, "you literally don't have time to run to the bathroom between acts because it's usually too far away. So most people keep pee jars in their bunks."

"I'm sorry—pee jars?"

"Yeah, it's just a jar that you pee in when you can't get to a bathroom," she says. "And there's all these strategies about the kind of nuts or trail mix you're going to buy at Walmart in order to get the right size jar." Tessa checks her costume in the mirror, adjusting the hem of her sparkly, low-cut dress. "I had no idea how hard this business was going to be," she continues. "There's a perception that any old meth head can do this job—and there are meth heads here, for sure—but the work is so physically demanding that you can't be strung out all the time." Tessa peeks through the curtain at Red, who is *tap-tap-tapping* a nail up into his sinus cavity with the handle of his microphone. "The end of a fair is the worst," she says. "On the last day, after you've been performing for twelve hours or more, you literally stay up all night dismantling your ride or taking down your tent. Then you load it all up, and you get in your truck and drive hundreds of miles to the next fair where you immediately start setting up for the next run, which takes many more hours. You might not sleep for two days between fairs. I mean, the actual physical labor is exhausting. And it doesn't matter if it's pouring rain or if it's 20 degrees or if it's 110 degrees, because the show's gotta go on."

While the nature and pace of the work are certainly demanding, it's the living conditions at the sideshow that really tests the performers' mettle. As a rock and roll roadie, I'd spend part of the week on a comfortable tour bus, and the rest of the time in a nice hotel, where things like pillow top mattresses, stocked mini-bars, rainfall showerheads, heated towel racks, and flushable toilets are taken for granted. But in the sideshow, there are no tour buses or hotel rooms. Instead, rudimentary bunks fashioned from slats of plywood are mounted in the back of the semi truck that hauls the show. "Red sleeps in his van, but the rest of us sleep in the truck," says Tessa. "There aren't enough bunks for everybody, so people sleep out on the stage in sleeping bags, or they just pile up next to each other on the ground." Making matters worse, the bunkhouse portion of the semi truck does not have air-conditioning or heat. "The trailer is made of metal, so in the summer it's like being in an oven," Tessa adds. "And in the fall, it's freezing. There's no insulation whatsoever. So you're really exposed to the elements."

Usually there are no toilets at the sideshow site, so when the performers need to relieve themselves, they must either use their pee jars — and there's nothing more delightful than a dozen mayonnaise jars full of urine splashing around on a hot summer day — or they must make the long trek down the midway to the public restrooms. This is particularly challenging for an older guy like Red, whose knees are so bad he can barely climb the stepladder up to the stage let alone walk a quarter mile in the heat to take a leak in a disgusting Porta Potty. And these public facilities are often locked when the fair closes at night anyway to prevent the carnies from using them.

Bathing presents its own difficulties when you live on the carnival midway, and the performers get creative with their limited resources. "We hang a vinyl panel behind our sideshow tent and run a hose to it, and that's our shower," Tessa explains. "So we basically take turns hosing off. When it's hot outside, it's not a big deal. But when it's cold, it's awful." Tessa pauses, listening for her cue from the stage—Red is about to introduce her for their electric chair act. "Gotta go—it's show time," she says, as she turns and bounds up the stepladder, disappearing through the curtain.

I'm now alone in the room with Red's personal effects—his laptop computer opened to his Facebook page, his pot of day-old instant coffee, his sequined American flag vest—and that's when it occurs to me: this is Red's home. He may sleep in his van, but this cramped, muddy area behind the stage is his kitchen, his living room, his dressing room, and his workshop. This is where he spends the majority of his time when he's not performing. And it makes me a little sad, because for a profession whose name conjures images of travel, adventure and freedom, his world seems pretty small. As I ponder this unsettling irony, I notice a 35-pound plastic bucket of *Tidy Cat* litter under Red's table, which strikes me as odd. Besides the snakes in the show, I haven't seen any animals around here—and certainly none of the feline variety. So why does a man without pets have cat litter in his dressing room?

Because he's doing the unthinkable.

The bathrooms are far away and Red's got bum knees. He can use a pee jar when he has to urinate, but what about *other* bodily eliminations? Can you buy a trail mix jar big enough to defecate in? Probably, but you'd have to get it at Costco. And your aim would have to be spot-on. But with a bucket of cat litter, you could sit on it like a toilet and do your business. Or as it's known in the rock roadie world, *Going Full Manson*.

Out on the stage, Red shish-kebabs a long needle through his Adam's apple, eliciting a smattering of uncomfortable applause from the crowd. He introduces the next act—a guy throwing knives at a pretty woman—then steps through the curtain and hobbles back down the stepladder. "Okay—where was I?" he says, plopping onto his chair.

"You'd just met the gypsy hermaphrodite, and she stuck a nail up your nose."

"Right, right," says Red. He lights up a cigarette and continues his story.

After mastering the torture acts he learned from Toni Del Rio, Red left the New Orleans carnival in the spring of 1967. Unable to find a job in a sideshow, he returned to the orphanage in Philadelphia at the age of sixteen. And this is where his life took a dramatic turn. He learned that a clerical error in his child welfare personnel file had erroneously switched his birth year from 1951 to 1948, making him appear to be three years older than he actually was. According to the state of Pennsylvania, Red was now nineteen, able-bodied, and eligible to join the military as the war raged in Vietnam. "The director of the orphanage told me he could get me into the U.S. Navy, and I said yes, because I needed a job," says Red. "I mean, I lived my whole life in institutions, and the Navy was just another one, as far as I was concerned. You get up at a certain time in the morning, shave, shower, and shit, eat breakfast, and go do whatever you have to do—in the orphanage it was going to school; in the military, it was doing drills."

Red enlisted in the Navy in 1967 at the age of 16 and was serving in Vietnam before he turned 17. He tells me that he became a Navy SEAL, but he provides few other details about his time in-country. At one point, though, he eludes to his abrupt ousting from the military. He clearly does not want to talk to about it, but after I push him, he tells me the incredible, gut-wrenching tale.

The year was 1968, the bloodiest year of the Vietnam War, and Red's experience as first mate on a riverboat when he was a teenager in Delaware was paying dividends on the waterways of Southeast Asia. "I could pilot any boat—I was good with navigation," says Red. "I could tell where I was within a couple of miles just by using the stars and my wristwatch." As a SEAL, Red participated in a number of missions—or sorties—sometimes to apprehend an "unfriendly" thought to be hiding in a particular village, other times to gather intelligence, destroy a particular target, or even conduct raids on suspected POW camps. "We'd do a sortie, and when we got done, we'd get three days R&R," says Red. "They'd put us someplace, and we could do whatever we wanted for those few days. And they supplied all the booze, beer, drugs, a horizontal woman, whatever we wanted. Anything. And then we would be sent off on another mission."

Red, who concealed both his real age and his homosexuality when he joined the Navy, became romantically involved with a fellow SEAL in his squad, an act so scandalous given the time and place that they kept the relationship a secret. In late 1968, Red's team was sent on a mission to extricate two American POWs from a North Vietnamese prison. Though the team was able to liberate the American prisoners, they took heavy fire during the operation. One SEAL was killed, and Red was seriously wounded. "The person who got killed was my lover," Red says. "And it was him that ended up getting blown to pieces. The whole lower half of his body landed on my legs." Red clears his throat and continues. "So that's... what happened. And I just snapped, screaming and carrying on like a crazy person. They taped my fucking mouth shut and gave me about four hits of morphine, and they carried me out of there."

At this point, Red is overcome with emotion: his body is visibly trembling, and he's doing his best to choke back tears. He gathers himself and continues. "They put me in the chopper to EVAC me out. But I was so high on morphine I thought the medic was my lover who had just been killed. And I was so out of it that I was trying to seduce the guy—I practically had my hand in his pants. So I basically came out of the closet, right there in that helicopter. And that just didn't happen in those days. They didn't like faggots in the service—*especially* in the SEALS."

Red takes a deep breath and rubs his eyes. "I was recovering in the Naval hospital when the they found out I'd lied about my age. They said, 'You gave us false information, which is a federal offense. That'll get you fourteen years in Leavenworth.'" But the Navy didn't send Red to prison. Instead, as Red tells it, they offered him a deal. "They said, 'What we can do here, is you can sign this paper that says you never existed in the service.' So I signed it. And they sent me home. According to the U.S. government, I was never there—it's like the whole thing was a bad dream."

Red returned to the United States in February of 1969, and like many combat veterans, he struggled to adjust to civilian life. "I was emotionally distraught and mentally screwed up from the war. I didn't get a welcome home parade or nothing. And I was called a baby killer and every other horrible thing. I was called everything but human," says Red. "I got messed up on drugs and alcohol real bad. And I went back to the carnival business because they don't care what you are—they had alcoholics and drug addicts, people with mental problems and physical deformities. I fit right in."

Over the next few months, Red's emotional state worsened as he struggled with depression, likely a byproduct of PTSD. "In August of 1969 I was close to committing suicide. I had a gun and I was ready to do it," says Red. "But a friend of mine heard about this big music festival and we decided to go to it. That festival was Woodstock."

Red and his friend hitchhiked to Woodstock, and once inside, they quickly gravitated to the Hog Farm area, a hippie collective founded by activist Wavy Gravy who operated the free kitchen at the event. "I was on the verge of killing myself, but the Hog Farm straightened me out," says Red.

"How did they help you?" I ask.

"The guys at the Hog Farm—*they listened to me*. The Navy didn't want to listen, the courts didn't want to listen, the director of the orphanage, the welfare department, the social workers and psychologists—nobody wanted to listen. But the people at Hog Farm did. All I had to do was vent out. And that's what saved my life." Red smiles as he shifts in his chair. "I don't remember much about the festival itself, but I did eat some of the brown acid. And I totally freaked out when Hendrix played the "Star-Spangled Banner" on his guitar. That blew my mind—I guess the acid might've helped. I still get flashbacks from time to time, and most of them are pretty good."

After Woodstock, Red returned to the carnival business but was unable to find work as a sideshow performer. "By 1970 there were only a handful of traveling sideshows left, so those jobs were hard to come by," he says. Instead, Red earned a living repairing carnival rides and doing electrical work on the fair circuit. "Eventually, I became the manager of a reptile show. I had a komodo dragon and some snakes and lizards and shit." Red would explore the darker corners of the sideshow business during his brief stint as a glooming geek, or gloomer—a shocking and controversial act where the performer bites into a live animal, killing and disemboweling it before a curious-yet-horrified audience. "We'd do the geek shows at small backwoods fairs, down in bayou country. I'd paint my skin brown, put on an afro wig, and wear a Native American breechcloth while communicating in grunts, like some kind of primitive tribesman. And then I'd bite the head off a live chicken, or maybe a snake," says Red. "But the show isn't about *me* biting into the animal—I'd just tear into its belly with my teeth and pull half its guts out. The show is watching the animal run around the pit with its intestines dragging behind it until it keels over and dies. Then you'd pick up the dead animal and spin it around so its blood and guts fly into the audience. People in the crowd would start puking, and you'd take the puke and rub it on your body and throw it back at them."

"So, it's a show for kids?" I say, trying to mask my revulsion with a moment of levity.

"Yeah—it's pretty messed up," says Red, laughing. "But a lot of people wanted to see that stuff, and they'd pay five bucks a pop. You'd fill up that tent with sixty people, multiple times a day—sometimes I'd make $1500 in an afternoon. And that was dead serious money back then. If you did three or four of those, you'd be set for the winter."

I should mention that today is not only the final day of the Volusia County Fair here in central Florida, but it's the final day of the entire carnival season for the World of Wonders sideshow. Tonight, immediately after their last performance, Red and his crew will take down the tents, dismantle the stages and props, and load everything onto the semi-truck where it will be stored in nearby Gibsonton until the spring. I want to see this end-of-season ritual, so I tell Red that I'll be back later tonight when they are taking down the show. I toss my notebook and tape recorder into my bag and slip away through a flap in the tent.

I've got some time to kill, so I stop at an unassuming sports bar called Gator's Dockside, best known for its deep-fried alligator tails and a drink called Swamp Water, a sugary, tooth-aching blend of sweet tea, vodka, and lemonade. As I gnash my way through a plate of fresh gator meat, I keep replaying portions of Red's interview in my head. For the most part, his incredible life story is just weird enough to be believable. But certain bits, specifically about his service in Vietnam, are troubling. Is it really possible that Red, an orphan sword swallower who learned his trade from a gypsy hermaphrodite, joined the U.S. Navy at the age of sixteen and became a member of the SEALs, the most elite fighting force in the U.S. military?

I'm not so sure.

According to Red, he joined the Navy in mid-September of 1967, and after eight weeks of boot camp, he would have graduated by late '67 or early '68. If he went directly into the SEAL program, whose incredibly difficult training took about seven months in those days and had an 80% failure rate, he would have finished in the summer of 1968, not long after his 17th birthday. At the time, he would have been the youngest Navy SEAL in history, and to date only one other seventeen-year-old has completed the program, and that was back in 1982. If Red was deployed immediately after his SEAL training, that would put him in Vietnam no earlier than August of 1968. As Red tells it, he was ousted from the military and sent home in February of 1969. This suggests that everything he told me about his time in Vietnam—witnessing his SEAL lover's horrific death, his own battle-related injuries, and the Navy learning that he lied about his age and that he was gay—all happened in a span of five months. While I suppose this is technically possible, it seems unlikely given the timeline he provided. And why would the Navy threaten to incarcerate him for falsifying information and then offer him a secret deal? Wouldn't they simply discharge him, which was the common practice whenever gay or underage soldiers were discovered in their ranks? The more you pull at the threads of his story, the more it seems to unravel. And conveniently, his statements cannot be verified because the Navy allegedly made him sign a document stating that he "never existed in the service." I mean, how do you fact-check the story of a man who never existed? It's like trying to get fingerprints from a ghost.

While certain aspects of his story seem implausible,

I don't discount everything he told me about his time in Vietnam. It's entirely possible that he joined the Navy and served in the jungles of Southeast Asia. But was he only sixteen? Was he really a Navy SEAL? I may never know. But I'm certain of this: as Red recounted the horrors he experienced in Vietnam, his anguished, visceral reaction was an authentic display of grief. His pain was palpable. So when he tells me that he witnessed the gruesome death of someone he cared a great deal about, I believe him. It's the circumstances surrounding this tragic event that remain foggy. I toss back another Swamp Water, pay my tab, and hit the road, but not before Instagramming a photo of my half-empty plate with the caption *Just ate gator tail in Florida—SO AWESOME!!*

It's just after midnight. The fair is closing down for the season and the last straggle of teenagers is being ushered towards the exit. The air, even at this late hour, is sultry and thick, creating a fine mist that settles on the Tilt-A-Whirl, the funnel cake wagon, the ring toss and milk bottle pyramid games, and all the other mid-century relics bathed in the flickering neon of the nostalgia factory known as the carnival midway. Outside the World of Wonders tent, there's a flurry of activity as the sideshow performers begin dismantling the bally platform. Red is back in his dressing room, packing up his personal belongings and loading them into his van. I still have many questions about his time in the military, so I press him for additional information.

"Hey Red—where in Vietnam did you serve?"

"Can't say, can't say," he responds.

"Can you give me *any* details about your time there?" I ask, trying not to sound exasperated. "Like, when you got injured, did they take you to the Naval hospital in Danang?"

"I don't like talking about it," he says, removing the cigarette from his mouth before draining the last swig of Mountain Dew from a can on the table. "At the time, I didn't really understand our involvement in Vietnam. Very few people did." He pauses, taking a long drag off his cigarette. "After I got home from the war, I met one of the guys I served with, and he gave me my fatigues back along with some of my pins and medals. By then, I could care less about the military or the political government. And I didn't want nothin' from them. So when I was at Woodstock, I gave everything away. The only thing I kept was my Vietnam Service Ribbon and one of my SEAL pins off my dress uniform." His eyes flash, as though he's just remembered something. "Actually, I still have a fatigue jacket somewhere in my van. But the SEAL patch on it with the trident and the eagle is starting to fall apart. Those jackets are made out of heavy denim, but the patch is so old it feels like silk now. You can almost see right through it. I cut the sleeves off the jacket, but I still have it."

I watch Red as he neatly folds his Royal Stewart kilt and places his Scottish belts and sporrans into a canvas duffel bag. Then he reaches under the table, grabs the *Tidy Cat* bucket by its handle, and drags it to the center of the room. He points to a couple of wrenches on the ground. "Give me those, will ya?" I hand him the wrenches, watching as he pries off the *Tidy Cat* lid and drops them into the bucket, filled not with kitty litter and human excrement, but with hammers and screwdrivers and drill bits.

He doesn't shit in the bucket—he keeps his tools in it.

"Come on—I'll see if I can find that jacket for you," he

says. I follow Red outside the tent to his 1990 GMC van. When he swings opens the back doors, the first thing I see are two sets of glowing feline eyes staring back at us from inside the vehicle.

"You have cats," I say flatly.

"The black one's name is Wednesday," says Red. "I got her from someone who was fired for drinking too much on the job. The other one is a half-breed ragdoll. She was born with no iris in her left eye—it looks like a cloudy blue moonstone. I named her Precious."

Red rummages through several piles of clothes, but doesn't find his military jacket. He looks back at me. "I coulda swore it was here. Maybe it's in storage back in Philadelphia."

Of course there's no jacket I think to myself, because it probably never existed in the first place. Or so I thought. A few months from now, Red will message me on Facebook to tell me that although he still hasn't found the jacket, he came across a picture of him wearing it at a sideshow convention back in 2003. When I open the photo attachment, I see Red, probably twenty pounds lighter, hair pulled back into a short ponytail, wearing a camouflage fatigue jacket with the sleeves cut off just as he had described it. Though it's a low-resolution image and somewhat pixilated, I can see the Navy SEAL patch with the trident and eagle on it above the left breast pocket. The jacket, which would have been 34-years old when the photo was taken, appears to be in excellent condition. There's no way to prove that it's really the same jacket he wore in Vietnam. But then again, there's no way to prove that it's not.

Back in his dressing room, Red takes the last drag off his cigarette—and I mean *the last* drag because he smokes them all the way down to their nubs—and stubs it out. I watch him as he carefully peels away the paper from the filter, drops the filter into the empty Mountain Dew can, and pops the paper into his mouth. He chews the paper, or rather gums it for several seconds until it gets soft and pulpy, and then he swallows it. "It's an old habit I picked up in the Navy," Red says. "By eating the paper, it removes my scent from the filter. That way, the VC's dogs couldn't track us in the jungle. I've been doing it so long that it's automatic now, just like breathing." And this is why talking to Red can be so maddening: just when I am convinced that much of his story has been fabricated, he offers an amazingly detailed anecdote like this. Honestly, it's hard to know what to believe.

At the far end of the tent, Tessa Fontaine is gathering props from the main stage to be loaded onto the truck. This is her last night in the sideshow business as she prepares to return to her normal civilian life. Aside from eating fire and charming snakes, Tessa is a gifted writer working on a book about her experiences in the sideshow as the dis-sertation for her PhD in creative writing. I tell her that I'm here gathering material for a book of my own and that I'm frustrated, because I suspect Red hasn't been entirely honest with me. Since Tessa spent most of the year living and working with Red and the other performers in this challenging and intimate environment, she has a unique perspective. "The sideshow is many things, but above all else it's a performance—it's a meticulously crafted story that the performers tell the audience," she says. "And they've been telling these stories for so long that nobody even knows what's real and what's not. And what's more important is that nobody cares."

This strikes an uncomfortably familiar chord. In this age of pervasive social media, many of us embellish or flat-out fabricate certain details of our lives so we can present the best possible versions of ourselves to our peers. Every Facebook post seems to feature an amazing gourmet meal we've just eaten, an exotic vacation wonderland we've visited, the antics of our adorably cute cats (guilty!), or the near-daily creative, athletic, and academic triumphs of our above-average children. Every photo we share captures us at our best possible angle—no double chins on my timeline! Have you ever untagged a photo of yourself because you thought you looked fat or because you had a zit on your nose?

Because I have. Lots of times.

But these carefully curated, hyper-idealized versions of ourselves that we present on social media can't be accurate, because no one's life is an endless parade of ultra-hip cocktail parties, amazing beach sunsets, and incredible personal accomplishments, unless you're a Scientologist or a Kardashian. If I really wanted to present a truthful account of my life, I'd post frequent status updates about my chronic constipation, or how I ate Pepperidge Farm Goldfish for dinner *again*, or how I'm self-conscious about the coffee stains on my teeth, or how sometimes I feel so fat that I wouldn't mind looking like the "before" picture in a weight loss commercial. On social media, I'll never be completely honest about my life and neither will you, because we all want to write our own story in which we're the hero—and the hero doesn't need Metamucil and a bran muffin to have a healthy bowel movement in the morning. My point is that many of us tell half-truths about ourselves to further the narrative that we're exciting and attractive and successful. And now a new study suggests that fabricating details about our lives on social media sites like Facebook can actually lead to the creation of false memories. According to Sarah Knapton, Science Editor for *The Telegraph*, "one-fifth of young people between 18-24 admit their online profile bears little resemblance to reality, and that their recollection of past events has been distorted by their own fabrications." And this is exactly what sideshow performers like Red have been doing for more than 200 years: *they've been telling these stories for so long that nobody even knows what's real and what's not.*

It's after 2 AM, and I have an early flight just a few hours from now. I tell Red that I'm heading back to Orlando and thank him for being so generous with his time. As we walk through the big tent towards my car, I ask him what he thinks is the public's biggest misconception about the carnival business. "They think we're a bunch of liars and thieves," he says without missing a beat. "But there's liars and thieves in every industry." Red pulls a fresh pack of cigarettes from his pocket and peels off the cellophane wrapper. "Everyone calls us freaks, but I prefer to call us anomalies. Really, we're just people. We're just sentient beings. And there's nothing special or different about us. We have ups and downs like anybody." Red motions to Short E. Dangerously, the legless half-man daredevil who walks on his hands. "Some of the anomalies I've known — bearded ladies, fat people, tall people, midgets, whatever you want to call them — they weren't freaks. They had educations and families and hopes and dreams just like anybody. My mentor, Toni Del Rio, could read and write seven languages, and she was from a family of Basque gypsies who lived in the Pyrenees Mountains between

Spain and France. I knew an armless and legless woman who studied penmanship and calligraphy. And she had no fucking limbs!" Red points to a pretty young woman carrying stage props to the truck. "That girl there—she has a speech impediment. And she's the talker out in front of the bally! And the guy outside selling tickets is mentally challenged. You know, he's a little *slow*. And he's the one who counts the money! As long as you can do your job here, nobody cares."

Red pauses to light up a smoke. He takes a long drag and exhales. "I was on a carnival in '71 and there were a pair of identical twins working the Sky Wheel ride. And those twins remembered me. You know where I first met them? At the mentally retarded institution," he says. "They could set up and tear down that expensive piece of machinery just as good as anyone, and they were both mentally retarded. You see, it don't matter if you're a rich man, poor man, beggar man, thief, doctor, lawyer, or Indian chief. It don't matter if you're ugly or pretty or strong or weak or even physically deformed. None of that shit matters. Because in the end, we're all just a drop of goddamn sweat on God's nuts." Red looks out at the twinkling lights of the midway, his eyes filled with a fiery pride. "In its own way, this place is sacred. Because all of humanity is represented here. It's all here. All you have to do is open your fucking eyes. And open your mind."

Smoke Gets in Your Eyes

I am afraid of flying. Deathly, shit-my-pants afraid. Yet my job as a writer requires frequent travel to faraway places. Fortunately, I'm not irrational in my fear: if my transportation options are a ten-hour flight in business class with free slippers and hot meals, or three weeks on a steam freighter bunking with a wild-eyed brute who calls himself "the Senator" and wears a necklace of human ears, I'll gladly take the plane. But I'll probably have a massive anxiety attack and spend the duration of the flight locked in the bathroom praying for a quick and painless end.

It's not that I'm afraid of the *idea* of flying—I often fly in my dreams like Superman or Neo in *The Matrix* and it's exhilarating, and the notion of jetting off to an exotic vacation wonderland is certainly appealing. It's like how I'm not afraid of the idea of Goliath Bird-Eating Tarantulas, those giant South American spiders that devour entire birds. Though technically, tarantulas don't eat their prey because they don't have teeth to chew flesh. Rather, they inject their victims with highly acidic digestive juices that break down the soft tissues to near-liquid form allowing them to effectively drink their meals, or what I call *the most horrific smoothie ever*. And in a badass *Animal Planet* kind of way, this is a cool idea. But if I was trekking the Amazon and I stumbled upon a Goliath spider actually slurping the guts of a dead parrot, I would probably soil myself. This disparity between an idea and its reality is not uncommon: things like JELL-O shots, threesomes, casino buffets, and a Jared Leto-fronted emo band may seem appealing in theory, but in the harsh light of day they're pure hell. What frightens me about flying is the very real act of being strapped to a chair in an aluminum death tube, hurtling through the atmosphere seven miles above the earth at speeds exceeding 500 miles per hour.

Given the vagabond nature of my profession and the fact that I enjoy collecting a paycheck, my aerophobia presents something of a dilemma. But I get through it the way any rational person does: I drink alcohol and take prescription drugs. Preferably Xanax, though Ativan, Klonopin, or Valium will certainly do in a pinch. These psychoactive pharmaceuticals take the edge off so I'm not white-knuckling the armrest through the entire flight and having panic attacks over Newfoundland, which is about as fun as having a freakishly large spider inject your skull with digestive juice so it can suck your liquefied brains into its Krazy Straw blood-funnel mouth.

Today I'm on a crowded flight to Amsterdam, and thanks to some nasty turbulence over the North Sea I am already on my third Xanax and my fourth mini bottle of chardonnay. Ostensibly, I'm going there to write a story about the 16th annual Cannabis Cup competition where I'll sample the world's finest marijuana and hashish and cast a ballot for the best strains in various categories. You know, *for journalism*. But there's another reason I begged my editor for this assignment: I'm hoping to find a revolution.

As a kid who came of age during the socially conservative and culturally vapid Reagan Era, I feel like I missed out on the counterculture movements of the 1960s. The youth of that time—the Beats and later the hippies—believed they could change the world. Rallying behind important, noble causes like the fight for civil rights and ending the war in Vietnam, they questioned everything from the authority of the United States government and the morality of capitalism to the value of traditional gender roles and the existing social paradigm. My generation, on the other hand, focused its energy on going to the mall and watching Wang Chung videos on MTV. Our idea of rebelling against the status quo was turning up the collars on our polo shirts, and we didn't question anything, except "Who shot J.R." and "Where's the beef?"

Much of the activism and experimentation of the sixties was cultivated at the great festivals of the time. Events like Woodstock and the Human Be-In were more than parties and rock concerts: they were places for young people to congregate and exchange ideas about culture and politics, providing fertile ground for movements to take roots and grow. Maybe an event like Cannabis Cup could be my generation's Gathering of the Tribes, a flash point of culture and activism where young people rally behind the important causes of today like marriage equality, climate change, and ending the wars in Iraq and Afghanistan. And besides, the sixties just seemed like more fun. While the flower children of the 1960s got to experience the hedonistic pleasures of free love, my generation reached sexually maturity during the burgeoning AIDS epidemic when the specter of casual sex hung over our heads like a dark, deadly cloud. And instead of experimenting with psychedelic, consciousness-expanding drugs like LSD and being encouraged to "turn on, tune in, and drop out," we got the scourge of crack cocaine and Nancy Reagan telling us to "Just Say No."

But on this trip, I'm saying *hell yes*.

And I'm not the only one: there are at least thirty drunken hooligans on my flight who are also headed to the epic stoner event. The trip from San Francisco is not unlike a mile high frat party, complete with beer bongs, projectile vomiting, and some libidinous under-the-blanket activity from a young couple seated next to me. After the bathroom smoke detector has been set off for the third time in as many hours, the pilot reprimands us over the loudspeaker, threatening to land the plane in Greenland if it happens again. It reminds me of my drunken stepfather behind the wheel of our wood-paneled station wagon when I was a kid, scolding my stepbrothers and me in the back seat: "You girls quit squabblin'—you want me to pull this car over? Now somebody hand me a goddamn beer!"

Upon arriving in the Netherlands, our group is met in baggage claim by Tad, an impish man holding a cardboard sign that reads "Cannabis Cup Judges" in a childlike scrawl. We follow Tad to a waiting bus, and as we climb aboard, we are each given a package containing a gram of weed, a small brick of hash, some rolling papers, and several disposable lighters. Free at last from the tyranny of U.S. drug laws, my jubilant comrades light up their joints in unison, raising a smoky toast to freedom.

When I booked my trip to Amsterdam with 420 Tours, an herb-friendly agency specializing in Cannabis Cup travel packages, I knew it was important to forego the insulating comforts of a luxury hotel for accommodations more in tune with the spirit of the event. I wanted to live, eat, and sleep with these modern-day hippies and counterculture revelers. The unnervingly perky travel agent said she knew just the place.

The bus drops me at a youth hostel in a crumbling pre-WWII building just outside the city loop adjacent to the Amsterdam Zoo. At 8:30 AM, the lobby is bustling with festivalgoers, mostly 18- to 20-year-olds, and the marijuana fog is thick enough to obscure the "No Smoking" sign hung prominently on the door. When I check in at the reception desk, the clerk gives me my key and indicates that my roommates have already arrived. I follow the echo of bongo drums up a narrow winding staircase and down a darkened, dormitory-style hallway. Wet, hacking coughs emanate from behind each door, conjuring visions of a turn-of-the-century tuberculosis ward. My room, only slightly larger than a prison cell, is an odiferous potpourri of urine, vomit, and stale pot smoke. Six rusted Hitler-era bunks with oily mattresses line the windowless wall, and a broken chair leans precariously in one corner. There is no television, phone, or radio. And in the lone shower stall, a small dead rat lies slumped across the hair-matted drain. I am fairly certain this is how the Black Plague spread across Europe in the 14th century. I make a mental note to check myself for ticks.

My new roommates are seated on the floor, passing around a cigar-sized joint. Lori and Donna are ravers from Milwaukee who have come to "get their smoke on." They have matching magenta pigtails and Lori is wearing a baby pacifier around her neck. Donna takes a pull on the joint and passes it to Pete, a lanky Texan with an impressive white boy 'fro. Pete tells us he smuggled some mescaline into the country to sell at the festival and that the profits will go toward his college tuition. When I jokingly suggest that he's the only person in history to smuggle drugs *into* the Cannabis Cup, he flashes a goofy smile and utters a single word in a lazy Texas drawl: "Groovy."

I say goodbye to the glazed, giggling trio and make my way across town to the Arena Hotel, the official Cup headquarters and home to all daytime festival activities. Though the Cannabis Cup has become a lucrative enterprise in recent years, its origins are humble. The competition was founded in 1987 by Steven Hager, former editor of *High Times* magazine, as a tribute to the California marijuana harvest festivals of the '70s. Originally, there were just four entries and three judges: Hager, a photographer who documented the event, and the grow master known as Dr. Indoors. In 1992, the sixth festival had 50 judges and introduced the sterling silver Cannabis Cup trophy that would be awarded to all future winners. By 1995, the Cup had become a major international attraction featuring 1,500 judges and 30 competition entries, drawing thousands of visitors from around the world. The judging has been open to the public since 1993—for a price. This year, *High Times* sold 1,700 judges passes at $200 each. Worn around the neck like a rock tour laminate, a pass guarantees free samples of pot and hash, access to all parties, concerts, and events, and the right to vote in the competition. After picking up my judge's credentials, I wander into the exhibition hall containing rows of booths hawking every type of marijuana paraphernalia. There are exotic, hand-blown bongs shaped like swans and blowfish, along with vaporizers, grow lights, and a pungent array of cannabis food products, from old school pot brownies to a Bavarian hash strudel. Noticeably absent, however, are the social, political, and environmental groups now ubiquitous on the music festival circuit. If you want to buy a water pipe fashioned from a rabbit skull, Cannabis Cup is the place. But if you want to save the whales or learn about sustainable energy, you'll have better luck cruising the concourse at a Dave Matthews concert.

Downstairs in the main room, lecturers pontificate on cannabis-themed topics, including "Hidden Knowledge and the Conspiracy Against the Psychedelic Mind" and my personal favorite, "Jesus Was a Stoner." According to the speaker, the anointing oils used by Christ were cannabis extracts, and application to the skin could induce hallucinogenic visions. As I ponder this bold theory, a heavy-set woman in the audience begins speaking loudly to no one in particular. "Jesus was a hippie?" she bellows. "Don't surprise me none. He got the long hair and the beard. And what about those sandals?" Then she looks over at me and adds, "Personally, I always thought he looked like Dan Fogelberg."

The main event of the Cannabis Cup, of course, is the contest to determine the best strains of weed and hash. Although complimentary samples of some entries are available in the Judges' Lounge at the Arena Hotel, the majority of the strains in competition must be purchased at the coffee shops that sponsor them. These establishments, each with its own vibe, clientele, and theme, are government-regulated and allowed to sell small amounts of marijuana and hashish for personal use. The term *coffee shop* is somewhat deceiving, however, since most of these places don't actually sell coffee. And if you try to order an iced caramel macchiato at one of these shops, the proprietor will likely pitch you into a canal. This year, the Cannabis Cup voters must visit 28 of these coffee houses scattered across the greater metropolitan area—an extraordinary logistical feat to accomplish over the three-day judging period. The task must be attacked with military precision and a clear head, not exactly strengths of your typical stoner.

Due to the volume of entries and the limited voting period, most judges only sample about half of the entries before they cast their ballots. And the ones they do sample are usually from shops near their hotels in heavily trafficked tourist areas, putting the smaller out-of-the-way coffee shops at a disadvantage. It is also common for judges to grade the first type of weed they smoke on a given day more favorably than the third or fourth because the effect of the initial high is more pronounced. These inconsistencies ultimately skew the results of the competition—a fundamental flaw of the Cannabis Cup. In an effort to maintain the integrity of the contest, I vow to sample all the entries during the impossibly short judging period and grade them to the best of my ability.

This year's Cup includes 36 entries, so in order to sample them all, I'll need to smoke twelve types of weed and hash a day for three consecutive days, which means getting stoned every two hours for 72 straight hours. As I soon discover, it is impossible to evaluate different types of weed when they are smoked in rapid succession. After a few tokes, I cannot taste the difference between the strains. After five or six, my judgment becomes clouded, and after eight or nine, I find myself wandering the city aimlessly, frightened, and unable to find my hostel. Aside from the obvious pitfalls associated with this type of deranged marathon — namely, the mental and physical strain of flooding one's system with a high-grade narcotic — there is a twist to this story: I do not use marijuana. Sure, I smoked a little grass in college. And I hit the bong pretty hard during my bohemian phase in the early '90s, when I lived near the Haight-Ashbury and wrote terrible poetry about ex-girlfriends and pretty leaves I found in the yard. And yes, I might've smoked some reefer during my freewheeling rock and roll roadie days: let's just say that Celine Dion's touring crew can really huff some doobage. But over the years, the giddy euphoria and soulful introspection induced by pot gave way to debilitating paranoia, fueled by an insatiable desire for chili cheese fries and Pop Tarts smeared with chocolate-chip cookie dough. If I'm going to find my revolution and hit my deadline for this story, I'll need to set aside my issues and soldier on.

I begin the judging process at Barney's Breakfast Bar, a popular coffee shop that took home the Cannabis Cup in 2001 and 2002. I purchase a gram of Barney's current cannabis entry, a saucy full-bodied herb called *Laughing Buddha*, and a gram of its hash entry, *Helter Skelter Ice*. Sitting at a table, I roll a *Buddha* joint and pack a small ceramic pipe with the hash. For the competition, we've been instructed to grade the entries based on taste, smell, strength, and appearance. I light up and take a deep drag of the *Buddha*, which goes down smooth, with a pleasant fruity aftertaste. It's strong, but not too strong.

Then I fire up the hash.

The first hit practically knocks me out of my chair and the room starts to spin. I have never been good with hash. Exhausted from jetlag and now very stoned, I head back to the hostel for a good night's rest, stopping at several coffee shops on the way, choking down samples of *Kali Mist*, *Shiva*, and *Gandhi Ganja*.

I barely sleep the first night. The maddening, relentless clamor of bongos from a hippie drum circle reverberates down the hall, through the air ducts, and into my skull. I drift off shortly before sunrise but am soon awakened by a wretched cacophony of inhuman screeches. Monkey screeches, to be precise. Mescalin Pete looks over from his bunk. "It's the goddamn zoo," he says. "Those furry bitches shriek like hell when the sun comes up."

The breakfast provided by the hostel reads like the menu from a Dickens novel: dry toast, an assortment of odd-smelling cheeses, and a large tub of gray mush that could be fairly classified as "gruel." I share a table with a mother and her 20-year-old daughter who have traveled from Florida to experience the Cup. They are wearing matching t-shirts that read FUCK THE RULES in bold print. I ask the mother, an accountant for a public school district, if she feels any conflict about doing drugs with her daughter. She flashes a crooked, toothy smile and offers this bit of advice: "The family that bakes together stays together." Then she fires up a fatty, takes a drag, and passes it across the table to her kid. The woman reminds me of my own mom, a free-spirited hippie-cum-New Ager who smoked a lot of weed back in the eighties. But that's where the similarities end. Even though my mom smoked openly in our apartment, she never encouraged me to partake and we never got high together. In fact, I was mortified at her behavior and constantly afraid my friends would find out. When I was a freshman in high school, she even tried to grow her own marijuana. She bought a handful of seeds, rigged up a grow light in her closet, and waited for the buds to flower. But the plants — two sad little emaciated twigs — failed to produce much of anything at all, let alone anything that could get you high, save for a few brown, brittle leaves that had dropped onto the carpet.

I spend the next 12 hours zigzagging across the city, sampling the likes of *NYC Diesel, Cinderella 99, Thaitanic, White Widow,* and *Knockout.* Because there are so many entries and it's difficult to keep track of them all, many judges take meticulous notes which is a valuable resource when it comes time to vote. Some judges have gone high tech, organizing their comments on hand-held computers and documenting each entry with a digital photograph. I begin the competition jotting my observations in a tattered, college-ruled notebook. Less than 24 hours into the judging period, the notebook has been destroyed in a bong water mishap and I've resorted to scribbling remarks on cocktail napkins and falafel receipts. By the third day, I will be scrawling comments on my jeans with a Sharpie, including such cryptic missives as *White Smurf good, My tongue feels fuzzy,* and *I am the chicken man.*

To the sponsoring coffee shops, the Cannabis Cup is a serious event with far-reaching financial implications. The winner is assured a substantial boost in tourist business, along with bragging rights for the next year and the privilege to display the Cannabis Cup trophy. With so much at stake, many of the larger coffeehouses have taken to lobbying the judges (read: bribing) by offering free T-shirts, hats, lighters, pipes, and of course generous servings of their finest marijuana in hopes of swaying voters. Earlier today I asked a woman named Tammy, a dental hygienist from San Diego, which entry she liked the best. "I don't know," she replied, "but Barney's had the best free shit."

Whenever large sums of money are at stake, corruption tends to follow, and Cannabis Cup is no different. In 1999, the 12th Annual Cup was marred by a vote-rigging scandal that threatened the credibility of the event. It was the first time that the seed and hash competitions were judged by the coffee shop owners rather than the public, and it was determined that the winners of the top three hash prizes had manipulated their votes to benefit each other. The Greenhouse, a wealthy and powerful player in the Dutch cannabis scene, was stripped of its Hashish Cup, and the other shops lost their second and third place medals. "Want to win a Cup? All it takes is money," said Eric Bosman, manager of popular coffee shop De Dampkring, in an interview with *Cannabis Culture Magazine* just three months after the scandal. "We saw our competitors ripping our posters down and making nasty statements. It used to be a harvest festival, but now there's a bad spirit in the Cup and with it has come fraud, greed, and division."

That evening I head over to The Melkweg, a popular club that is home to all the late-night Cannabis Cup activities and concerts, including a performance later that night by George Clinton and P-Funk. Beyond the small clusters of festival attendees I've encountered in various coffee shops across the city, this is my first real exposure to the Cannabis Cup crowd en masse. As I survey the room, I note that they are predominantly white men, under 25, and almost exclusively American. I'd assumed that mostly hippie-types would be attending the Cup, and I prepared myself for an abundance of tie-dye, dreadlocks, and the overwhelming stink of patchouli. Instead, there is a distinct hip-hop and rap rock component to the Cannabis Cup crowd, its fashion and attitude (fashitude?) owing more to Eminem and Limp Bizkit than Wavy Gravy and the Grateful Dead. At one point, I am the only man at the bar *not* wearing an Adidas tracksuit. I've also seen a caustic, aggressive streak running through the crowd. In the short time since I arrived, I've already witnessed two fights and overheard slurs against Arabs, Asians, and gays—a far cry from Woodstock's "Three Days of Peace and Love" in the summer of 1969.

George Clinton delivers a predictably unintelligible set. In between songs, he urges the crowd to smoke pot but avoid hard drugs. "Smoke the dope but not the coke!" he yells repeatedly from the stage. Nine days later, Clinton will be arrested in Tallahassee, Florida and charged with a felony count of cocaine possession when police find a bag of crack and a glass pipe in his car.

After the show, I meet a 19-year-old kid from Montana who introduces himself as Keith, but says, "Everybody calls me Frog." Frog is wearing snowboarder goggles even though it's not snowing, and he has an odd verbal tic that causes him to make periodic grunting sounds at the end of his sentences. We talk about the competition entries, discussing our favorites and how we might vote. "I really liked *Kali Mist-Bubble Hash*," he tells me, "and those *Reefer's Peanut Butter Cups* were the bomb… GRRRNT." I am finished smoking pot for the day, but when Frog offers me a taste of a hard-to-find entry called *AK-47*, I acquiesce. In my estimation, there are four basic types of marijuana: those that make you giggly, sleepy, paranoid, and hungry. *AK-47* is the last variety, *big time*. I say goodbye to Frog shortly after 2 A.M., and that's when the deep, insatiable munchies kick in. I crave nachos. I yearn for Cinnabon. I need Cap'n Crunch. As I scour the city in search of an open restaurant or market, I encounter one shuttered shop after another. Amsterdam is not a 24-hour city like New York and most places close by 10 PM. I return to my hostel and make a beeline for the lone vending machine in the lobby, but the old-timey snack dispenser has a handwritten "out of order" sign taped over its coin slot. I can see the beautiful candy just out of reach behind the tempered glass, calling to me like a sugary siren in the night.

Must. Have. Candy.

I begin rocking the machine, attempting to jar a Snickers bar from its coiled grip, but it won't come loose. "Damn you!" I scream at the cruel metal beast, pounding my fists on the glass. The disinterested clerk at the reception desk looks up from her magazine, shrugs her shoulders, and goes back to reading. Dejected, I head up to bed.

As I lay in my bunk, kept awake by the familiar din of bongo drums, it occurs to me that after two full days at the Cannabis Cup the only example of activism I've witnessed is a guy in a Darth Vader mask handing out leaflets to decriminalize marijuana in America, and the extent of the political discourse I've encountered is a group of fantastically baked college guys chanting "President Bush Sucks Ass" and "Free Tommy Chong." The moment I drift off to sleep, I am jolted back to consciousness by a chorus of screeching chimpanzees and howler monkeys.

In the morning, I force down a bowl of lukewarm gruel and begin plotting my day. There are approximately 12 hours until the voting booths close and I still have 20 entries to sample. I frenetically toke my way through small amounts of *Hawaiian Snow, Yumbolt, Pot of Gold,*

Biddy Early, and *Euforia*. This pace, however, does not bode well for my mental and physical health: I haven't slept in 72 hours and am close to a meltdown. I decide to take a break and do some souvenir shopping in the touristy area between Prins Hendrikkade and Centraal Station. I buy several gifts for people back home, including two pairs of tiny Dutch wooden shoes because I think my cat will look funny in them.

With a dozen entries still to sample and only a few hours left to cast my votes, I need an aggressive strategy if I'm going to complete this psychotic marathon. So I head over to the Kashmir Lounge, an atmospheric, Indian-themed coffee shop with hookahs and pillows on the floor and park myself at a long table with all the remaining Cannabis Cup submissions fanned out before me. I lay out 10 overlapping rolling papers, licking the edges so they form a single massive sheet—a trick I learned from an Aerosmith roadie named Pot Party Paul—and roll a cigar-sized joint with bits from all the remaining strains: a dash of *White Rhino*, a pinch of *Killer Bud*, a sprinkle of *Arabica Hash*, and so on. In my sleep-deprived stupor, it makes perfect sense. I finish rolling the green monster and fire it up. As the tornado of smoke billows through my lungs, I brace myself for the inevitable psychedelic shock wave.

And I wait.

But nothing happens. With less than an hour until the polls close, I hop the next tram toward the Arena Hotel to cast my votes. As the train snakes its way through the city center, I feel my pulse quicken as a warm wave rushes through my veins. I'm somewhere between Vondelpark and Liedesplein when the drugs kick in. "Just be cool," I tell myself. But I am pretty fucking far from cool. And that's when the paranoia takes hold: it gathers deep in my belly, twisting up through my chest and around my heart, writhing upwards and wrapping its bony fingers around my throat, squeezing. "Good God," I say aloud. "Not here! Not now!" I nervously scan the crowded commuter car, searching the pale Dutch faces around me for any trace of disapproval or misguided rage. Would these herring-eaters come at me? An old woman near the back of the train glares at me, and for a brief second, our eyes meet.

And that's when things get freaky.

I watch in stunned horror as the skin on the woman's forehead and cheek begins to bubble and peel away like the rind of an orange, revealing the grotesque face of a tarantula-like creature underneath with bulbous bug-eyes and vicious, hairy fangs. Her geriatric body twists and contorts, bones bending at impossible angles, spine popping, flesh ripping, as eight bristly arachnid legs burst through her ribs and abdomen into the fading daylight, the final act of an enormous spider molting its withered human exoskeleton. And when the creature's hideous transformation is complete, it looks directly at me with those eight horrible eyes as if to say, *"Come closer so I can drink your delicious brains."* I frantically search my pockets for anything I can use as a weapon, but all I muster is a tube of lip balm and a fistful of rolling papers. Then I remember the shopping bag of Dutch souvenirs at my feet. I rifle through the trinkets, mentally cataloguing the wound-inflicting value of each item: *I'll bet this snow globe could do some damage.* Though I'm at a clear disadvantage in this fight—the influx of THC in my system has slowed my reflexes considerably—I'll go down with dignity, flinging windmill-shaped salt and pepper shakers and tiny wooden shoes at the head of my anthropodal attacker. Luckily, I'm able to hop off the train at the next stop and take to the streets before any blood is spilled. Although the details are hazy, I vaguely recall eating Austrian funnel cakes from a pastry wagon in Museum Square and urinating over the banks of the Amstel River in full view of a crowded tour boat.

I arrive at the Arena Hotel Judges' Lounge as the polls are closing, make my selections for the best overall cannabis, local hash, coffee shop, glass piece, and expo booth, and drop my votes into the secured ballot box. Mission complete, I return to the hostel and drift into a deep slumber. I sleep straight through the awards ceremony that night, through the bongo drums, and through the symphony of baboons at daybreak. I later learn that the Greenhouse's *Hawaiian Snow* entry took the top honors. I had voted for *Laughing Buddha*, which finished a distant third.

As I'm packing for the long trip home, it becomes apparent that the leftover mescaline my roommates took at breakfast has finally kicked in: Donna insists there is a dragon in the bathroom and Pete is stroking my hair, because "it feels like a pretty pony." I say my goodbyes to the tripping trio and head out.

On the ride to the airport, I replay the events of the week in my mind, trying to make sense of what I experienced at Cannabis Cup, or more to the point, what I hadn't experienced. And I think T.S. Eliot's line from his 1925 poem "The Hollow Men" comes closest to describing it:

> *Between the idea And the reality*
> *Between the motion And the action*
> *Falls the shadow*

As a kid, I'd been enamored with the idea of revolution—the idea that people can come together, triumph over the powers that be, and change the world for the better. But the reality of revolution is a different story, because affecting social and political change is hard work. It's hard canvassing a neighborhood, knocking on doors, and registering voters. It's hard organizing a protest and marching in the streets on a cold winter night. And it's hard dodging tear gas, rubber bullets, and the swinging batons of overzealous law enforcement. Like many well-intentioned people, I want to be part of a movement that changes the world. But my commitment to the cause, any cause, rarely goes beyond drinking ethically sourced, Fair Trade lattes and separating my recyclables on garbage day, because frankly, I'm too lazy to do the hard work. I want a better and more just society for all people, I just don't want to break a sweat trying to make it happen. Or as political activist and reggae legend Peter Tosh said so eloquently, "Everybody want to go to heaven, but nobody want to die."

And in revolutions, people *do* die: historically, they're bloody, brutal affairs that leave behind a trail of corpses. And the revolutions of the late-sixties were no exception. In 1966, Chairman Mao Zedong launched his own Cultural Revolution in China to purge the country of those who favored reform over ideological purity, and more than 1.5 million people were killed and millions more beaten, tortured, and imprisoned over the next decade. In 1968, the Soviet Union and its Warsaw Pact allies invaded Czechoslovakia to quell the liberal student uprising known as the Prague Spring, leaving more than 600 Czechs and Slovaks dead. And right here in America, Alameda County Sheriff's Deputies killed one student protestor and hospitalized 128 more in People's Park at the University of California Berkeley in 1969, and National Guardsmen opened fire on unarmed students at Kent State University killing four and wounding nine others in 1970, a stark reminder that our own counterculture revolution was not a bloodless endeavor. After this week, well, after the last thirty-five years, really, it's become clear that the revolution I've been searching for no longer exists, or maybe it only existed in the fever dreams of those who lived through the sixties and in the idealistic fantasies of those who came after. It turns out that Cannabis Cup is just a party with a $200 cover charge, and there's nothing wrong with that, but there's nothing really right with it either.

On the flight home, I find myself seated next to an earthy, impassioned young woman sporting purple dreadlocks and a tie-dyed *Morrison Hotel* T-shirt. We begin talking — or rather she begins talking — and in one breakneck diatribe, she tells me how much she enjoyed Cannabis Cup ("The herb was righteous") and details her unwavering support for Greenpeace, hemp, the rainforest, and Trey Anastasio of Phish. These may not be earth-shattering convictions, but at least she cares about *something*. And this gives me hope. After a few minutes of friendly banter, she asks if I want to split an 8-ball when we land because she knows a guy in Berkeley "with some kickin' powder." That's when I notice her severely dilated pupils and the nervous amphetamine twitch I used to see in rock and roll tour bus drivers in the days before mandatory drug testing. I politely decline her invitation and turn away, feigning exaggerated interest in the life-sized Yeti garden statue featured in *SkyMall* magazine. "Why yes, this enormous mythical snow ape *would* be perfect in my yard," I mutter to myself. When no one is looking, I wash down two Xanax with a tiny bottle of Chardonnay and stare out the window into the heavy clouds, waiting for the shadows to lift.

Fur Your Eyes Only

The bouncy house sits alone in the middle of the hotel ballroom with a sign over its narrow doorway that reads, "Must Remove Paws Before Entering." It's one of those big inflatable jumpers, the kind you might rent for a carnival fundraiser or a child's birthday party. But these aren't kids queuing up for a raucous tumble inside: they're adults, and they're dressed as wolves and otters and other woodland creatures. One by one, they enter the blow-up house, joyful, uninhibited, as they bounce around with childlike glee. I watch for a few minutes, but the novelty of seeing a grown man in a giraffe suit flail around like a spastic eight-year-old quickly wears thin. As I turn to leave, the purple raccoon next to me raises its fuzzy arm and points to a commotion brewing across the room. "Oh shit," he says through his muffled headpiece. "I think it's collapsing."

And that's when the screaming starts.

I push my way through the crowd towards the bouncy house, the hiss of escaping air growing louder as I approach. The once-rigid structure is rapidly deflating, its walls tilting, roof sagging, shriveling into itself like a post-coital phallus gone flaccid. Nervous, excited chatter sweeps through the crowd: from what I gather, one of the jumpers got knocked unconscious and is trapped inside. I step closer, and as I peer into the house through its slumping mesh window, I see the motionless figure of a blue fox—or maybe a coyote—lying prostrate across the spongy vinyl floor. A beefy staff member dressed in cargo shorts with bunny ears and a clip-on cottontail pushes past me, yelling for everyone to stand back. He drops to his knees, reaches into the bouncy house through its wilting, lopsided doorway, grabs the creature by its fuzzy turquoise ankles, and drags its limp body to safety. After a few tense moments, the fox regains consciousness and the crowd cheers. The guy next to me removes the head of his chipmunk suit and says loudly to no one in particular, "So. Fucking. AWESOME." This surreal scene takes place at Furry Weekend Atlanta, a four-day convention celebrating the furry fandom—or simply *the fandom*, as they call it—and I've come here to explore this odd and misunderstood subculture.

The furry fandom is a sub-genre of science fiction and fantasy, similar to Trekkies or fans of the Harry Potter franchise, but with a few key differences that I'll get to later. So what exactly is a furry? In the simplest terms, a furry is someone who enjoys watching, reading about, and even dressing like anthropomorphic characters—that is, animals who walk upright and behave like humans: think Bugs Bunny, Mickey Mouse, the Care Bears, or Rocket Raccoon from *Guardians of the Galaxy*. But there's more to it than that. "The furry fandom is about an aesthetic, really," says Kyell Gold, an award-winning author of erotic furry literature. "There are people who wear costumes and people who don't; people who like cartoony animals and people who like realistic animals; there are people who wear tails and collars in public and people who don't; there are people who are openly sexual and people who are privately sexual and people who aren't sexual at all; there are people who perform and people who create and people who just like to read and watch. But the one thing that most everyone in the fandom agrees on is that we like the *idea* of these fuzzy animal-people."

While the furry fandom largely exists in the digital realm where its members interact using online forums, virtual environments like Second Life, and furry-specific social networks like FurNation and Furtopia, it's the furry conventions of the natural realm that really brings the community together. Each furry convention has its own theme—this year, ours is *Moulin Rouge*—and most offer a full program of events, including a fursuit parade and dance contest, a marketplace of Furry-related products, 24-hour video and tabletop gaming rooms, furry-themed classes and panels, an area where you can commission and purchase furry artwork, furry speed dating, stand-up comedy, and more.

At present, there are more than 50 furry conventions worldwide, many of them in exotic places like Brazil, Finland, South Africa, New Zealand, and Wichita. And the number of people who attend these conventions each year is surging. "The furry fandom has benefited from an accelerating intersection of the geeky and the mainstream," says Alex Osaki, writer and author of The Furry Survey. "Five years ago, no one could have predicted that HBO's epic fantasy series *Game of Thrones* would successfully blend dragons and incest, that *My Little Pony* "Bronies" would be popular enough to warrant their own convention, or that the television adaptation of an indie comic like *The Walking Dead*—a series about flesh-eating zombies— would become one of the biggest shows on TV, smashing the coveted 18-49 demographic and averaging two million more viewers than *Sunday Night Football*."

As Osaki suggests, much of the current cultural landscape is dominated by geek culture: Superhero movies based on comic books like *Batman*, *Iron Man*, and *The Avengers* consistently rule the box office, *Th e Bi g Bang Theory*, a sitcom about four nerdy scientists, is the most-watched TV show in America, tech entrepreneurs like Mark Zuckerberg of Facebook and Sergey Brin of Google have become global celebrities—and more baffling— they've made it cool to be a computer programmer for the first time since NEVER, and astrophysicist Neil deGrasse Tyson, the best-selling author who revived Carl Sagan's *Cosmos: A Spacetime Odyssey* for network television and hosts his own late-night talk show on the National Geographic Channel, has 3.68 million Twitter followers and gets a rock star's reception wherever he goes. Right now, geek is chic and the furry business is booming.

At 10 AM on my first full day at the convention, the lobby of the Sheraton Atlanta Hotel is buzzing with activity that might seem strange anywhere else but is perfectly normal here. Though I haven't even had breakfast yet, I've already seen a moose in assless chaps leaning against the valet podium checking his Twitter feed and two chubby teens dressed as cats rolling on the floor, purring, and batting a toy mouse. I wander through the crowded lobby past an eagle, a llama, and Sonic the Hedgehog who is wearing a Hello Kitty backpack and sipping a latte, to the registration table to pick up my convention packet and ID badge. Most attendees use their furry name on their badge instead of their real name—mine says *Rodger Rabbit* because Bugs Bunny was my favorite cartoon character as a kid.

Not everyone at the convention has a furry persona, or *fursona* in fandom lingo, but the vast majority do. Some people choose their favorite animal as their fursona, while others choose an animal with personality or behavioral traits that are similar to their own. "Animals in classic literature and mythology like Aesop and Reynard have a particular set of humanlike traits that are unique to them. It's the same with furries," says Kyell Gold. "For example, some people are big cats that are more solitary and physically imposing. Some people are wolves, who are more social and enjoy traveling in a pack. I'm a fox. And foxes tend to be clever, witty, and not physically gifted, with a tendency toward vanity, though I try not to let that one out."

Most people have a single fursona that they use in the fandom—*once a lemur, always a lemur*—but some have fursonas that evolve over time, and some have multiple fursonas that they change based on their mood. "For most of us, our furry persona is an idealized version of our self," says Kyell Gold. "A lot of people select their personas based on what they aspire to be, and they actually begin to take on the characteristics of the animal they choose. I've heard people say, *I was going to do that, but it's not very wolf-like. So I decided not to do it.*"

Many furries think you can make accurate predictions about a person based on the animal they've chosen. So your fursona not only represents how you see yourself, but it's also a way for others to easily identify you. "It's a kind of tribal mark," adds Kyell Gold. "It's a way to say *I'm part of your group.*"

I'd assumed that most attendees would be wearing elaborate full-body costumes known as fursuits, similar to those worn by Disney theme park characters and sports team mascots. Instead, the majority of people are wearing simple, economical costumes, like a set of fuzzy ears with a dog collar and a clip-on tail. Only around fifteen percent of attendees are wearing full fursuits, in part because they're expensive: a quality ferret suit can set you back more than $1000.

Because it's difficult to move around in the full costume, most fursuiters have handlers to help them navigate stairs, escalators, and other challenging terrain. "At conventions, the fursuiters are quite visible, and there is a certain respect for them because the suits are incredibly challenging to wear and maintain," says Alex Osaki. "Many people make their own fursuits by hand. And like any similar exhibition—classic cars, say—there's a certain appreciation for those who work many hours to produce something."

In many ways, the tradition of constructing your own fursuit is emblematic of the fandom's do-it-yourself culture, not unlike the DIY ethos of the punk rock community. According to Alex Osaki's extensive, multi-year demographic furry survey, 96% of people in the fandom are creatively involved in some way, with the furry aesthetic driving their music, their storytelling, what they draw, or what they talk about. Unlike most fandoms that are primarily consumers of preexisting content, the furries actually create the things they celebrate. For example, if you're a fan of *Star Trek*, it's the TV shows and movies that are of primary interest you. If you're a fan of Harry Potter, it's the books and movies. If you're into anime, you might be interested in a particular artist or drawing style. "In most fandoms, there's a baseline of content that you can be familiarized with," says Osaki. "But in the furry fandom, there is no shared cultural experience because there is no canon of work." Besides a few eclectic touchpoints like Larry Nivens' *Ringworld*, Richard Adams' *Watership Down*, and certain Disney films, there is no source material from which to draw. "So if you are interested in a particular interaction of characters or a particular story, you have to create it yourself," says Osaki. "The shared experience, then, is not a particular film series or a particular author, or analyzing who would win in a fight between Wolverine and Superman—it's this overarching creativity." Osaki pauses, then adds, "I'm not aware of any other subculture that is so singularly focused on self-expression, and I suspect that it draws people who are looking to indulge that without being judged."

Arguably, the most revered people in the fandom, above even the fursuiters, are the artists who create the furry-themed drawings, paintings, and illustrations that are so integral to the community. Each convention has a specially designated area called Artists Alley, where 50-100 illustrators offer their creative services on a commission basis. The Artists Alley at Furry Weekend Atlanta has rows upon rows of artists seated at long tables, each with his or her portfolio displayed so you can view samples of their work. The idea is that attendees can find artists whose style they like and commission them to create an illustration of their choosing. For example, you might commission an artist to illustrate your furry fox avatar wearing medieval armor and fighting a dragon. For many furries, commissioning a piece of artwork is more than just a souvenir of their weekend at the convention: it is a way to see the animal version of themselves brought to life. "You get to see your furry persona fully realized," one artist tells me. "At first, it's something that only exists in your imagination, and then with our help, it appears on the page."

Back in the conference center, I stop to watch a green cheetah breakdancing to Nicki Minaj's "Starships" while a blue penguin and a trio of enthusiastic Klingons cheers him on. All around, there are groups of young people—some costumed and some not—sitting on the floor in small clusters, talking about comics and movies and music. They're laughing, playing games, and flirting with each other. The relaxed social vibe reminds me of a college dorm, and for good reason: the median age of a furry is 22, and nearly a third of the fandom is under the age of 19. However, there are plenty of furries who skew older, known within the community as *greymuzzles*. It's also worth noting that furries are predominantly white and predominantly male, and in the 2008 Furry Survey, only 32% identified as heterosexual, while nearly 60% identified as bisexual or homosexual. "I think in many ways it's a safe place for people to explore their sexuality," says Osaki. "Especially for things that are a little bit fringe."

I continue through the conference center past two heavyset geeks with unruly Hobbit beards, their skin stained pallid by the light of a computer monitor. One of them is dressed as a wizard, and they're having a spirited conversation about a Dungeons & Dragons-like role-playing game. "Oh yeah? Well *we* have arrows with silver tips that can kill werewolves," the first guy says.

"No DUH," the second guy says. "*All* goblins have silver arrows."

These young men are the purest embodiment of the geek archetype that I've seen in a long time, and coming from a guy who once spent his entire Spring Break making an Imperial TIE Fighter out of Legos *and* a papier-mâché wampa, that's really saying something. Though I don't know much about the two men, except that they play fantasy games involving dragons, elves, and magic, I'd be willing to bet that they didn't run with the popular kids in high school and that they have more than a cursory understanding of what it's like to be bullied. But here, among all the sublime geekery and brightly-colored fur, they have found acceptance. "Can you name a single place where literally nobody will give you shit about being unattractive? Or uncool? Or gay? Or transgendered? Or autistic?" says Osaki. "And no, the answer is not high school. It's the furry fandom."

This inclusiveness has always been a core component of the furry community. In its early days, many of the strongest personalities were gay couples, which made the fandom attractive to people of all sexual orientations. "I see it as a safe passage thing," says Kyell Gold. "Early on, they made it unequivocally clear that sexual orientation makes no difference in this fandom. And that attracts all sorts of people who feel as though they've been marginalized by their communities."

Additionally, the lack of source material makes it easy for new people to come to the fandom. "If you go to a Trekkie convention and you haven't watched any *Star*

Trek, eventually you're going to feel like you're missing something and you won't have much to talk about," says Kyell Gold. "People will come up to you and say, *Which series do you like?* And you won't have an answer. But you can go to a furry convention basically cold. It's very easy to be a casual fan. I go to the conventions and hang out just because they're fun."

And the fandom's inclusiveness seemingly extends to everyone, regardless of how or why they've been marginalized by the rest of society. As I'm walking through the conference center to attend a panel called "Chainmail for Beginners," I get a Facebook message from Melissa, an old friend from college. She knows I'm at the convention, and she proceeds to tell me about her girlfriend's twenty-year-old son who is a furry and has high-functioning autism. In the fandom he goes by the name Kumori and identifies with the wolf spirit. Kumori's story is both fascinating and heartbreaking: he's a good kid who is intelligent and kind, but he's also a little shy and socially awkward. Because of his autism, he'd always been a little different from the other kids, and that made him a target of cruel jokes and bullying. "When I was growing up, back in elementary school, I was always seen as the odd one. And no one really wanted to talk to me," says Kumori. "But the furry fandom has made me more outgoing. And I think that's had an impact on my life."

As a kid, Kumori always felt a special kinship to animals. He loved going to zoos and animal parks, and particularly enjoyed animated Disney movies with anthropomorphic characters like *The Fox and the Hound* and *The Lion King*. When he was a teenager, after being bullied for years, Kumori started having recurring dreams about wolves. "The dreams were usually about me, as a person, transforming into a wolf. And not a regular wolf, but one that could walk on two legs and talk like a human." In the dreams, Kumori's transformation often took place in a public area in full view of others. "Sometimes I'd transform into the wolf in front of my school where all my classmates could see me," says Kumori. "Some of the people were afraid of me, and some were just staring at me in disbelief." As the wolf, Kumori projected strength, and the classmates who had rejected him or treated him cruelly now cowered in fear. "I had the dreams because my brain was trying to tell me something," says Kumori. "It was a side-effect of being bullied for years. As the wolf, I was finally able to get revenge—not with violence, but with a show of strength. I was able to say, once and for all, that I'm not willing to take it any more."

Amazingly, not long after Kumori started having the wolf dreams, the bullying came to a stop. When he graduated from high school, he told some friends about the recurring dreams and they directed him to the furry Wikipedia page. It was the first time he'd heard of the fandom. "When I started reading about the furry community, I immediately knew it was the place for me. It was almost instantaneous," says Kumori. He soon purchased a partial fursuit consisting of a clip-on tail and a hat with animal ears, and he describes the first time he wore the costume with a certain confidence and warmth: "It just felt *right*, if you know what I mean."

As Kumori delved further into the online community, he began making friends and building relationships with other people in the fandom. Today, the furry community is a big part of his social life and his identity. "I think the furry community has been incredibly supportive of his quirkiness as a high-functioning autistic person," says my friend Melissa. "For a kid who had a tough time growing up, it's been a really positive thing for him."

When I look around the crowded conference center, what I see is largely a gathering of social outsiders. One young woman I speak to who is wearing fuzzy tiger ears with painted-on whiskers and a sharply-kinked tail, refers to the furry subculture as "the fandom of misfit toys," which seems apropos. "You're dealing with decent people, many of whom feel they aren't respected or have been somewhat ostracized by their communities," says Alex Osaki. And some of them, like Kumori, surely experienced cruelties because they were just a little different from their peers.

Near the back of the room, I notice a chubby kid with freckles and a bad haircut wearing a vintage R2-D2 t-shirt that's at least a size too small, his full round belly stretching the thin material to its breaking point. As I watch him flit through the crowd, an oddly familiar sensation starts to bubble deep in the pit of my stomach. At first, I can't quite figure out what it is that I'm feeling, or more accurately, what it is that I'm remembering. And then it hits me: *I was just like these kids.*

* * *

When I grew up in the late seventies and early eighties, it was during the rise and eventual peak of the *Star Wars* cultural phenomenon, and I was a devoted fan of the science fiction film series. I carried a Darth Vader lunchbox to school, I trick-or-treated as both Luke Skywalker *and*

Boba Fett, I collected nearly every action figure and toy related to the films, and I would have cheerily renounced my standing in the Catholic Church to become a disciple of the Force. There were no fan conventions in those days and this predated the internet, so you had to get creative if you wanted to meet other kids who shared your interests. Instead of road tripping to Comic-Con like the geeks of today, we'd dress up as our favorite sci-fi characters and go see the latest genre movies on opening night — movies like *Raiders of the Lost Ark, Star Trek II: Wrath of Khan,* and *The Road Warrior.* In retrospect, those impromptu gatherings outside the cineplex were *our* fan conventions.

On May 25, 1983 — dressed as Han Solo — I camped out for sixteen hours with hundreds of other pale chubby virgin nerds to see *Return of the Jedi,* the final film of the initial *Star Wars* trilogy. The three-year wait between *The Empire Strikes Back* and *Jedi* had been excruciating for this wookie-loving 14-year-old, so when I finally got to my seat and the theater lights dimmed, I was giddy with anticipation. At the film's 17-minute mark, I had what can only be described as a sexual epiphany: that's when Princess Leia appeared onscreen as Jabba the Hutt's prisoner wearing an erotic metal bikini. By today's standards, Leia's *Jedi* slave outfit was tame. But in 1983, to an auditorium of undersexed, horned-up teens, it was scandalous and titillating. I remember staring up at the screen, eyes wide, pulse racing, as three single words escaped my quivering lips: *"Oh. My. God."* But I wasn't the only one entranced by Leia and her seductive attire, evidenced by the collective groans of a hive mind nerdgasm echoing in the darkness around me. Less than 24 hours later, I would masturbate in an old woman's yard.

These events are not unrelated.

The old woman, Mrs. Heidelberg, was a stern, stout widow in her seventies who lived in a regal estate on the wealthy island town of Belvedere perched at the edge of the San Francisco Bay. Once a week I'd go to her house and water the plants on the grounds of her elaborately terraced property, admiring her panoramic view of the Golden Gate Bridge. She would pay me seven dollars for my work, which was enough to rent three movies at our neighborhood video store. I used my wages to see every French New Wave film in their collection and had recently segued into Italian Neo-realism and the seminal works of Fellini.

I was a very lonely teenager.

The *incident* occurred over Memorial Day Weekend when Mrs. Heidelberg was away visiting her ailing sister. In her absence, she asked me to collect the mail and leave it in a basket on the porch. As I walked the stack of letters, catalogs, and junk mail up the long private drive to the house, I noticed the glossy new issue of *People* magazine buried in the pile. Carrie Fisher was on the cover, dressed as Princess Leia in the now-iconic metal bikini. And based on the sudden tightening of my trousers, the white-hot passions that had burned so brightly just hours earlier in that darkened theater still smoldered in my fleshy loins. Finally, overcome by the bursting deluge of adolescent hormones, I ducked behind a hedge in Mrs. Heidelberg's yard and took matters into my own hands, as it were.

It wasn't the first time I'd become aroused by a scantily clad woman in a movie or TV show. There was Phoebe Cates undoing her red bikini top and baring her breasts in *Fast Times at Ridgemont High*. There was Anita Ekberg frolicking in the Trevi Fountain in *La Dolce Vita*. And there was Randi Oakes, best known as Officer Bonnie Clark on *CHiPs*, all wet and nipply in the *Battle of the Network Stars* dunk tank. But Princess Leia in that outfit *moved* me. I mean, Phoebe Cates was hot, but she never compelled me to pleasure myself in shrubbery.

It's not that I was a pervert—not *totally*. It's just that sexuality was very confusing for me at that age. Most kids learned about sex from an older sibling or from their friends, but that wasn't an option for me: I was an only child and I was fantastically unpopular. And this was more than a decade before every curious, horny teenager would have a pipeline of free unlimited hardcore pornography flowing directly into his or her bedroom on the internet, which probably isn't the healthiest way to learn about sex, but at least it's *something*. Instead, I had to rely on other sources for my education, like the *Cosmo* magazines I'd swipe from our neighbor's mailbox, or sneaking downstairs late at night to watch scrambled R-Rated movies on Cinemax: *I think I see some pubic hair! Oh wait—it's just Gabe Kaplan's neck beard.*

* * *

"You know how the Hulk would grow extremely large when he got angry because of his exposure to gamma radiation?" the wiry moderator asks. "It's kind of like that, but if *only* his dick got big." This statement occurred in the first three minutes of a seminar called "Hyper-Anatomy 101," an introduction to the erotic art genre featuring illustrations of normal-sized furry characters that have enormous genitals. And when I say "enormous," I don't mean *12-inch pornstar big*—I mean an anthropomorphic lion with a cock the size of a Volkswagen, or a penguin with testicles the size of hot air balloons.

Though there are other more family-friendly workshops on the schedule like "Fursuit Construction" and "Make a Furry Tail Keychain," many of the seminars at Furry Weekend Atlanta—and most furry conventions, for that matter—are of a sexual nature. Besides the hyper-anatomy class, they offer an introduction to bondage and discipline seminar called "BDSM 101" and "A Beginners Guide to Navigating Kink," among others. In fact, you don't have to spend long exploring any part of the furry fandom before you'll come across sexually graphic material. For some people, both inside and outside the furry community, the dichotomy between the fandom's innocent reverence for the beloved cartoons, comics, and Disney characters of its collective childhood and the prevalence of furry-themed pornographic material associated with the fandom is difficult to reconcile.

This is where things get tricky.

If you're trying to describe the furry fandom in a manner that is fair, you shouldn't dwell on the sexual aspect of the community because it's just one small slice of a much larger pie. At the same time, it's impossible to create an accurate depiction of the furry fandom without acknowledging the enormous fuzzy elephant in the room. "You have to address the sexual aspect of the fandom because it exists," says Kyell Gold. "And to say that it doesn't exist is just as dishonest as saying that the subculture is *only* about sex."

At the conventions, perhaps no place has more sexually explicit material on display than Artists Alley. When you look through many of the artists' portfolios, the vast majority of the illustrations are sexual in nature. One portfolio I flip through contains only images of anthropomorphic wolves with engorged human cocks. Another portfolio contains only images of a sexy female fox dressed in a Girl Scout uniform, striking various erotic poses. One artist tells me that 80-90% of the illustrations he's commissioned to draw are sexual in nature. "The point of our jobs is to make your fantasies come true on the page. It's what people want and they're willing to pay for it," he says with a shrug.

Down the hall in the furry marketplace known as the Dealers Den, you'll find a number of authors hawking their furry-themed books, most of which are filled with sexually graphic material. And if you go online and Google "furry," it won't take you long to find an endless trove of hardcore anthropomorphic porn. "The fandom is about sex to the extent that *people* are about sex. Which is to say, quite a lot," says Kyell Gold. "In the mainstream, sex tends to be tucked into dark corners or sublimated into acceptable venues. For example, the reason certain actors are popular isn't *only* because of their dramatic stagecraft, but because they look good in a bikini or in a tight muscle shirt. The fandom is about the same thing; it's just more honest about it."

Additionally, there is a very small percentage of furries—less than 1%, according to the data—who like to engage in sexual activities with other furries while dressed in their fursuit costumes. "You can argue that there is a fetish component to the fandom because there are certainly people who have it as a fetish, but there also people who do not," says Kyell Gold. "And your participation in the fandom doesn't rest on that distinction at all."

Many people in the fandom complain that the media unfairly focuses on this rare fetish aspect of the community, which hurts the public image of the group. And they're right. I'd never heard of the furry fandom until six weeks before the convention, when I happened to see an old episode of *CSI: Crime Scene Investigation* called "Fur and Loathing." It was about a murder that takes place in a strange community of people called furries who have orgies dressed in plush, full-body animal costumes. *This is some freaky shit,* I thought to myself. Unfortunately, many people learn of the fandom as I did: from seeing unfair portrayals of it on popular TV shows like *30 Rock, ER,* and *Entourage,* or from reading poorly-researched stories about it in newspapers and high-profile magazines like *Vanity Fair.* "I know there are *some* people who have sex in fursuits. The problem is that it's often depicted as the main reason for joining the fandom, and it's just not true," says a furry woman who goes by the name Talarus. "People have sex dressed as schoolgirls, French maids, flight attendants, nurses, clowns, and other things. But those outfits don't elicit the same negative reactions that fursuits do, mostly because of the way the media has portrayed us." She adds, "I wear a fursuit to entertain children, to promote businesses, and to fundraise for charities. I work hard to cultivate a positive image for the fandom, and it's difficult because there's always some idiot who says *Hey, I saw you guys on CSI.* It makes it hard to be treated as a professional. So yes, for many furries, this is a controversial subject."

One furry, who asked to remain anonymous, adds, "A

lot of us don't want the fandom being presented as *People Who Have Sex in Animal Costumes*. It's like how you wouldn't want all of humanity being presented as *People Who Have Spanking Fetishes*. It's upsetting that we have to think this way, because it isolates the people here who do enjoy those things. And I feel like, as a fandom, we should accept all of us, just like we want non-furs to accept us."

Whether it's because of the "fursuit orgy" trope so often perpetuated by the media, or the proliferation of sexually explicit material attributed to the subculture, the idea that the fandom is the enterprise of perverts and weirdos will persist. But there's a certain hypocrisy that comes with taking a moral position like this—just have a look at the burgeoning genre of erotic furry literature. Why is a novel about a randy anthropomorphic fox who wants to fuck a sexy penguin considered more deviant or offensive than something like *New York Times* bestseller *Fifty Shades of Grey*, a book that spawned the genre known as "mommy porn" and single-handedly introduced bondage, handcuffs, and spanking into the consciousness of bored housewives everywhere? I've seen *Grey* fans on airplanes, on trains, and in cafes reading their dog-eared copies of the book, barely able to contain their arousal as they follow the masochistic exploits of Christian Grey, fantasizing about the snap of his riding crop across young Anastasia Steele's taut, naked bum. Why is the furry book considered fringe pornography while the other is a heralded global phenomenon spawning numerous sequels, feature films, and a tidal wave of merchandising opportunities? Perhaps on some level it has to do with the fandom's large and well-documented lesbian, gay, bisexual, and transgender population that forms the core of its constituency.

"Portraying something that is largely non-heterosexual as being hedonistic and sex-positive is itself a highly subversive act," says Alex Osaki. "On its own, the idea of having sex dressed in a purple furry animal suit is just sort of ridiculous. But people having *gay* sex—that's something very real that you have to acknowledge, whether you want to or not."

While I'm researching the furry community online, I meet a greymuzzle who goes by the name Old Cow, and the way he describes his sexual journey to the fandom is both eye-opening and heart-wrenching. "When I was a kid, I discovered that certain animal features were very pretty to look at, much the way people find wolves or eagles beautiful in a way that's hard to define," he says. "As a teenager, I was exposed to media that portrayed female humanoids with animal-like traits, including certain mutants in the Marvel Universe like Wolfsbane and Feral, Disney's *Robin Hood*, and certain animal-people in the *Ninja High School* comic book series. And I thought they were pretty darn cute. Like *sexy cute*," he says bluntly and with no trace of shame. "I had a lot of problems in my home life, but I was able to lose myself in an imaginary world where human problems were left behind—a world where it didn't matter what people looked like on the outside, and where everyone saw each other as beautiful," he says. "These were fantasies, of course, because we don't live in that world. But at that age, it was my only escape." He pauses for a long moment as if searching for the right words, his silence hanging heavy in the air. "What really appeals to me is the depiction of romance between those who are somehow different from each other, and how those partners learn to accept those differences," he says.

"As a lonely little kid, it was just easier to imagine a relationship with an anthropomorphic fox than with the cute girl who lived next door. Looking back, I realize it was about replacing the complexity of human emotions with the simple motivations of the animal kingdom."

This greymuzzle, like so many of us when we were young, was just a scared and confused kid trying to navigate the labyrinthine world of love and lust and human connection. The fact is, sexuality exists in the furry community because it exists everywhere. And yes, some people in the fandom may be aroused by the image of a seductive lioness in thigh high stockings and garters, and some people outside the community will think this is shocking. But before you pass judgment on the fandom, consider the following: though a guy in a squirrel suit with a hankering for cartoon animal porn might *seem* like a pervert, I'll bet he never sexually violated a hydrangea in a senior citizen's yard. *Ahem.*

In my last conversation with Kumori, I asked him why he so closely identifies with the spirit of the wolf, and his answer was profound in its basic truthfulness and universality. "Wolves are pack animals," he said. "And I feel that I work better in a group than by myself." This sentiment is not only at the heart of the furry fandom, but ironically it's the very thing that makes us human: on some primal level, don't we all want to be part of a pack that accepts us as we are?

It's the last night of the convention and I'm watching the fursuit dance contest, one of the most beloved events in all the fandom. The raucous, ebullient crowd is cheering for a 300-pound black and white wolf furry named Oreo who is shaking his considerable booty to a techno beat, and his freeform goofiness is contagious. After the winner of the contest is announced, the ballroom becomes an impromptu dance club for everyone in attendance.

Everyone but me.

I used to love dancing when I was younger, but over the years something inside me changed: I started over-thinking everything, including my physical appearance and how others perceived me. Eventually, I became so self-conscious that I stopped dancing altogether. But here in this ballroom, *in this moment*, as I watch these people in their ridiculous fuzzy animal costumes shaking and shim-mying to the beat of this terrible music, it becomes clear that they're radiating what can only be described as pure and unbridled joy. And it's this realization that starts to move me in a deeply unexpected way. Suddenly, I'm feel-ing things I haven't felt in years, decades even: freedom, a lack of inhibition, and yes, even joy. So I push my way through the crowd to the center of the ballroom, I untuck my shirt and roll up my sleeves, and I start dancing. I just let it all go, and I dance. And tonight, I don't care what anyone thinks, because it just feels *right*, if you know what I mean.

Apokalypse Nein!

A Spiritual Journey in Three Acts

Act I:

THE TIME TRAVELING MONK

I'm so fucked. And not because the world will come to a fiery, apocalyptic end just four days from now on December 21, 2012. You know, because of the ancient prophecies and vast government conspiracies and all. No, I'm fucked because my cruise ship is scheduled to sail from Galveston in less than two hours and I'm nowhere near the terminal. In fact, I'm clear on the other side of the island, looking for a gift to buy a Mayan shaman. But what do you get a jungle-dwelling spirit man you've never met? More specifically, what do you get him from an unremarkable East Texas Walgreens? Would he enjoy a three-pack of diabetic compression socks? How about a bottle of mustache dye? Or maybe a plastic reindeer that poops candy? *I'm so totally fucked*. And I can't just blow it off, because *not* bringing a gift is considered a sign of disrespect. And the last thing I want to do is piss off a Mayan witch doctor, because we all know how *that* horror movie ends.

My wife suggests we get him a candle, which is a much better oblation for a holy man than the comically oversized calculator I was about to purchase. It bears mentioning that my wife is both the brains *and* looks of this relationship, whereas my main responsibility is to reset all the digital clocks in the apartment after a power outage.

We make it to the cruise terminal as the last few stragglers are boarding the Carnival *Triumph*, a glitzy floating monument to unchecked decadence and Las Vegas-style depravity complete with casinos, hard liquor, all-you-can-gorge buffets, and round-the-clock entertainment. Unfortunately, an overzealous security guard named Ronn (spelled with two N's) confiscates the shaman's candle when he spots it in my backpack going through the x-ray machine. He mutters something about open flames not being allowed on cruise ships. When I ask him if that includes Bruce Vilanch, I'm met with stony silence. We scurry aboard before further action is taken.

After a brief stop at the ship's lobby bar, I'm directed to the Club Rio Lounge where an earthy silver-haired woman, clad in a flowing Emperor Palpatine-like robe ensemble, greets me with the Hindu-come-hippie salutation *Namaste* and asks if I'm ready to begin my spiritual transformation. I take a sip from my enormous strawberry-mango frozen daiquiri and tell her that I am. She checks my name off a list and gives me a bright purple wristband and ID badge. Then she runs her hand slowly up and down my forearm in a soothing, healing motion, looks deeply into my eyes, and says with a warm, beatific smile, "Welcome to the Mayan Galactic Cruise."

This New Agey seminar-at-sea, billed as "the peak spiritual event of the Millennium," celebrates a rare confluence of interstellar phenomena occurring on December 21, 2012, including the end-date of the Mayan calendar, the sun aligning with the center of the Milky Way Galaxy, and the winter solstice. The five-day cruise features an esoteric panel of psychics, spiritual healers, and alien aficionados hosting a variety of lectures and workshops, including "Becoming an Angelic Human," "Spacecraft of Ancient India," and "Ascension: Meet the Immortal Masters and Beings of Light." Additionally, we'll travel to Mexico's Yucatan peninsula, the heart of the ancient Mayan world, and visit the Kukulkan Pyramid at the sacred site of Chichén Itzá where a shaman will lead us in a traditional Mayan ceremony. A shaman for whom I no longer have a gift. *Dammit, Ronn!*

While there are some three thousand passengers on board the Carnival *Triumph*, only about two hundred are here for the Mayan Galactic event. And it's definitely an eclectic group. Many of the attendees are retirement-age hippies still basking in the Age of Aquarius. Described by Hunter Thompson as "refugees of the Love Generation," these perennial seekers are proudly decked in the psychedelic threads of their era, including tie-dyed shirts, sun-bleached denim *everything*, and the occasional Native American fringed deerskin vest. The other attendees are mostly middle-aged women dressed in the mystical New Ager style that I've come to know as *Stevie Nicks chic*. These holistic enchantresses drape themselves in billowy, earth-toned linens with an ethereal gypsy flair. They're also known to incorporate both leather *and* lace into the same outfit, which always includes dangly feather earrings. *Just like the white winged dove.*

We're all gathered in the big showroom, waiting for the Mayan Galactic orientation to begin, which is now 25 minutes behind schedule. This will be a recurring theme over the next five days, as most of the events are chronically, habitually delayed for a variety of technical and logistical reasons. Most of the Galactic Cruisers, however, are oddly at peace with the late starts and numerous glitches that continually plague the event, blissfully accepting that it's "All in Divine Order." This oft-repeated mantra of the New Thought movement suggests that whatever happens, good or bad, is the sublime will of the universe and that we should all just relax and go with the flow. Fortunately, going with the flow becomes decidedly more palatable when the showroom bar fires up its slushy margarita machine.

After forty minutes, Linda, the organizer of the Mayan Galactic Cruise, takes the stage to kick off the opening orientation session, which begins with a bit of bad news. She informs us that keynote speaker Sean David Morton, a well-known psychic and UFO researcher who claims that Nepalese monks trained him in the art of time travel, missed his flight from the Northeast and consequently missed the boat, both literally and metaphorically. She's hoping he'll be able to meet us when we dock in Cozumel and join us for the last two days of the cruise. And no, the irony that he missed his flight even though HE KNOWS HOW TO TIME TRAVEL is not lost on me.

Linda continues the orientation, assuming the role of professor for what is effectively a *New Age 101* community college course whose sweeping curriculum includes the mind-body-spirit connection, the Mayan prophecies, and the pseudo-Jungian notion that we are all part of a universal consciousness. Noticeably absent from her comments, however, are any references to the end of the world, either by cataclysmic event or social unrest that some have spuriously attributed to 2012. "There are Fundamentalist Christians who believe the Rapture is happening on December 21st, but I don't think any of us here believe that," Linda says. In other words, the New Age community does not have an apocalyptic bone in its macrobiotic, yoga-toned body. Instead, they believe that December 21st marks the beginning of a grand spiritual transformation, or what Linda's website calls "the end of the old world of darkness and the beginning of a new world of light!" She notes that this transformation is already underway, as evidenced by the Arab Spring uprisings that began in 2010 and America's progress on issues like gay marriage. "We're heading into an unprecedented period of peace and light," she says. "But with big changes, there is always resistance." This resistance, she suggests, is the reason for the global uptick in violence and turmoil in the days and weeks leading up to December 21, 2012. As evidence, she points to the recent escalation of the Israeli-Palestinian conflict and the spate of mass shootings in America, specifically mentioning the horrific Sandy Hook Elementary School massacre which occurred just three days earlier. Though I find it brazenly distasteful that she would evoke the Newtown tragedy to bolster her own quasi-religious agenda, I remain hopeful that it's a momentary error of judgment and not a portent of things to come.

It's worth noting that Linda is a Doctor of Divinity and bestselling author who studied more than 20 years with Maharishi Mahesh Yogi, founder of Transcendental Meditation and guru of the Beatles and Deepak Chopra. By any standard, her resume is impressive. But she seems rather tightly wound for a self-described "spirituality expert." When her microphone doesn't work, or the lights are too bright on the stage, or there's been a misprint in the Mayan Galactic itinerary causing everyone to show up an hour late for a morning session, she becomes flustered and short with her staff, which is odd for a person who teaches meditation and affirms that we're all filled with angelic light and the eternal love of the universe.

As Linda attempts to get her slide show underway, she realizes that she forgot the cable that connects her laptop to the digital projector. Sensing her frustration, I approach the frazzled doctor and offer my assistance.

"Would you like to borrow a USB cable?" I ask. "I have one back in my cabin."

"It's *not* a damned USB cable," she snaps. "It's something else—I don't know what it's called. It came with the stupid computer." Flustered, she turns away in a huff.

I am *so* not feeling the angel light right now.

There is a brief break in the action while additional microphones are positioned on the stage. My wife, upon returning from the restroom, sits down next to me with a bemused look on her face. She motions to a woman at the back of the room who is wearing a green Indiana Jones-style fedora and a billowy tunic that appears to be fashioned from surgical gauze.

"She was in the bathroom stall next to me," my wife says. "And she was chanting in a strange, unidentifiable language."

"What do you mean by strange?" I ask. "Like Chinese or something?"

"Like, *not from this world* strange," she replies in a conspiratorial whisper.

I glance over at the mysterious woman in the green fedora. Her head is tilted back, eyes tightly closed, and she's silently mouthing a series of oddly unrecognizable syllables. It appears that she's in some kind of celestial trance, though the half-empty margarita glass in her hand might suggest she's simply got a good buzz on.

As the orientation continues, we're introduced to the panel of Mayan Galactic guest speakers. One man was abducted by aliens as a child and is now the world's foremost crop circle expert. Another man, after succumbing to terminal cancer, had a near death experience in which he ventured into the light and met benevolent spirit beings at the center of the universe. And there's Heaven, a self-described SpiritDancer™ who facilitates Goddess Ceremonies and Shamanic Dance Journeys with her sensual "prayerformances." Other speakers include a pet psychic, a past life researcher, and a fringe pseudoscientist who believes that "Nazi-derived off-world colonies" used a "torsion field weapon" to shoot down a Russian test missile over Norway in 2009. Curiously, this isn't the last I'll hear of space Nazis on this trip.

The welcome program ends abruptly when a chipper Carnival *Triumph* staff member informs us that we've run past our scheduled time and must leave the lounge immediately as they need the room for their *Rockin' Karaoke Dance Party*. Because our orientation is cut short, many of the guest speakers did not get to introduce themselves and several express frustrations as tempers begin to flare. Evidently, getting bumped for karaoke is a hard pill to swallow, even for the spiritually enlightened. When one of the psychics starts getting lippy with the Mayan Galactic organizers, I know it's time to call it a night.

Like many of my fellow Galactic Cruisers, and most everyone of a certain age, for that matter, I began to contemplate the nature of my existence—the big *why am I here* question—sometime last year around my 43rd birthday. Inevitably, this type of big-picture contemplation leads to questions of faith. And so, with a clichéd but wholly genuine mid-life crisis looming, I began searching for my spiritual place in the universe. Over the years I've had flirtations with Catholicism, Judaism, Buddhism, and even Scientology, so it makes sense that I would eventually test the esoteric waters of the New Thought community, especially since I grew up in the tony granola San Francisco suburb of Marin County, long-time enclave of the hippie scene in the 1960s and one of the epicenters of the New Age movement in the 1980s.

Growing up in the Reagan Era was strange enough with its pleated jeans, Jazzercize, and the ever-present threat of nuclear annihilation at the hand of the Soviets. But being a kid in Marin County during the eighties was exponentially weirder for a whole variety of reasons, like the fact that we had more tarot card readers than Taco Bells, and because a trip to the colon irrigator was as commonplace as a trip to the dentist.

But the New Age hippie strangeness didn't end there.

Though most suburbanites in the 1980s spent the weekends doing "normal" things like attending their kids' soccer games, cruising neighborhood garage sales, or shopping at the mall, Marin County residents marched to the whistle of a different pan flute player. Their idea of a lazy Saturday involved getting their chakras aligned, their auras read, or their chi flow regulated by a self-anointed guru in his Mill Valley studio located above a Himalayan restaurant whose specialties were tofu rice bowls and positivity.

My mother was at the forefront of this movement.

In 1985, she became a professional masseuse, a body worker, and a healer, and to this day believes whole-heartedly in the mind-body connection. Between the years of 1983 and 1987, she dressed exclusively in flowy, Stevie Nicks-inspired gowns, and there was hardly a moment when or Steely Dan's *Aja* or Air Supply's *Lost in Love* weren't playing on the hi-fi in our living room. Energy crystals and burning incense were strategically placed all over our apartment, and a dog-eared copy of Shirley Maclaine's *Out on a Limb* was a permanent fixture on the coffee table, alongside well-worn editions of Dr. Wayne Dyer's *Your Erroneous Zones*, *The Tibetan Book of the Dead*, and perhaps most disturbing for a curious 13-year-old, the *Kama Sutra*. Because you never want to think of your mother as a sexual being, let alone one who has mastered the standing wheelbarrow position.

My mom, who fled the Catholic Church back in the seventies, spent a lifetime searching for her own spiritual place in the world. Searching for something pure, decent, and true. And for the most part, I think she's found it. I'd like to find that too, as long as it doesn't involve attending services on Sundays during football season or wearing ceremonial underpants. While I've always envied the sense of community that people get from their churches, I could never reconcile the hateful dogmas associated with many of those institutions. But at the age of 44, it might be nice to feel like I'm a part of *something*.

It's 8:30 AM on December 18th, our first full day at sea, and just three days before humankind's great spiritual transformation *or* our descent into an apocalyptic hellscape, depending on your religious bent and level of paranoia. I begin my day with a session called "Peering into the Mind of God" with Dr. Fred Alan Wolf, a well-known theoretical physicist who has taught at prestigious schools like the University of London and the Hahn-Meitner Institute for Nuclear Physics in Berlin. In 1982, he won the National Book Award in Science for *Taking the Quantum Leap: The New Physics for Nonscientists*, and he has appeared in a number of documentary films, including *The Secret* and *What the Bleep Do We Know?* Wolf, who also goes by the name Doctor Quantum, is mainly known for his fringe theories on quantum mechanics and parallel universes, with an emphasis on the relationship between physics and human consciousness. Though some of his ideas are controversial within academic circles, he *is* a respected scientist, and I suspect his presence on the Mayan Galactic Cruise will lend an air of credibility to the panel of speakers.

After a brief delay, Dr. Wolf—sporting a silvery shock of unruly hair, an untamed beard, and rumpled bohemian clothes—steps onto the stage looking more like a 1960s Haight Street radical than a renowned physicist. He gazes at the audience and says with an addled, mischievous grin, "I'm going to take you on a quantum journey into the bubbles of your own consciousness."

Oh Christ.

The stage goes dark as Jefferson Airplane's "White Rabbit" blasts over the loudspeakers. Images of Lewis Carroll's *Alice in Wonderland* flash on the large projection screen, and the entire room is bathed in a psychedelic light show that would not be out of place at a 1967 Vanilla Fudge concert. And then, quantum physicist Fred Alan

Wolf starts dancing. But not just *any* dancing: he's twirl-ing like a Deadhead during a Jerry Garcia guitar solo. And he's singing along with the iconic Jefferson Airplane track, belting the hallucinogenic lyrics at the top of his lungs: "One pill makes you larger, and one pill makes you small. And the ones that mother gives you, don't do anything at all. Go ask Alice, when she's ten feet tall."

For fuck's sake.

It's too early in the morning for a burned-out hippie acid trip of this magnitude, so I decide to blow this hookah stand and get some breakfast. On the way, I pass the casino where one of the Mayan Galactic psychics is seated at a blackjack table, puffing on a cigarette, with an enormous pile of chips neatly stacked in front of him. Our eyes meet, but I quickly look away. It can be awkward when you see a person outside of the environment where you are famil-iar with them, like when a kid sees his math teacher at the grocery store (*they eat food too?*), or when you walk into a strip club and see an old college girlfriend onstage gyrating to an Aerosmith song. But this subversion of social context is precisely what makes theme cruises appealing: the ability to see the subjects of the cruise away from the stage in a public setting. On the Freedom Cruise, a Republican Party event, you might be able to take a hot tub with a conservative luminary like Karl Rove, or join Oliver North in a karaoke duet of "Islands in the Stream." Last year, I was on a theme cruise featuring nightly concerts by hair metal bands from the 1980s, and its main attraction was the possibility of meeting RATT at the buffet, or playing shuffleboard with Slaughter. But for me, the idea of socializing with a psychic in his or her private time seems inappropriate, especially one on a suspicious roll at the blackjack table. The psychic and client relationship should remain in the professional sphere, like that of doctor and patient. That's why I would never have lunch with my proctologist: no matter what the topic of conversation, the only thought in my head would be, *"This man had his finger in my ass, and now he's eating a chicken panini."*

I spend the rest of the day bouncing between lectures with titles like "Crop Circles: The Message is Known" and "Karma Science and Reincarnation." During one particularly surreal three-hour stretch, I overhear the following statements:

- *"Of course* there are fairies, elves, and gnomes!"

- "We are stardust becoming conscious. Literally, the calcium in your bones came from the residue of dying stars."

- "All of us here? *We are the hundredth monkey.*"

In a break between sessions, I start chatting with a gruff, intuitive healer named Azure Skye. She tells me that in addition to offering services like Numerology, Reiki, and Flying Dragon Qigong, she also performs something called "soul retrievals," which sounds absolutely horrifying. I'm still unclear if this involves *her* retrieving *your* soul from the clutches of evil, which I suppose is a good thing, or if she retrieves the souls of others at your behest, which sounds overtly sinister. Either way, I'm fairly certain this dark practice is the basis of a creepy fairytale that Scandinavians tell their children to keep them from misbehaving: *Jørgen, Törvald—if you don't clean your rooms, the Soul Retriever will get you in your sleep!*

It's just after dusk, and I'm out on the ship's deck for a "Sky Watch" session that entails strapping on military grade night vision goggles, staring up at the stars, and looking for extraterrestrial spacecraft. The nightly gathering is led by an unofficial Mayan Galactic guest speaker named Ed, a disheveled, fifty-something conspiracy theorist who is somewhat famous in the shady realm of anti-government chat rooms. Using a laser pointer aimed at the sky, Ed directs our attention to a number of "space critters" as he calls them, but everyone in our group just looks confused.

"You can't see that?" he says swirling the laser pointer, exasperated. *"It's right there!"*

"I'm pretty sure that's a satellite," my wife replies, squinting through her night vision goggles.

"It's *not* a damned satellite. It's an alien space ship!"

I keep scanning the horizon, but I'm not finding any of his space critters. Ed grows visibly upset when no one else in the group can see them either.

"Most people think there are only a handful of alien ships that visit the earth. In fact, there are twenty million UFOs around the planet at any given moment," he tells us in a frustrated, patronizing tone. "When we look up in the sky, what we are seeing is ambient light from the stars reflected off millions of alien spaceships."

For the record, I am not a UFO denier. In fact, there are E.T. believers in my immediate family. My aunt Cynthia, a devout Buddhist whom I adore, believes she communicated with beings of extraterrestrial origin back in the eighties when strange messages came to her through "automatic writing." And I just learned that my father, a retired Army Captain who is fully grounded in logic and easily the most intelligent person I know, believes that aliens visited the earth thousands of years ago and brought certain technologies to early humans. While I personally find that a bit far-fetched, I do think it's highly likely that there are other intelligent life forms in the universe, especially since there are potentially millions of planets with the ability to sustain life. And to even suggest that we earthlings are the only intelligent creatures in the universe is both arrogant and disheartening. We are, after all, the species that invented parachute pants, the Pet Rock, and line dancing. But to suggest that there are twenty million individual alien spacecraft hovering above the earth at this very moment? Well that's a special kind of crazy.

Tomorrow we travel to the sacred Mayan site of Chichén Itzá, and I still don't have a gift for the shaman. Since I'm on a ship, I really only have two options: I can get him something from the onboard gift shop, which mostly has Carnival-branded t-shirts, junk food, and toiletry items, or I can try to win him a stuffed penguin from the mechanical claw arcade game in the children's Fun Zone. Ultimately, common sense prevails (translation: I ran out of quarters in the arcade), and I find myself in the gift shop purchasing a pair of toenail clippers and a giant Slim Jim. Back at our cabin, my wife empties the contents of the shopping bag onto the bed.

"Really?" she says incredulously. "You got nail clippers for a Mayan shaman?"

"You can't overestimate the value of proper podiatric maintenance," I tell her.

"And the Slim Jim?"

"Everyone loves processed meat snacks in tube-form. It's a universal truth."

Act II:

PLASTIC SHAMANS

In the 48 hours since the Mayan Galactic event began, I've heard a great deal about space aliens and crop circles, cosmic vibrations, Divine Light, and universal consciousness. In fact, I've heard a lot about everything *but* the actual Mayans. And this gets me thinking: what exactly *is* the Mayan connection to the 2012 phenomenon? Because in all the lectures I've heard, and in all the New Age materials I've read, the correlation seems tenuous at best.

We know it all begins with the Mayan Long Count calendar, which appears to have an end-date of December 21, 2012. I say *appears* to have an end-date because the Mayans viewed time as cyclical and not linear like we do, which means that their calendar does not "end" on the last published date — December 21, 2012 — but instead resets to zero after a period of 5,125 years, the way a car odometer rolls back to zero after 999,999 miles. But how did we get from this benign piece of time-keeping minutia to the New Age idea that December 21, 2012 is the beginning of humanity's great spiritual transformation? How exactly was that leap made?

There are many threads that connect the New Age community to the 2012 phenomenon by way of the so-called "Mayan prophecies" and there are many key players in the movement such as Terence McKenna, John Major Jenkins and Carl Johan Calleman. But when you wade far enough into the slough of New Age literature, you find that all roads lead back to one man: Jose Arguelles.

In 1969, the seeds of the 2012 phenomenon were planted when Jose Arguelles, an art history professor at University of California Davis, learned about the mysterious cycle of Aztec prophecies called the "Thirteen Heavens and Nine Hells of Increasing Doom" from New Age writer Tony Shearer. According to Shearer, the period of Thirteen Heavens—each lasting 52 years—began in 843 AD with the completion of the Quetzalcoatl pyramid at Teotihuacan and ended in 1519, the year Spanish conqueror Hernan Cortez landed on Aztec shores. The violent, bloody arrival of Cortez and his army marked the beginning of the cycle of Nine Hells, a 468 year period of darkness and suffering. The Ninth and final Hell began in 1935 with Hitler's rearmament of Germany in the lead-up to World War II and ended 52 years later on August 16, 1987—and *this* prophetic date was the key to everything.

Arguelles, who had been one of the originators of the Earth Day concept and organized the first Whole Earth Festival in 1969, was savvy enough to understand that a successful movement needed a fixed date to coalesce around. The Age of Aquarius movement in the late 1960s had stalled partly because there was no consensus on exactly *when* the Age of Aquarius would begin. Its nebulousness did not bode well for sustaining participation or enthusiasm. But Shearer had *an exact* date—August 16, 1987—and Arguelles could use it to rally and refocus the floundering Aquarians along with a younger generation of New Age seekers. Arguelles would ultimately fuse *Mexico Mystique* author Frank Water's pseudo-Jungian notion of the collective unconscious as viewed through a mystical Mesoamerican lens with Shearer's prophetic date into a single unified event called the Harmonic Convergence, which took place in locations across the world on August 16-17, 1987. It was both a celebration of the end of the Ninth and final Hell cycle, and Earth's first globally synchronized meditation. By all accounts, it was a fantastic success and catapulted Arguelles to international stardom.

"I remember the Harmonic Convergence," my mom tells me, laughing. "I went to this nudist camp out by Harbin Hot Springs with this guy I was dating, and we took ecstasy and wandered through the forest tripping out on nature. I think there was a band playing, and there were naked people meditating everywhere—it was quite a weekend."

Just prior to the Harmonic Convergence, Arguelles released his groundbreaking book *The Mayan Factor*. For the very first time, he brought the December 21, 2012 end-date of the Mayan Long Count calendar into the public sphere, fueled the imaginations of millions, and effectively launched the 2012 phenomenon. Much of the book came to Arguelles in visions he had while taking psychedelic drugs and from channeling the spirit of a 7th century Mayan prophet named Pacal Votan, and many of the resulting concepts have become classic New Age tropes, including the notion that the Mayans came from another planet, have "star-bases," and are able to travel between dimensions.

Perhaps most significantly, Arguelles wrote that the Harmonic Convergence in 1987 was the beginning of a twenty-five year transitional period counting down to the end of the Mayan Long Count calendar, ushering in a spiritual golden age on December 21, 2012 that he called "a unified field of planetary consciousness." This, essentially, is the 2012 phenomenon as we know it today.

There's only one problem with all this: none of it is

even remotely based on any actual Mayan history or mythologies. If you comb through all the ancient Mayan texts that exist today, if you analyze every inscription and pictograph on every existing Mayan structure, you won't find a single mention of star-bases, interdimensional spirit beings, or even a grand metaphysical shift in consciousness. This means that nearly all the information surrounding December 21, 2012 with any purported Mayan connection, beyond the actual "end-date" of the Long Count calendar, comes from undocumented Aztec prophecies, the channeling of ancient spirits that might be of extraterrestrial origin, and visions from hallucinogenic drug trips in the 1970s. In other words, it sounds a lot like my freshman year of college. It also sounds like a number of clever American writers co-opted the Mayan calendar to cloak their New Age ideas in Mesoamerican mysticism for profit. People can and should believe in whatever they want: Jesus, Buddha, Mohammad, magical elves, or even yes—interdimensional spirit beings with off-planet star bases who are trying to transform human consciousness into a synchronized oneness with the rest of the universe. But call it what it is—because what it *isn't* is Mayan. And appropriating the culture of an indigenous people who have been brutally oppressed since the Spanish arrived in the 16th Century and twisting their beliefs into something that resembles science fiction, well that's just being a dick. I'm hopeful that tomorrow's journey to one of the most sacred sites in Mesoamerica with an actual Mayan holy man is informative, respectful, and indicative of their rich culture. I also hope they have churros, because they are a delicious treat.

It's December 19th and the Carnival *Triumph* is docked

in the Mexican port city of Progreso in the Yucatan Peninsula. Before we disembark, we're briefed on the details of our Chichén Itzá tour and given some helpful tips for surviving an afternoon in the jungle, including "Stay hydrated," "Bring sunscreen," and "Don't pet wild monkeys because they're aggressive and riddled with disease." We're also asked *not* to refer to the sacred site of Chichén Itzá as "Chicken Pizza," a phrase commonly used by American tourists that is considered disrespectful by the locals. Additionally, the shaman sent out an email requesting that we dress in all white for the Mayan ceremony, and everyone in our group complied. I don't know what's more disconcerting: that we look like a deranged suicide cult with our matching white outfits and purple wristbands, or the fact that THE SHAMAN HAS EMAIL. As we're shepherded off the ship and onto waiting tour buses, we're each given a bagged lunch and a photocopy of a prayer to Hunab K'u—the Mayan supreme deity—that we'll recite during the ceremony.

It's a two-hour bus ride to the archeological zone at Chichén Itzá. About fifteen minutes into the trip, I hear a series of strange, singsongy chants echoing from the seat behind me. I crane my neck and see that it's coming from the mysterious woman in the green Indiana Jones fedora. The language—if you can call it that—sounds like an odd mashup of Tibetan, Navajo, and Hindi. It's familiar, and yet it's not.

"Excuse me," I ask during a lull in her incantation. "I heard you chanting and I'm wondering what language that is you're speaking in?"

"It is a combination of all languages," she replies dreamily. "It is the universal language."

"And were you praying? Or was that some kind of meditation?"

"What if I told you that I was channeling the Pleiadians?" she says with a faraway glaze in her eye.

The Pleiades is one of the nearest star clusters to Earth and a staple of New Age lore as many believe it is the home of multi-dimensional beings that wish to aid us with our spiritual transformation.

"Pleiadians—you mean, *like aliens*?" I ask.

"Aliens. Spirits. Angels. Whatever you want to call them," she says. "I am their vessel. They communicate through me every day." She leans towards me and whispers, "Did I just *totally* blow your mind?"

Our group of sixty-odd Galactic Cruisers arrives at Chichén Itzá and is immediately hustled to a spot in front of the large Kukulcan pyramid where we're introduced to the shaman, a small grey-haired man named Hunbatz Men. He's dressed in white like the rest of us, with a bright red bandana around his forehead. At first he seems confused, like he's not sure what he's supposed to be doing with us. After several awkward minutes he begins speaking, but his voice is low and soft, and it's difficult to hear him over all the space-age chanting. He points to a gnarled tree and tells us that, according to Maya mythology, it is the sacred Tree of Life or *Yaxche*, and that all life on Earth originated from it.

Hunbatz Men attempts to position our unwieldy group into two parallel lines that face the pyramid, which is like trying to herd drunken cats in a rainstorm. And he insists that our lines be *exactly* straight, because anything less than geometric perfection is an insult to the Gods.

This goes on for half an hour.

Eventually, Hunbatz Men, visibly frustrated by our line-forming ineptitude, begins telling us the history of his Mayan ancestors. Within minutes, a park security guard informs Hunbatz that he does not have the proper permit to perform a ceremony at this location, and he directs us to another spot a quarter mile away. And so we march through the archeological zone in two not-very-straight lines, past the throngs of camera-toting tourists and vendors hawking cheap sombreros and mass-produced "Mayan" trinkets.

"Two lines! Keep moving!" the shaman screams at us in broken English. One woman in our group, who left her shoes on the bus because she "wanted to feel the sacred Mayan Earth between her toes," now limps along, dragging her bloody naked feet over the coarse, unforgiving gravel. It's like the Trail of Tears, if you replace "thousands dead from disease and starvation" with "mildly uncomfortable toe blisters and general irritability."

We arrive at a small alcove situated between two crumbling Mayan structures. It's almost noon, and because we wasted so much time at the other location, we only have a few minutes until we have to board the buses so we can get back to the ship for a 2 PM sailing. Hunbatz Men is desperately trying to position our group in a perfect circle so he can perform the Mayan ceremony at its geometric center. He walks around our lumpy, oblong perimeter, directing some people to move forward and others to move back, because the egg-shaped ring we are forming is an insult to Hunab K'u.

At this point, the crowd is growing restless, and several of my fellow Galactic Cruisers begin voicing complaints. One man groans about the lack of air conditioning in the bathrooms: *"It's like a urine sauna in there!"* A heavy-set woman rails against the poor selection of sugar sub-stitutes at the Java Jungle Espresso & Smoothie Bar in the Chichén Itzá Visitor Center: *"How am I supposed to drink my latte without Splenda? Do they think we're savages?"* Another person, a Mayan Galactic guest speaker who is a medium that talks to the dead and goes by the name of Spirit Man, is concerned that we're behind schedule and that the ship will sail from Progreso without us.

"Don't worry—they won't leave us behind," Linda assures him. "It's all in Divine order."

This only seems to infuriate Spirit Man. "Every one of your events has been chronically late and incredibly dis-organized," he growls. "So I don't have faith in anything you're saying."

It's a tense situation, bordering on ugly. That's when Heaven, the SpiritDancer™, steps into the center of our misshapen egg-circle in an effort to calm the increasingly hostile crowd.

"Okay everyone, let's take a big, deep breath of Divine Revelation," she says in a soothing voice. "Breathe in the light. *Thaaat's it.*"

It seems, at least for the moment, that the riot has been quelled. Hunbatz Men now joins Heaven at the center of the circle to begin his Mayan ceremony. To be honest, I have no idea what to expect from this type of Mesoamer-ican ritual. Would he walk through fire? Perform a cer-emonial dance? Dismember a live chicken? Or would it be more subdued, like a church service? Hunbatz starts by telling us that we are only just beginning our spiritual journey, and that we have all returned to this sacred place because we've been here before in other lifetimes. At this point, Linda steps forward to speed things along—realizing that we really *are* behind schedule—and asks that we take out our copies of the prayer so we can read along with him. When she hands Hunbatz a copy of the prayer, he looks as though he's never seen it before. He clears his throat and begins reading the lengthy passage aloud, but after a few sentences he hands it off to one of the tour operators to read for him. While this other man who is decidedly *not* a shaman reads the prayer, Hunbatz walks around our circle, hands clasped over his heart, seemingly lost in holy thought, but not really doing anything that I would describe as "ceremonial" or "shamanic."

And then it's over, almost as quickly as it began.

Many in our group are confused about the abrupt ending of the ceremony, and some are outright angry. After all, they paid a hefty sum to participate in a ritual performed by a Mayan shaman and instead got a Xeroxed poem read by an American tour bus driver. Adding further insult, Hunbatz's assistant walks through the crowd with a large cloth sack, collecting the gifts people brought for the shaman. When he gets to me, the bag is already overflowing with offerings. I stuff the toenail clippers down into the sack but keep the giant Slim Jim for myself, as I don't feel he really deserves it. I walk back to the buses in silence, gnashing at the meat stick with my teeth until it's been whittled to a glistening, slobbery nub.

Back on the ship, I'm nursing a glass of overpriced Pinot Noir and feeling somewhat dejected, as today hadn't gone as I'd hoped. I wanted to experience a bit of authentic Mayan culture on our journey to Chichén Itzá, but all I got was a lesson in Pleiadian mind-melding and an "I Survived Chicken Pizza" t-shirt whose collar tag is stamped MADE IN CHINA. And I can't seem to shake my nagging feeling about Hunbatz Men, our shaman-for-hire. He was presented to us as an authentic Mayan Elder and Wisdom Keeper, but something about him just seemed *off*. After a few Google searches, I learn that Hunbatz Men's real name is César Mena Toto, that he's worked as a commercial artist in New York City, and that he promotes a wide range of New Age beliefs that have little to do with the actual culture and tradition of the Mayan people. He teaches, among other things, that the Mayans came from Atlantis and that their ancient civilization was in contact with space aliens. Right now, my dad is like, *"See, I told you. How else do you think they moved those giant Easter Island heads? Aliens!"* It should be noted that there are no references to Atlantis or extraterrestrial contact anywhere in Mayan mythology, written, archeological, or otherwise.

Hunbatz Men is also one of the main perpetuators of the crystal skulls phenomenon, the supposedly magic and possibly extraterrestrial artifacts that served as the basis for the movie *Indiana Jones and the Kingdom of the Crystal Skulls*. In 2011, Hunbatz Men took the crystal skulls on tour across America, beginning in New York City and ending in the banquet room of a Los Angeles airport Sheraton on November 11, 2011 (that's *11-11-11!!!*), where it was rumored that the "mysterious Atlantean Orb" might also make an appearance. Additionally, he's the founder of the Cosmic Mysteries School, a New Age academy in Cold Springs, Kentucky whose courses include "Ninja Energy Secrets," "Firewalking," "Jungle Cat Flexibility," and the curiously titled "Female Sex Magic."

In other words, it's like Hogwarts for hippies.

My concern is not *what* Hunbatz Men teaches and

writes about, but rather that he's marketed as an authentic Mayan Elder and shaman. Many foreign tourists who procure his services are likely to assume his teachings are representative of actual Mayan culture when in fact they are a distortion of the beauty and sophistication of the real Mayan people, which only diminishes their immense contributions to the ancient world. And this problem has increased exponentially over the last decade as the public's fascination with the so-called 2012 phenomenon has grown to a fever pitch. Dr. Robert Sitler, a respected Mayan scholar and author of *The Living Maya*, describes the 2012 phenomenon and its relation to the "Mayan Prophecies" as a profitable niche for a number of self-proclaimed shamans whose claims to Mayan ancestry are often dubious. "Their contributions often blend traditional Mayan beliefs with an amalgam of New Age spirituality that includes visits from extraterrestrials, prophetic crystal skulls, and origin stories going back to the lost city of Atlantis," he writes.

This is basically a checklist of Hunbatz Men's teachings.

Looking back on it, much of what he told us didn't seem very Mayan-like at all. His numerous references to "the new cosmic age," "returning to the light," and "the universal consciousness" sounded like they were ripped right from Jose Arguelles' New Age playbook. Which, of course, they probably were, because Hunbatz Men and Jose Arguelles had known each other since 1985, and each had a tremendous influence on the other's work.

But this is what's really maddening: the reason Hunbatz Men was even *allowed* to perform a ceremony at Chichén Itzá is precisely because he *isn't* considered a

Mayan spiritual leader by the Mexican government. In fact, The National Institute of Anthropology and History, the government office that operates the archeological parks in Mexico, has banned all *actual* Mayan spiritual leaders from performing ceremonies at their ancestral sites, including Chichén Itzá. The Mexican government cites "visitor safety" and "preservation of the sites" as reasons for the ban, neither of which have much credence and only seem to reinforce the continued oppression and marginalization of the indigenous Mayans. "We would like to do these ceremonies in the archaeological sites, but unfortunately they won't let us enter," said Mayan priest Jose Manrique Esquivel in a statement to the Associated Press. "It makes us angry, but that's the way it is. We perform our rituals in patios, in fields, in vacant lots, wherever we can."

Essentially, any self-designated New Age guru can come to Chichén Itzá, get a permit, and perform an alien channeling session or a holistic soul migration at the foot of the great pyramid for a group of tourists whose pockets are filled with strong American dollars. But if a person of actual Mayan descent wants to perform the solstice ceremonies of his ancestors, he must do so in a Wal-Mart parking lot in nearby Merida.

But that's not the worst if it.

Two days from now during the *End of the World* party at the Tikal archeological site in Guatemala, apocalyptic revelers will cause "irreparable" damage to one of its iconic stone pyramids. "Sadly, many tourists climbed Temple II and caused damage," said Osvaldo Gomez, a technical adviser at the site, in an interview with local media. "We are fine with the celebration, but the tourists should be more aware because this is a UNESCO World Heritage Site."

Temple II, also known as Temple of the Masks, was built in the 8th century and has survived more than thirteen hundred years of strife, including the invasion of Hernan Cortez and his army of Spanish conquistadores, the collapse of the entire ancient Mayan civilization, and brutal civil wars that crippled Guatemala in the 20th century. But the structure would prove to be no match for the hordes of drugged-out, patchouli-stinking tourists who would illegally climb its steps to twerk and do the *Nae Nae* on its ancient sacrificial platform. Apparently, absolutely *nothing* is sacred.

It's 9 PM and I've made my way to the Oxford Lounge for the evening's "Psychic Demonstration," where Spirit Man, the temperamental medium who communicates with the dead, and the pet psychic, a tiny Eastern European woman who claims to come from a long line of gypsies, will put their awesome intuitive powers on display. From the outset, there is a palpable tension between Spirit Man and the pet psychic. At one point, during a heated exchange over who will perform first and for how long, it seems like they might actually come to blows.

Please God, let there be a psychic rumble. Please.

Later, Spirit Man tells the audience that, while at Chichén Itzá earlier in the day, he saw the apparition of an ancient ancestral Mayan warrior on top of the pyramid, "wearing a wild head dress, and a majestic flowing red robe." Spirit Man ends his presentation with a sales pitch for his private sessions, where he'll help you communicate with your long-deceased Nana at the low-low cost of $130 for twenty minutes.

Next, the pet psychic takes the stage to tell us about her book *Celebrity Pets Tell All* (available on Amazon!) in which she telepathically communicates with the pets of celebrities to get insider gossip about their famous owners. Some of the celebrity pet pairings include Paris Hilton and her dog Tinkerbell, Britney Spears and her dog Bit-Bit, and George Clooney and his pot-bellied pig Max. The hog-channeling gypsy then performs several live psychic readings of audience members' pets. To do this, she fixates on a photograph of the animal and telepathically channels its thoughts, which she then relays to the audience. During one memorable reading, she tells a woman that her dog "likes to chase things," "would rather eat people food than dog food," and "does not like cats or squirrels." If she'd added, "likes to lick his own balls," I would've marched out to the deck and thrown myself overboard into the glassy sea.

Act III:

ARMAGEDDON IT

It is Thursday December 20, 2012, just one day until the Mayan Long Count calendar resets to day zero after 5125 years. We're docked in Cozumel for the morning, and the Mayan Galactic Cruisers are busy prepping for the grand spiritual transformation they believe is just hours away. And when I say "prepping," I mean drinking piña coladas at Carlos 'n Charlie's, shopping for duty-free liquor and cigarettes, and getting towed around the harbor on large, inflatable water weenies.

Elsewhere in the world, Christian fundamentalists and other doomsdayers are counting down the minutes to what they believe will be Armageddon. But aside from a handful of vendors selling t-shirts that read *"Sobrevivientes el 'Fin del Mundo'"* or *"I survived the end of the world,"* which is rather optimistic considering the apocalypse isn't supposed to happen for another seventeen hours, there doesn't seem to be any sense of panic out on the streets. Most of the people we meet, both tourists and Mexican locals, seem dispassionately indifferent to the 2012 phenomenon.

We stop in Jimmy Buffet's Margaritaville Restaurant and Bar, a soulless, culturally void tourist hell pit, for an order of their trademarked Apocalypso Tacos, which seems fitting on this supposed eve of destruction. My wife orders a drink called *The Last Mango in Paris* that the menu says is "not to be confused with the movie of a similar title." Margaritaville is a corporate chain restaurant whose meticulously calculated schlock has been focus-grouped and refined for maximum financial gain, which makes it all the more interesting that they would purposely and knowingly name an alcoholic beverage after a soft-core Marlon Brando movie mainly remembered for its butter-lubed anal sex scene. I suppose Applebee's and Chili's will follow suit by offering their own line of suggestively titled drinks, beginning with *Golden Shower Tequila Poppers* and ending, I fear, with the *Pasadena Mudslide.*

When our meal arrives, I ask the waiter, a Yucatan local, if he thinks the world will be destroyed or human consciousness will be transformed in less than twenty-four hours when the Mayan calendar supposedly ends.

"No, but it's good for business," he says laughing.

"So you don't believe any of it?"

"Honestly, we don't really pay attention to the old calendars here," he says. "All of this—it's mostly for the tourists. It's a great excuse for them to have parties and drink some cervezas. That's really all it is."

And these parties, most of them English-speaking events and none of them cheap, are scattered all over the Yucatan and Guatemala. In Pisté, the tiny town just outside the gates of Chichén Itzá, there's *Synthesis 2012*, a massive three-day electronic and world music dance festival. In Playa del Carmen, there's the *Day Zero* techno rave at a newly-opened Mayan theme park. At the archeological ruins in Palenque, there's the *International Rainbow Gathering*. And in Guatemala, there's the *End of the World Party* at the Tikal Mayan ruins, and the *Cosmic Convergence* at Lake Atitlan.

Beyond the clubby, ecstasy-fueled festival scene, there are hundreds of tour groups just like the Mayan Galactic Cruise all descending on the Yucatan to be part of the 2012 experience. There are *End of the World Jungle Bike Tours*, *End of Days* package tours to Mayan archeological sites across Mexico and Central America, and even a December 21st event with Star Johnsen-Moser, an American "seer" self-described as "an open channel for the Ancient Ones," who will lead a *Crystal Skull Light Activation Ceremony* on top of the Kinich Kakmo pyramid in Izamal. The interest in 2012 is so significant that *Businessweek* projects a ten percent increase in tourism to the region over the previous year, which could translate to billions in additional revenue.

And it's not just Latin American interests hoping to ride the Mayan prophecies money wave. T.G.I. Friday's encourages you to "Go Out With a Full Stomach" at its end of the world themed "Last Friday" celebrations, featuring *The Final Sip* Mayan margarita and *The Last First Bite* warm pretzels with beer-cheese dipping sauce. Not to be out-gluttoned, Carl's Jr. touted its new nine thousand calorie burger, posting on its Facebook page: "If it's not the end of the world, then it's definitely the end of your hunger. #burgergeddon #baconpocalypse." A Denver hotel is offering a "Party Like There's No To-Maya" package that comes with radiation tablets, freeze-dried food, and gas masks all for $12,021 (that's 12-21—*get it?*). And a Russian company is selling *Apocalypse Go Kits* that include a bottle of vodka, a can of fish, and a rope to hang yourself should the eternal hellfire of Armageddon become too unbearable.

But not everyone is happy about the commercialization and monetization of the 2012 prophecies, particularly the Mayans who still reside in the region. Alberto Marroquin, an indigenous Mayan leader, said that his community was feeling marginalized by its lack of participation at Guatemala's official 2012 events. "This is illogical," he told the AFP news organization. "It's like celebrating something when the main person has not been invited." And just two months ago, Felipe Gomez, leader of a Maya alliance group, urged the Guatemalan Tourism Institute to reconsider the doomsday celebrations they have been promoting, insisting that they are just performances for the tourists that are disrespectful to the Mayan culture.

"We are speaking out against deceit, lies, and twisting of the truth, and turning us into folklore-for-profit," Gomez said in a statement to the AFP. His pleas were ignored, and the government-sanctioned end of the world festivities continued as planned.

It's late afternoon, and we're back on the ship making the return journey to Galveston when I start thinking about missing Mayan Galactic keynote speaker Sean David Morton. Remember him? He's the time-traveling psychic who missed the boat back in Texas and was planning to meet us in Cozumel. But he was a no-show today, and the event organizers didn't say a word about it.

So, funny story about that.

Tonight I learned that Sean David Morton was indicted by the U.S. Securities and Exchange Commission and charged with investor fraud in what has been described as a "Psychic Ponzi Scheme," placing him somewhere between Bernie Madoff and the Amazing Kreskin. The SEC claims that Morton used his clairvoyant celebrity status to scam nearly one hundred clients out of $6 million between 2006 and 2007. According to the official Litigation Release, "Morton falsely told potential investors that he has called all the highs and lows of the stock market, on their exact dates, over a fourteen-year period," and "falsely asserted that the alleged profits in the accounts were audited and certified by PricewaterhouseCoopers LLP who he claimed certified that the accounts had profited by 117%." In other words, Sean David Morton is a liar and a carnival huckster. And now I'm even beginning to question his time travel capabilities. But here's the topper: the U.S. District Court Judge filed the legal summary against Sean David Morton on December 17, 2012, which is *the same day* we sailed from Galveston when he conveniently "missed" the boat. *Fucking perfect.*

Tomorrow's "end-date" of the Mayan Long Count calendar takes place at exactly 11:11 UTC, or 5:11 AM here in the Caribbean. In less than twelve hours, the Mayan Galactic Cruisers will gather on the ship's forward deck in the early dawn hours to celebrate the impending transformation of human consciousness, or "the end of the old world of darkness and the beginning of a new world of light."

Oh, and there's also that whole apocalypse thing.

We don't have any doomsday believers in our group, but there really *are* people out there who think the world will come to its fiery end just a few hours from now. Last May, the Reuters news agency cited an international poll that showed one in ten (10%) global citizens believe the end-date of the Mayan calendar marks the end of the world. Parse the data any way you want: that's still a lot of people, perhaps millions, who are bracing for the apocalyptic hellfire they believe is about to be unleashed upon us all. Though I do not personally give credence to any of the half-baked doomsday scenarios floating around out there—including our destruction by super volcanoes, reversal of the earth's magnetic poles, massive solar flares, or collision with the mysterious Planet X—it *does* make me wonder how I should spend my last night on earth if the end is nigh. I'd like to think that my final hours would be spent contemplating my spiritual place in the universe, making peace with some of the more regrettable decisions I've made in my life, and being thankful for all the love and friendship I've experienced in my precious time here. The reality, however, given that I'm stuck on this garish, floating liquor repository, is far more corporeal in nature. Rather than an evening of intense self-reflection, I'll likely be gorging myself on multiple plates of warmed-over chicken fingers from the poolside grill, performing a terrible karaoke rendition of Bon Jovi's "Blaze of Glory," and drunkenly groping my wife back in our cabin as we reenact the "Let's Do it For Our Country" musical number from *Grease 2*.

But before we get to all *that*, I decide to attend one last "Star Watch" session with Ed, searching the sky for his "space critters." The sea is choppier than usual tonight, and the dark billow of menacing thunderclouds can be seen gathering on the horizon. When I meet the group outside, Ed is in a tizzy, ranting incoherently about two alien ships in the sky that are battling each other in some kind of interstellar dogfight. I ask him why the aliens are fighting each other, which seems like a logical question, and his voice gets low and serious.

"Why are the alien factions at war with each other?" he asks somewhat incredulously, as if it's beneath him to have to answer such a pedestrian question. "It's because of the Nazis."

"The Nazis?"

He nods. "The Nazis are descendants of an advanced alien race who came to earth thousands of years ago. In World War II, they conducted experiments on the Jews where they fused their alien DNA with human DNA to create alien-human hybrids. When the war ended, the top Nazi officers fled to outer space, setting up colonies on Mars, where they've been waiting until the time is right to come back and conquer earth."

Space Nazis. Got it.

"The offspring of these alien-human hybrids still live among us today, and many are now in high-ranking government positions." Ed looks around the deck nervously before continuing in a hushed tone. "You see, Barack Obama and Hillary Clinton are both alien hybrids."

Ah, crap. Here we go.

"And you know the Sandy Hook Elementary School shootings that just happened in Connecticut? Obama and Hillary used alien mind-control on the killer to make him shoot all those kids."

Fuck. Me.

"That way, they'd be able to use the shootings as propaganda to abolish the Second Amendment and take away all our guns. So when the Nazis come back to take over the earth, they won't face an armed resistance. That's their whole plan. It's real, and it's already happening."

I'm so livid and disgusted by Ed's horrific, inexorably deranged comments that I'm physically shaking, almost at a loss for words.

Almost.

"YOU ARE FUCKING BATSHIT CRAZY," I tell him, the two of us on the deck bathed in starlight.

Ed just shrugs, raises the night vision goggles to his eyes, and goes back to scanning the sky. I grab my wife's hand and lead her back inside the ship. "Stay away from that guy," I tell her. "He's a depraved lunatic, and he's dangerous."

In need of a stiff drink or three, we head over to the casino lounge where a cheesy musical act, inexplicably dressed like Sgt. Pepper's Lonely Hearts Club Band, offers their take on a variety of smooth '70s jams. I'm still seething from crazy Ed's vulgar and irrational diatribe, but the tequila shots combined with the band's oddly effective reggae version of Bread's "Everything I Own" featuring a wild-eyed Filipino on keytar seems to be taking the edge off, at least for now.

As the tequila gets its hooks into me, I find myself thinking about our shaman, Hunbatz Men, and feeling more than a little guilty. Perhaps my initial assessment of him was too harsh. After all, it's not like he's *really* hurting anyone with the fantastical stories he tells about the Mayans, aliens and Atlantis. He's just a guy trying to make a living in a challenging country that's short on opportunities, and people seem to enjoy his work. The bigger question is when did I become so judgmental? Is it just a byproduct of middle age, like excessive ear hair and having to pee in the middle of the night? Because I wasn't always this way. As a young man, I was open and accepting of everyone and everything, because that's how my mom lived her life and that was the example she set. And I fear if I continue down this path, I'll soon be a crotchety old man, standing on my porch, shaking my fist at the neighborhood children and yelling, "You kids stay off my lawn!"

It seems like most spiritual journeys are about moving forward and evolving. But I'm beginning to wonder if my journey isn't about *going back*—back to the person I used to be before judgment and cynicism clouded my heart. Perhaps I'm the *Benjamin Button* of seekers, progressing in reverse, vainly attempting to reclaim the innocence and wonder of childhood that inevitably gets trampled asunder by the rigors of life. A boat against the current, as Nick Carraway says in *The Great Gatsby*, "borne back ceaselessly into the past." And maybe, just maybe, Hunbatz Men is not *intentionally* misrepresenting the Mayan culture for the benefit of his paying clients, because in the words of *Seinfeld's* frugal sage George Costanza, "It's not a lie... if you believe it."

When I go to get us another round of drinks, I meet a woman seated alone at the bar who is wearing a purple Mayan Galactic wristband. We start chatting, and eventually the conversation turns to her thoughts on this five-day spiritual event.

"I've talked to quite a few people who feel ripped off from this whole experience and have a lot of anger about it," she says. "There were just so many negative feelings."

"How do you mean?" I ask.

"I had lunch with one of the panel speakers, a short eastern European woman," she tells me. "I think she was a pet psychic. And she said Spirit Man insulted her the night they had their program together. He said, 'I'm a *medium*, but you're just a psychic who talks to cats.' And she was very hurt by that. I just thought, *My god—what is going on here?*"

As I head back to the table with our drinks, the band's lead singer is introducing their next song from the stage.

"Who wants to party like it's the end of the world?"

The crowd of maybe fifteen people lets out a half-hearted cheer.

"Then let's blow the roof on this boat!" he yells, as the band launches into an oddly melancholic, slow jazz version of Def Leppard's "Armageddon It."

My god—what is going on here?

We finish our drinks and head back to our cabin since we have to be up early for the December 21st festivities.

At some point in the pre-dawn hours, a massive storm system that had been wreaking havoc in the Midwest for much of the past week was now moving south through Texas to the Gulf of Mexico, right into our path. We're awakened around 3 AM when the Carnival *Triumph* starts to pitch back and forth, getting severely hammered by heavy winds and high surf. Soda cans and toiletries fly off the shelves in our cabin, and the ship is swaying with such force that it's difficult to even remain standing. My wife, who does not do well in turbulence of any kind, starts popping Xanax like they're Skittles.

At 5 AM we head outside to the deck for the Mayan Galactic celebration. The winds are now gale force, clocking in near 60 MPH, and the rain, blowing in sideways, stings as it pelts our faces. About fifty of the most diehard Galactic Cruisers are gathered on the deck to celebrate the end-date of the Mayan Long Count calendar which marks the winter solstice, the Earth aligning with the center of the Milky Way Galaxy, and what they believe will be the grand transformation of human consciousness. The event organizers had scheduled a laser light show, and they were going to project a live video feed from space on the big outdoor screen, but the severity of the inclement weather nixed all those plans.

And the weather really *is* bad.

Like, *Perfect Storm* bad.

My wife and I are huddled in a corner by the beverage station, our faces red and raw from the wind's vicious lashing, and the raging sea tosses the Carnival *Triumph* about as if it were a child's toy in a bathtub. Water splashes out of the Jacuzzis, creating an ankle-deep deluge of funky, sudsy liquid all around us, as the empty lounge chairs slide across the deck, crashing into each other with a dull, metallic thud.

It is 5:09 AM, just two minutes until the supposed end-date of the Mayan calendar, which some believe will be the end of the world. The rational part of my brain knows that our planet is not about to explode in a cosmic fireball. But the part of my brain that makes me afraid of exorcism movies, spiders with hairy legs, and a mustache-free Alex Trebek, *is kind of freaking out.* Because as the final seconds tick away, the storm *appears* to be growing in strength. Almost as though the earth is thrashing and seizing in its final death throes.

I should have seen this coming, because in the days and weeks leading up to December 21, 2012, there were a number of rare and frightful occurrences, some natural, some manmade, and some just plain-ass crazy, that could be interpreted as signs of the end times. Climate change gave us an elbow smash to the groin with 2012 registering as the hottest year on record. A massive hurricane hit the mid-Atlantic seaboard in late October and leveled portions of New Jersey and New York. A 6.1 magnitude earthquake struck off the coast of San Diego not far from where I live, and North Korea successfully tested a rocket that could hit the United States *and* claimed to have found a secret unicorn lair in Pyongyang. I'm sure all of this is just happenstance, but *come on* — unicorns? *Fuck.*

We're all watching the big countdown clock as the last few seconds tick off:

5...

4...

3...

2...

1...

As the clock hits zero, I close my eyes and squeeze my wife's hand.

And nothing happens.

We're all still here.

People all around us are hugging and crying. The Mayan Galactic tech guy, wearing what appear to be clown pants and a horned Viking helmet, runs across the deck in the rain screaming, "It's happening! It's finally happening!" as his sparkly gold cape flaps in the wind behind him.

In the outdoor DJ booth, an older woman introduced as a "Mayan priestess" takes the microphone and says, "As of this moment, we are in alignment with Hunab K'u, center of the galaxy, essence of life, love and consciousness. This moment only happens once every twenty-six thousand years, so we must revel in it."

I do my best reveling with some coffee in me, so I head over to the poolside bar and order a cup. While I'm waiting, I start chatting with a cheery, wide-eyed Galactic cruiser named Cheryl.

"So what did you think of this whole event?" I ask her.

"Well, it was kind of disorganized. And the technical difficulties got somewhat old," she says. "But this is my fourth cruise with this group. And each time I am transformed. How could you *not* be? I mean, look at all these beautiful, enlightened souls."

Cheryl seems relatively moderate in her beliefs. I don't think she channels alien deities or thinks that mythical creatures like Sasquatch actually exist, so I ask her how she reconciles the more extreme aspects of the New Age community, like the fascination with benevolent extraterrestrials or the wildly offensive, unhinged rants of a guy like Ed.

"Just because these things seem far out to you, doesn't mean they are to everyone. I bet there are people here who were just eating that stuff up," she tells me. "I personally can't get into the conspiracy theory stuff, but a lot of people do. I thought the celebrity pet stuff was entertaining."

I push her just a little bit, telling her what I learned about Hunbatz Men and that many of his teachings aren't based on the Mayan culture at all.

"I liked him and felt he was genuine in his love for the Mayan culture and his respect for the sacred ceremony, though I wish we hadn't been so rushed at the end," she says. "I am not familiar with the crystal skulls phenomenon, but it doesn't matter. His beliefs make no difference to me."

The Mayan Priestess asks us all to form a "sharing circle" on the deck for a final group prayer. Cheryl and I join the others in a large, misshapen circle, arms interlocked, ankle-deep in fetid hot tub water. The priestess guides us through a short meditation, which gives way to the chanting of *Oms*, all fifty of us in unison, arms joined as the sun rises behind us. I look over at Cheryl, whose eyes are wide and filled with pure joy. "So you've been on four cruises with these people," I ask her. "Why do you keep coming back?"

"Because it's a place we can go where no one thinks we're crazy," she says, the rainwater streaming down her cheeks like a waterfall of tears.

A place to go where no one thinks we're crazy.

And that's when I finally *get* it. Because really, isn't that what everyone wants? A place where they're totally accepted, regardless of age, status, or belief system? For the most part, these are kind and gentle people with open hearts and open minds, which is a great deal more than I can say of myself right now. Without question, my spiritual journey is going to be a long and difficult slog.

It's just after 6 AM. My wife and I are back in our cabin getting warm and dry, and I begin to wonder how the rest of the world is holding up—after all, a lot of nervous people bought into the apocalyptic hype. Is there chaos in the streets? Did the fabric of society begin to unravel as we approached the zero hour? When I flip on the news, I half expect to find the CNN studio converted to a *Mad Max Beyond Thunderdome*-style ring, with Wolf Blitzer fighting a retarded leather-clad giant before a crowd of post-apocalyptic mutants. *Two men enter, one man leave!*

To their credit, CNN's reporting of the December 21, 2012 celebrations is kept to a minimum, instead focusing its coverage on what's really important: the five funerals taking place later today in Newtown, Connecticut, where two staff members and three young children from Sandy Hook Elementary School will be laid to rest. It is a sad, sobering jolt of reality, which makes all the talk about galactic alignments and universal consciousness seem insignificant and quaint.

But my instincts weren't completely off: in its coverage of the Newtown burials, CNN is replaying footage from the immediate aftermath of the December 14th shootings—footage of police officers leading small children away from the school to safety, of SWAT teams in assault formations, and of panic-stricken parents unable to find their kids—and I'm reminded of the moment when we first began to understand the magnitude of the atrocities that had been committed, and the realization that we, as a nation, might never be the same again. As it turns out, there *is* unfathomable chaos in the streets, and it does seem as though the fabric of our society is unraveling right before our eyes. These things indeed happened, just not for the reasons I thought.

The last Mayan Galactic session starts in a few minutes, but we decide to skip it. Because really, it's just a final desperate money grab, a New Age infomercial imploring us to buy the books, DVDs, crystals, and potions that will expand our consciousness. But right now, my consciousness feels as though its been stretched to its limit. So we quietly undress in our cabin, crawl back into bed and pull the covers over our heads, holding each other in the darkness, clinging to the only thing that really matters. Something pure, decent, and true.

After the Glitter Fades

It's 10:30 AM on a Friday in Little Rock, Arkansas, and Connie Hamzy is sitting at the bar of the Sticky Fingerz Rock 'N' Roll Chicken Shack, telling a story to a small audience of busboys and cocktail waitresses: "So I'm out on the tour bus, smokin' dope and blowing roadies," she says in a lazy Southern drawl. "And who comes into the back lounge? *Neil fucking Diamond*." A man pulls up a stool next to her. He is wearing a hat shaped like the snout of hog. "So Neil looks me up and down and nods his approval," Hamzy continues. "Then he gets high with us and disappears backstage. A few minutes later, his manager says he wants to see me in his dressing room. So I knock on the door, and there's Neil waiting for me in a blue robe. And I didn't just suck him—there was fucking too."

At first glance, Hamzy could be any middle-aged woman half-drunk in a bar on a Friday morning. But a closer examination reveals she's different somehow, maybe even important. Customers, mostly men, approach her from all directions. They seem to know her name. They say hello and want to shake her hand. The man in the pig hat buys her a drink. Why is she the object of all this attention? Because she's a rock and roll legend immortalized in the opening verse of the song "We're an American Band" by Grand Funk Railroad:

Out on the road for forty days
Last night in Little Rock put me in a haze
Sweet, sweet Connie, doin' her act
She had the whole show and that's a natural fact

But Connie Hamzy is more than a two-line cameo in a 30-year-old song: she's the world's most notorious rock and roll groupie, with a sexual resume that dates back to 1970. Her list of conquests reads like the selections on a biker bar jukebox, including, she claims, members, of the Who, Led Zeppelin, the Eagles, Bad Company, the Allman Brothers Band, ZZ Top, the Doobie Brothers, and more. In 1974, when Hamzy was 19, her groupie escapades were detailed in a *Cosmopolitan* magazine profile, and in 1992 she wrote a tell-all article for *Penthouse*. She's been interviewed by Geraldo Rivera, Joan Rivers, Sally Jesse Raphael, and Maury Povich, and she recently appeared on *Insomniac with Dave Attell*. Though most of her groupie contemporaries like Pamela Des Barres and Bebe Buell had drifted out of the scene by the mid-'80s to raise families or cultivate book deals, Sweet Connie continued her exploits into the new millennium, and today she can be found lurking backstage at nearly every gig in central Arkansas. Connie Hamzy is 50 years old.

"She's a legend in Little Rock," says Sticky Fingerz owner Chris King as he wipes down the bar. "Whenever there's a good concert at the amphitheater, she likes to come in before the show, have a glass of chardonnay over ice, and tell us these wonderful stories about her life." He turns and points at two handcrafted figurines sitting on a shelf behind the bar, adding, "And she made those dolls." The infamous "Sweet" Connie Hamzy, then, is a groupie, a rebel, a boozer, and… *a doll maker*? If that last one seems surprising, it shouldn't. Because Connie is anything but predictable.

Though I'd spoken to Hamzy on the phone several times in preparation for my October visit, I didn't know what to expect when I met her in person. As I discovered early on, she is prone to outbursts that teeter precariously between the profane and the bizarre. During one conversation, Hamzy, upon learning that I had briefly been a roadie for Dan Fogelberg, said with a hint of detached bemusement, "Yeah, I blew him. And his manager, too," as if recounting the first time she ate string cheese or listened to a Josh Groban CD. As a journalist, the real challenge is crafting a response that is neither demeaning nor judgmental. "Well," I said evenly, "That sounds like a tasty treat."

I pull up to a modest white house with green trim at the end of gently sloping street and turn onto the dirt patch masquerading as a driveway. Unlike the carefully groomed yards of the surrounding homes, this one is wild and unruly, with tall grass and colorful flowers growing wherever they please. I park behind a rusted-out Toyota Tercel covered in cobwebs and dried pine needles. Its hood is tattooed with small animal footprints, and there appears to be a bullet hole in the windshield. For a moment, I feel like I've stumbled onto an episode of *COPS*, half-expecting a naked man to bolt from the underbrush in a meth-induced rage.

As I walk up the muddy path, the screen door swings open and Connie pads down the steps towards me with the boundless energy of a girl half her age. She takes me by the hand and leads me inside. "Come on now, we got a lot to talk about."

When I step inside Connie's house, I am instantly transported back in time to the glory years of rock and roll, when big hair, tight pants and eight-minute drum solos reigned supreme. Appropriately, Whitesnake's "Fool for Your Lovin'" blasts from the stereo. The décor is 1970's garage sale chic, and the smell of marijuana and unchanged cat litter hangs heavy in the air. Every wall in the house is adorned with rock memorabilia from her adventures over the last 35 years, including hundreds of ALL ACCESS tour laminates hanging from hooks in every room and numerous framed, autographed photos of artists such as REO Speedwagon and Def Leppard, each with a dated backstage pass from the show. In one dusty corner of the living room, there's an enormous pile of drumsticks on the floor. Most of them are autographed, faded and yellowing with age—I pick one up and the signature reads "Ringo Starr." In another corner, a small wooden baby crib is filled hundreds of CDs. I spend a few minutes wandering through the house, admiring the artifacts as if I am in a grand museum. This exhibit, however, owes more to Eddie Money than Monet, more to Van Halen than Van Gogh.

Connie points to a photo of herself with Rick Springfield from 1985. He towers above her five-foot frame and his arms are wrapped around her. She looks radiant, with flowing mocha hair and large, chocolate-brown eyes. "I never actually *did* Rick Springfield," she says, "but I had sex with his masseuse on the massage table and he video-taped it. He got off on voyeurism. You know, he was Dr. Noah Drake on *General Hospital*."

Today, Hamzy looks remarkably healthy for a woman whose life has been riddled with booze, drugs, and indiscriminate sex. She is thin, but not sickly. Her hair still flows to her shoulders, though the dark roots are evidence of a neglected dye job. There are more lines in her face, and at times she looks tired. But there are also flashes of radiance, particularly when a song comes on the radio that she likes, and this morning her eyes are full of life. Connie brings me a warm 40-ounce can of Old Milwaukee Light and pours herself a glass of Franzia chardonnay over ice. She motions to a tray on the cluttered coffee table containing a glass bong, some rolling papers, and a small amount of weed: "You mind if I get high?" Before I can answer, she takes a deep hit off the bong and slowly exhales a plume of smoke. "I know it sounds crazy," she says. "But I wanted to be a groupie since I was a little girl."

Connie was born an only child to working class parents in North Little Rock in 1955. Her mother was a housewife and her father did auto-body and fender work. According to Hamzy, he was a womanizer and a gambler.

"Being an only child, I guess I was a little lonely," she says. "So I gravitated to bands and concerts. I loved it, because everybody was so happy there. In a weird way, it almost seemed like a family."

When she was in grade school, her parents took her to see *Dick Clark's Caravan of Stars*, a popular concert series featuring bands such as Herman's Hermits, Little Richard, and Paul Revere and the Raiders. "I would see these girls going backstage. They were always dressed up, and they looked so glamorous," she says. "And they got to hang out with all these famous people while everybody else was stuck outside. But I didn't want to be outside—I wanted to be back there too."

Hamzy had her first groupie experience in 1970 when Steppenwolf played Little Rock's Barton Coliseum. "I knew where the backstage door was because I'd go back there to get autographs when I was kid. So my girlfriend and I walked around back, and there was a limousine sitting there. Steppenwolf's road manager saw us and invited us back to the hotel to pick up the band. And we said *Sure!* My girlfriend was with their lead singer in one room, and I was with their drummer in another room. We didn't have sex, but he got me out of my shirt. I was only 15." A month later, Hamzy lost her virginity to the drummer of Frijid Pink, a Detroit band that had minor success with covers of "Heartbreak Hotel" and "House of the Rising Sun."

"She was such a sweet kid when I first met her, wide-eyed and innocent," recalls Jonnie King, a DJ at Little Rock's KAAY in the early 1970s, who met Hamzy when she was a freshman in high school. "For her, being a groupie was about belonging. She needed attention and affection, and maybe that was the only way she knew how to get it. When I saw her a couple of years later, she wasn't the same little girl. The sweetness had dissolved and there was a harshness."

By 16, Hamzy was backstage at nearly every concert that came to Little Rock, from Three Dog Night to the Carpenters. She had blossomed into a dark-haired beauty and was becoming known for her willingness to experiment with drugs and sex. Looking to expand her popularity in the music world, she had stickers printed with her name and parents' phone number on them and handed them out to managers and roadies at shows. "I did it so they could stick 'em on their road cases, like a backstage pass," she says. "And that way everybody knew my name."

As her reputation in the music industry grew, managers and promoters began flying her to shows around the country. "They'd leave prepaid tickets at the airport, and I'd get on a plane and go. I did that with Grand Funk and Alice Cooper. One time I left on a private plane with Leslie West of Mountain. I was only 16."

"While the other high-school girls were trying out for cheerleading, Connie was hanging out with Cheech & Chong and Humble Pie," says Constance Canfield, Hamzy's longtime friend. "Being a groupie gave her an identity. Even today, it defines who she is."

I ask Connie if she dated or had any boyfriends while she was in high school. "Not really," she says. "I fooled around with a few guys that reminded me of my friends in the music business, like the quarterback of our football team. He looked just like Bobby Lamm in the band Chicago." She takes another hit from the bong, adding, "We never like, *dated*-dated because he would've got in trouble with the football team." She smiles as the memories come flooding back. "Yeah, I pulled a few of the football players. They were like the rock stars of high school. And I always liked the rock stars."

It's a few hours later, and Hamzy and I are sitting at the bar in Coulton's Steakhouse finishing lunch. We're discussing *Almost Famous*, Cameron Crowe's autobiographical movie about '70s rock and roll in which Kate Hudson plays a beautiful groupie named Penny Lane. I ask her if she thinks *Almost Famous* is an accurate portrayal of the era.

"I thought they did a marvelous job," she says, "although, they did sugar-coat it. You know, the drugs and the sex and all." She pauses for a moment, scraping her leftovers into a Styrofoam take-out box. "Keith Moon once fucked me with a banana in a backstage dressing room while a bunch of people watched. They should put *that* in a movie." Connie drains the wine from her glass and orders another. "You know, I never pretended to be anything other than a groupie," she says proudly. "Remember how Penny Lane kept saying, *We're not groupies, we're Band-Aids*? I met so many gals like that." The bartender hands her another chardonnay and she takes a long sip. "I'm sorry, but if you're backstage sucking dick, you're a groupie. And that's not a bad thing. Not a bad thing at all."

Connie sees a woman she knows in the restaurant and invites her to join us at the bar. Her name is Dovie Mitchell, but she cheerily introduces herself as "Lovie Dovie" and tells me she works for the local Department of Motor Vehicles. "You never have to question what Connie thinks because she'll tell you exactly what's on her mind," Dovie tells me. "That's one good thing about Connie—you always know where you stand, for good or bad." Dovie flags the bartender and orders a white wine spritzer. "Connie is a very determined person," she adds. "And when she decides she wants something, she usually gets it."

By the time Hamzy was a senior in high school, she had a solid reputation as *the* premier groupie in the Deep South and was becoming famous in the music industry for her oral sex skills. When I ask if there's anything special about her technique, Hamzy replies, "Swallow it. Swallow it all. And don't think twice about it. Don't be all mealy-mouthed."

During this period, Connie's conservative parents realized she wasn't *just* going to concerts, and they were determined to curb her increasingly outrageous behavior. The Osmonds were scheduled to play Little Rock, and her parents, out of touch with popular music, didn't want her to go to the show.

"My mother took me to Memphis for the night, to prevent those Mormon boys from corrupting me," Hamzy says laughing. "We stayed at the Holiday Inn Rivermont in Memphis, and the Allman Brothers happened to be staying there too. I met them in the lobby, and I went up to Gregg Allman's room and we had sex while my mother was wondering where the hell I'd disappeared to."

In 1973, Grand Funk Railroad released "We're an American Band," featuring "Sweet, sweet Connie" in the opening verse. "I had fooled around with Don Brewer and Mel Schaeffer of Grand Funk two or three times before the song came out. But I didn't know they were writing it. I had no idea." The song became a colossal hit, effectively launching Hamzy into the national spotlight. "The phone started ringing a lot after that," she says. "I'd come home from school and there would be a list of messages about a mile long my mother had taken from promoters, managers, and guys in bands."

That fall, Hamzy attended the University of Arkansas at Little Rock. While her peers were going to keg parties and cramming for midterms, Hamzy was ditching class to meet Foghat in New Orleans or the Who in St. Louis. In 1974, Hamzy claims that Don Henley booked her a ticket on a commercial flight to see the Eagles play in Chatta-nooga. When the plane was delayed at a stopover in Knox-ville, Henley picked her up in his private jet. "So I get on the plane and it's just me and Henley and the pilot," she says. "Henley and I are in the back, fooling around and making out. We're up in the air and my eyes are half-closed. Then I feel another set of hands on me, and I real-ize it's the pilot. So I raise up and say, 'Who's flying the plane?' And Henley says, 'Don't worry, it's on auto pilot.' So I just went with it."

It's mid-afternoon, and we decide to head over to the University of Arkansas campus. Hamzy recently learned that her 1974 yearbook photo is on display in the alumni office and wants to see it. She marches up to the elderly woman at the reception desk and in her boozy, booming drawl, says, "My name is Connie Hamzy. I went to school here a long time ago and I heard you had my picture up on the wall."

The woman comes from behind the counter and leads Hamzy to a display of notable and controversial students from the '70s. In addition to Hamzy, who is described as "The Little Rock groupie immortalized in Grand Funk's song 'American Band,'" there are photos of the universi-ty's "resident Communist" and the editor of the school's first and only underground newspaper. Hamzy's college photo is stunning: her long dark hair cascades around her shoulders, a hint of mischief and world-weariness in her gorgeous brown eyes. Unfortunately, the alumni office incorrectly spelled her name as "Hamsey" on the placard beneath her photo. When Connie catches the error, she launches into a tirade, screaming at the elderly reception-ist. "How could you fucking misspell my name? Don't you have me in your records somewhere? Couldn't you look it up? This is so fucked!"

Hamzy has been drinking wine all day, and the smell of liquor is strong on her breath. Clearly frightened, the elderly receptionist grabs the phone on the desk, announcing in a shaky voice, "I'm calling campus security." But Hamzy continues her vicious diatribe: "You cashed my parents' tuition checks, but you can't fucking spell our name right? What kinda shit is that?"

The receptionist speaks into the phone, keeping one eye on Connie. "Yes, I have a *situation* here in the alumni office."

At this point, I'm certain we will both end up in jail, and I'm wondering if my magazine editor will pay to bail me out. "Come on," says Connie. "Let's get the fuck out of here." As we're pulling away from the building, I hear the wail of sirens in the distance, getting louder and louder.

Hamzy left college before finishing her sociology degree. To support her groupie lifestyle, she's always worked part-time jobs that allow her the flexibility to travel and go to shows because, as she repeatedly tells me, "the gigs have always been the most important thing." Over the years, she's done clothing alterations for J.C. Penney, slung chicken at KFC, handed out food stamps to the needy, and bred Persian cats. Throughout much of the 1980s, Connie was a substitute teacher at an elementary school. "I would bring my students tour books and t-shirts and guitar picks from gigs. I even had them write letters to KISS." Until recently, she worked weekends at the Little Rock Zoo, renting out baby strollers for "extra beer and weed money." When I ask her what she's doing now, she replies, "I'm on disability for being bi-polar."

"Wait—you're diagnosed bipolar?" I say. "What does that mean?"

"It means I'm off my rocker, I guess," she tells me laughing. "I have good days and I have bad days. It's not easy being me. It's not easy being famous for sucking dick. But the government sends me a check every month, and that helps pay my bills. I call it my crazy check."

Hamzy never married, but she was briefly engaged to a Little Rock man in the early 1980s. "I told him up front that I wanted to keep going to shows and partying with rock stars, and he said okay, but ultimately he couldn't handle it. He was too jealous." They called off their engagement and Hamzy continued her groupie exploits, enjoying liaisons with such Reagan-era luminaries as the Hooters, Loverboy, Huey Lewis & the News, and Ratt.

"We were playing Little Rock, somewhere around 1985, and we'd heard the famous stories about Connie," recalls Ratt singer Stephen Pearcy. "So me and Robin Crosby, our guitar player who passed away two years ago, were out on the bus with her after the show. She's blowing Robin, and she looks up at me and says, 'You want some of this too?' She's a force, man. You gotta have some big nuts to hang with Connie."

"I loved the '80s hair bands," Hamzy says. "That was my favorite time in music. It was so glamorous—lots of sex, drugs, and rock and roll. But mostly sex and drugs." She would continue her backstage antics throughout the decade, enjoying sexual encounters with Peter Criss of KISS, Edgar Winters, and Rick Allen of Def Leppard, or as she describes them, "the cat man, the albino, and the one-armed drummer."

In a journal entry dated December 2, 1982, Hamzy

details a playful incident in which rocker Billy Squier spanked her with a hairbrush. Squier issued the following response via email: "I liked Connie. She was quite different from what her reputation might lead you to believe: smart, well-groomed, and kind of classy... and very friendly, as you'd expect. Of course, since ours was a strictly platonic relationship, she was always on her best behavior."

By her own admission, Hamzy's had hundreds of back-stage affairs with artists as diverse as Vanilla Ice, Richard Carpenter of the Carpenters, and the Oak Ridge Boys. Given her rich libidinous history, and at the urging of my editor, I am compelled to ask her a blatantly sensational question: "Who has the biggest penis in rock and roll?"

"Huey Lewis," she says without skipping a beat. "For a white guy, he's just got a huge cock. *Huge*. I love Huey. He's a great guy. Very well-endowed."

Hamzy's famous lovers weren't confined to rock and roll. In 1984, Connie alleges she had a steamy make-out session with then-governor Bill Clinton in a laundry room at the Little Rock Hilton, a claim the former President has adamantly denied. Hamzy detailed the incident in a January 1992 *Penthouse* interview, but Clinton press secretary Mike Gauldin was tipped off about the story before the issue hit newsstands, calling the allegations "baseless and malicious lies." The Clinton team moved to discredit Hamzy by getting signed statements of denial from the members of his entourage who were present that day in 1984. Hamzy pleaded her case on numerous tabloid talk shows, but the legitimate press refused to run her story. On January 25, 1997, Hamzy took a polygraph test arranged by the conservative political magazine *The American Spec-*

tator. She passed. "I may be a slut," she says, "but I'm no liar."

In late 1992, Hamzy got a book deal from a small Buffalo publisher. She was paid an advance of approximately $20,000 and she used the money to purchase her house. The book was to be based on Connie's detailed diaries, which she had kept since 1972. Coincidentally, the deal was brokered by Mike Pope, a friend of Bill Clinton's, whose company MP Productions did sound and lights for much of the 1992 Presidential campaign. Hamzy never met with the publishers, and though she received a rough copy of the manuscript, which was nothing more than a transcription of her journal entries, she claims she's never even seen a printed copy of the book. "The Clinton White House was looking for a small company to front this thing," says Hamzy. "They didn't want this book to come out. I guess they thought if they gave me some money, they could keep me quiet and keep my story squelched." Hamzy adds, "Good luck trying to find the book, because it don't exist." The book, titled *Rock Groupie: The Intimate Adventures of Sweet Connie from Little Rock*, has a publishing date of February 1, 1995 and an official ISBN number, but is listed as "out of print" or "currently not available" from every major retailer and used book outlet I contact.

It's just after dusk, and I'm driving Hamzy home after her rampage at the university. On the way, she points out the various neighborhood bars from which she's been banned for some combination of reckless inebriation and public nudity. There seems to be one on every block: the Press Box, the White Water Tavern, Pizza D'Action, the Oyster Bar. "If you can't get drunk and show your tits, what fun is that?" she says.

I park in front of Connie's house and walk her to the door. We're working out the logistics for tomorrow's main event: an '80s hair band festival at the Riverfront Amphitheater, featuring L.A. Guns, Slaughter and Firehouse in concert. I ask Hamzy if I should purchase tickets in the morning. She shakes her head incredulously. "*Puh-leaze*," she drawls. "Sweet Connie does not *buy* tickets." She unlocks the front door, then adds: "Don't worry, I'll take care of it." And I know that she will.

She steps into the house, but before she closes the front door, she looks back at me and says flatly, "If you want to come inside, I could suck your cock. I mean, I'll do it if you think it will make the story better." For me, this is a journalistic first. And I have to wonder: *would* getting a blowjob from her make the story better?

Maybe.

Though I'm sure my editor would love it, I can't bring myself to accept. I thank Connie for the generous offer and tell her that I'll see her in the morning. As I'm walking back to the car, I notice a two red eyes glaring at me from under the porch, tracking my every move. I hope they belong to a cat and not a rabid armadillo.

The next morning, I meet Connie back at Sticky Fingerz, a few doors down from the amphitheater. She's at the bar with a plastic tumbler of wine. When she sees me, she greets me with a big smile and places an L.A. Guns all-access tour laminate around my neck. "Told ya I'd take care of it," she says with a grin. Then she chugs the rest of her wine, and we head out the door into the blinding sun.

At the venue, Hamzy leads the way through an employee entrance. The guard at the gate knows her name—in fact, every worker at the amphitheater seems to know her, from parking attendants and beer vendors to the production crew and promoter. As we walk past the stage, a roadie looks up from the drum kit he's assembling and waves at her. Another guy in a cherry picker hanging lights yells, "Sweet Connie in da house!" She's clearly in her element, and she loves every minute of it. You might even say she's glowing.

I ask Connie if she can explain her enduring popularity with musicians and roadies. "I've always been more direct than the other girls," she says. "I don't play the games. Most bands are only in town for a few hours, so there isn't time for dinner and a movie. There isn't time for romance." She taps the face of an imaginary wristwatch. "My attitude has always been, *Time's a-wastin'—let's get it on!*"

Though most groupies will have sex with band members, hooking up with roadies is considered distasteful and demeaning. Hamzy, however, is the ultimate egalitarian. She makes no distinction between a sweaty lighting rigger and the lead singer of a band, treating everyone with the same amount of sexual zeal. "I love roadies, from the truck drivers all the way up to production. Hell, truck drivers are the backbone of the business. Why not show them a little love?" Tim Walker, a swag seller from Texas, recalls: "I was out with Tanya Tucker in '94, and Connie walked right up to me in catering and grabbed my balls. She said, 'If I give you head, will you give me some t-shirts?' So I said, 'Let's go.' And she did it, right there in the back of my truck."

Many of today's younger musicians and roadies know about the legend of Sweet Connie and consider a blow-job from her the ultimate rock and roll badge of honor. Jack Knoebber, a sound engineer I know from my roadie days, says, "I was in Little Rock about three years ago with Tesla, and Connie was making the rounds backstage, asking if anyone wanted a blowjob. I thought about doing it, just so I could say my dick was in the same mouth as Keith Moon and John Bonham."

But Connie's largesse didn't stop backstage: she would send nude photos of herself in Christmas cards to roadies she met across the country. "Then I got a threatening letter from some merch guy's wife," says Connie. "She said if I ever sent another naked picture to him, she'd jump a plane to Little Rock and stab me in the neck."

Hamzy even used her celebrity status to try to enter politics. In 1996, she wanted to run for the Second Congressional District seat in central Arkansas as "the candidate of the working poor" but couldn't get on the ballot. She did, however, run for the city board of directors in 1992 and 1996. And in 1998, she ran for mayor of Little Rock but her campaign derailed when she was arrested for public intoxication. She received 4068 votes in a losing effort to incumbent mayor Jim Dailey.

"Was running for office a positive experience?" I ask.

"Yeah," she says, "but I thought there'd be more cocktail parties."

Connie and I head backstage to the loading dock where members of L.A. Guns and Slaughter are climbing out of an airport taxicab. The bands have flown in for the show, which means there won't be any tour buses on the premises. "Dammit," she says. "Where am I supposed to suck dick?"

Hamzy says she prefers performing oral sex to having intercourse at a show because she "can cover more ground sucking cock." Given the history and breadth of her libidinous exploits, I ask her if there's any sexual act she *won't* do.

"Well, I don't want anybody peeing on me," she says. "And anal sex is mostly off limits."

" Mostly?" I ask.

"I don't take it anally. But I did know this one guy who was a manager at Barton Coliseum and he showed me the finer points of doing it to another person."

"So you fucked him with a strap-on?"

"Beads," she says smiling. "Large anal beads."

And while most of her sexual antics are quick and dirty liaisons accomplished with a methodical, workman-like precision, there have been moments of genuine affection. This is apparent when she describes the time she spent with men like Jon Bonham, Waylon Jennings, and Keith Moon, legendary drummer of the Who. In a 1992 interview, Connie says of Moon, "Back at the hotel, he hauled out his 45 record collection and we sang "This Diamond Ring" and "Love Potion No. 9" at the top of our lungs. And then we made love for the rest of the night. That was wonderful, weird Keith. We were probably a perfect match."

"Did you ever fall in love with any of your famous partners?" I ask.

"Believe it or not," she says, "when I was 16, I fell hopelessly in love with the saxophone player from Rare Earth." She unwraps a stick of gum and pops it into her mouth. "I cared about Waylon Jennings. He was a good man. And Bobby Lamm from the band Chicago. I always carried a torch for him. But he was into models and actresses. I guess in the long run he was out of my league."

L.A. Guns take the stage for their sound check, blasting into their 1989 hit "Rip and Tear." Hamzy sits on a road case at the edge of the stage, her feet not quite touching the ground. As the song builds to a pristine metal crescendo, an odd transformation in Hamzy takes place: she appears to be getting younger. And I don't just mean her attitude or demeanor—I mean *physically*. She actually looks younger. The lines in her face have smoothed and the sparkle returns to her eyes. *The gigs have always been the most important thing.* And 35 years later, they still are.

The gates have been open for nearly two hours, and the tattooed, mullet-sporting crowd is slowly trickling in. Connie seems disappointed with the atmosphere backstage, perhaps because the artists have barely acknowledged her presence. L.A. Guns pose for a photo with her but only after I ask them, and then they quickly retreat to their dressing room where a trio of younger girls have positioned themselves outside the door. When local band Bombay Black finishes its set, we decide to head home. On this night, sweet, sweet Connie will not be doing her act, perhaps an indication of a disappointing trend. "At Van Halen last Friday, I didn't suck one dick," she says. "Not a single one."

I ask her if she considers that a step up or a step down.

"I think it's a step down, to tell you the truth."

Back at Connie's house, she pours a glass of wine, drops Foreigner's *Agent Provocateur* into the CD player, and fires up the bong.

"Now that you're in your fifties, do you plan to continue your backstage antics?" I ask.

"I hope so," she says laughing. "As long as I don't get arthritis in my jaw." She takes a deep pull on the bong. "I've been a groupie for almost 35 years, and I still love it. I love the camaraderie with the musicians and the roadies and everyone who works in the business. A lot of these people are my friends. Some of them I even consider family." I've spent three days with Connie, trying to understand who she is, and why she has chosen this path. And now I finally get it. Her mission since she was a little girl, and the thing that her critics say has debased her, is the very thing that makes us human: it is her desire to be accepted. As I look around at all the band photographs adorning the walls of her house, many scrawled with personal notes of warmth and gratitude from the artists themselves, it's clear that Connie's mission has not been in vain.

Foreigner's "That was Yesterday" comes on the stereo, and Connie cranks up the volume. "I love this song," she says, mouthing the words: *"Goodbye yesterday. Now it's over and done. Still I hope somewhere deep in your heart, yesterday will live on."*

She gets really quiet now, and there's a faraway look in her eye. It might be the effect of the weed, but it also might be some kind of defining moment, where a middle-aged woman takes stock of a life lived beyond convention. "I really thought I would end up marrying a rock star, a musician," she says. "I really did, until I was about 25. And then I realized it probably wasn't going to happen. I'm probably better off anyways. I've seen so many of them go through such bad divorces, because of goddamn California."

I ask her if she regrets not settling down with a husband and raising a family, if she regrets not building a life and a home with someone. "Oh, hell no," she says defiantly. "Every day I thank my lucky stars that I had sense enough to stay single." She motions to her cats. "Besides, I've got family—Bubbles, and Georgie and Patch and Stuart." Connie takes a final hit off the bong. "It's been a great ride, and I wouldn't change any of it. And there's lots more living to do." And I can tell that she means it. You might even say she's glowing.

A Little Bit Country

Each summer when I was a kid, my dad took me camping in the Sierra Nevada Mountains. Together we'd hunt vermin with a pellet gun and fish in pristine alpine lakes. I loved those trips. But as I got older, the notion of sleeping on dirt, waking up with fire ants on my balls, and shitting in a hole in the ground would lose its romantic luster. By my thirties, I was a full-fledged creature of the city, specifically San Francisco, where sashimi, hot Pilates, and high-pressure colonic irrigations are part of the everyday experience. Today, the only hunting I do is for a parking space or a free Wi-Fi signal; the only fishing I do is for a compliment. It's not that I don't have a profound appreciation for nature—I do. But nothing sets my heart aflutter like quality air conditioning and a flushable commode. Also, I rarely get attacked by bears in the city. So there's *that*.

Paradoxically, I'm standing on the muddy banks of the Oconee River near the astonishingly rural hamlet of East Dublin, Georgia. It's only two and a half hours from Atlanta, but if you squint your eyes it could easily be mistaken for Mozambique or Katmandu or some other steamy, exotic locale. By late-morning, the air is warm and damp as a newly soiled diaper. The sky swarms with hummingbird-sized mosquitoes and the trees buzz with the sound of locusts.

Then, of course, there are the swamp leeches.

I'm at the river's edge, ankle deep in muck, with producers from the *Tonight Show*, CMT, and a local news station out of Macon. We're watching with morbid fascination as Melvin Davis, a 68-year-old self-proclaimed redneck, dunks his head into a barrel of murky river water. Finally, after a great deal of gasping and thrashing about, he emerges with a gnarled pig's foot clenched in his brown, decaying teeth.

"I'm good at three things," says Davis, choking up pints of stagnant water. "Lyin', chasin' women, and fetchin' these pigs feet." He tosses the hoof aside and dunks under for another go 'round. Davis is demonstrating the fine art of bobbin' for pigs' feet, one of the marquee events at tomorrow's Summer Redneck Games, the backwoods parody of the Olympics that draws thousands of fans to this remote region every year.

I've come here to do a story on the Redneck Games, and my editor wants me to focus on "local color," which is code for *find the weirdos*. With any magazine assignment, especially a travel piece like this when I might only have one or two days on location, I'm always concerned that I won't get enough material to write the story my editor is expecting, thus creating a domino effect in my life that invariably ends with me working the drive-thru window at a fast food joint, wearing a paper hat, and taking burger orders from a clown head microphone. I've been in East Dublin the better part of a day, and I've yet to find much local color beyond Melvin and his soggy pigs' feet. My notebook thus far is empty, my tape recorder blank. It may sound like an exaggeration, but I feel like I'm one small step away from asking if you want to supersize those fries.

As I'm kicking the muck off my shoes and pondering my next move, I notice a shirtless grizzled man with a long ZZ Top beard in cut-off denim short-shorts wading into the river behind me. I watch him as he flips over a rock, reaches into the mud beneath it, and grabs a live craw-fish with his bare hand. Then, to my surprise, he jams the entire flailing, snapping creature—head, claws, and all—into his gaping mouth and bites down with an audible crunch. He chews for a moment, grimaces, and swallows the whole thing down. I keep watching, slack-jawed, as this bearded wonder of nature catches and devours several more thrashing crustaceans until his ample belly has been filled. In Missouri, they call it *Ozark sushi*. But here, it's just lunch.

With his hunger satiated, the man wades out of the river, climbs onto a mud-spattered ATV, and rides away. "Thank Christ," I mutter to myself, furiously document-ing the scene in my notebook as I try to suppress my tears of joy. I will not be slinging Happy Meals—not today, any way. Because as I'll soon discover, the local color here is so vivid that at times it's like staring directly into the sun.

Since the end of the Civil War, rednecks have been characterized as conservative, working-class Southern whites with a rebellious nature and a near-fanatical sense of patriotism. But in recent years, there has been a renewed fascination with their throwback culture that extends well beyond the Mason-Dixon line. Thanks in large part to Jeff Foxworthy, the comedian who built an empire on "You

Might Be a Redneck" jokes, his protégé Larry the Cable Guy, and their wildly popular *Blue Collar Comedy Tour* and TV show, the redneck phenomenon has achieved mainstream appeal. Last year, Gretchen Wilson's "Redneck Woman" ruled the country and pop music charts and nabbed a Grammy, while NASCAR continues to deliver blockbuster ratings, and not just in the Deep South: this year's Daytona 500 was watched by more than one million people in Brooklyn, Queens, and Manhattan alone. But if you think America's interest in redneck culture is just a fleeting curiosity, think again. By the year 2012, redneck-themed reality shows will dominate the cable television landscape with a slew of wildly successful titles like *Swamp People*, *Hillbilly Handfishin'*, *Redneck Island*, *Lady Hoggers*, *Duck Dynasty*, and *Here Comes Honey Boo Boo*. The redneck lifestyle, it seems, has never been so popular.

East Dublin is a quaint, postcard-pretty village nestled halfway between Macon and Savannah, and on my first afternoon in town, I stop at local radio station WQXY to meet with program director and Redneck Games founder "Mad" Mac Davis. Davis is a menacing wall of granite and muscle, with a head shaved bald and a sinister-looking goatee. I shake his cartoonishly large hand, and he tells me about the origin of the Games.

"Back in '96 when Atlanta was hosting the Olympics, a lot of people were saying that we were just a bunch Southern hillbillies who couldn't pull it off," says Davis. "So I said, 'If that's what they think, let's give it to 'em.'"

Davis and then-program director "Big Charlie" concocted an Olympic-style festival that would play upon redneck stereotypes. "We expected 500 people to show up, and instead we got 5,000," says Davis, as he unconsciously

wrings his big ham fists. "After the first year, I started seeing families coming from all over the country. They'd plan
their vacations around this weekend, and it amazes me,
because it ain't Disney. It ain't Six Flags. It's the freakin'
Redneck Games."

In the first nine years of the Games, more than 95,000
people have attended, and media from countries including Holland, Chile, and Australia have covered the event.
Perhaps more importantly, the Redneck Games have
brought much-needed revenue into an economically dev-
astated community where 23 percent of Dubliners exist
below the poverty level, more than double the national
average. "These Games bring a lot of money to the businesses in Dublin," says Davis. "It's a huge financial boost
for all the hotels, restaurants, and convenience stores here,
especially the ones that sell ice and beer. That's money this
town never would've seen."

Towards the end of our conversation, I notice a gaudy,
bejeweled championship belt hanging in a glass case on
the other side of the room. When I ask Davis about it, he
tells me that in addition to his duties at the country music
station and managing the Redneck Games, he is a professional wrestling champion with the fledgling Georgia
Independent Wrestling Alliance. He invites me to *Redneck Rampage*, a popular wrestling event happening later
tonight at the County Farm Bureau in Dublin. It's the official kick-off to tomorrow's Redneck Games, and one of the
city's most anticipated entertainment events. I'm initially
ambivalent about going, but when Davis tells me that
grown men will climb into a steel cage and beat each other
with folding chairs, I have a change of heart and decide to
attend.

I should probably mention that I know very little about the redneck lifestyle and Southern culture in general, except that it is wildly different from my own experience. The disparity between my culture (urban, West Coast) and theirs (rural, Southeast) is on full display when I stop at an East Dublin coffee shop near my hotel and attempt to order a chai soy latte. "You want a Chachi *who*?" says the pubescent waitress, snapping her gum. With the Games less than 24 hours away, it's clear that I need a crash-course on the finer points of redneck culture. I decide to seek guidance from the Godfather of all rednecks, Jeff Foxworthy. Unfortunately, Foxworthy declined my request for an interview because of a long-standing feud with the founders of the Redneck Games. I've never been privy to a feud, and I'm intrigued by the Hatfield & McCoy vibe of the situation. When I ask Jeff Kidd, the events coordinator of the Redneck Games, about the origin of the dispute, he tells me they've invited Foxworthy for a number of years and he always refuses to attend. "He's just a prude little rich boy from Atlanta," chides Kidd.

With Foxworthy unavailable, I go to my backup plan and contact redneck expert Ben Jones, who played "Cooter" on the original *Dukes of Hazzard* TV series. Today, Jones is the proprietor of Cooter's Place, a museum in Gatlinburg, Tennessee featuring memorabilia from the show, including pants worn by Catherine "Daisy Duke" Bach. "The redneck movement is a return to the pioneer spirit of America," says Jones. "There's not much difference between the Duke boys and Roy Rogers and Gene Autry. It's the same American mythology, and those are the ideals America was founded on. Even if you're a dusty old cowboy, you can still live your life how you choose." He adds, "It's a wonderfully politically incorrect movement, a reaction to the sermonizers and the holier-than-thou folks who are trying to tell us what's right. We know how we're going to be portrayed in the media, and we just don't give damn."

Jeff Kidd adds, "We're down-home people, but we're not backwards hillbillies. We've got the internet and digital cameras just like everybody else. It's a return to simple values that people are looking for in this day and age. And that's what being a redneck is all about."

But even a culture boasting simple values has layers of complexity. Tawnya Tully, from nearby Cochran, Georgia, explains the caste system that exists within the redneck universe: "There's different degrees of rednecks," says Tully. "There's *town rednecks* who wear rebel flag T-shirts and listen to Charlie Daniels on the 8-track. There's *county rednecks* like us, who get out there and have grill-outs and porch parties with the neighbors. Then there's *dirt road rednecks*. Them folks don't take a bath for a week and they never wear shoes. Most of them live off the land. And they got four teeth, and two of them's in their pocket." She pauses to light up a menthol cigarette, taking a deep drag. "There's poser rednecks, too. You can spot 'em because they don't know how to ride a four-wheeler or shoot a gun."

Tawnya chugs down the remainder of her cocktail, a sugary mixture of vodka and grape Kool-Aid that she calls a *Purple Panty Pull-Down* because "after three of these, you'll be pullin' down your panties, all ready to get it on." She wipes her mouth with her sleeve, takes another deep pull off her cigarette, and continues. "If you grow up poor on a farm like I did, you have to invent things to do," she says. "So I'd go in the corral after daddy had wrangled up the cows, and of course there's poop everywhere. So you grab onto the cow's tail, barefoot in the manure, and you slide across the barn in it. We called it cow skiing. Now *that's* being a redneck."

My next stop is the Dublin-Laurens County Historical Society housed in the old Carnegie Library. Outside the turn-of-the-century building, a 35-foot tall marble statue of a Confederate soldier has stood watch over the town square for nearly 100 years. Inside the small museum, Trudy Lord, the elderly woman who runs the facility, gives me a personally guided tour. The collection features Civil War medals, muskets, and uniforms, and old photographs of the city and its forefathers. As I study the numerous artifacts, I notice that there is only one reference to a black man in the entire collection. His name was Ten Cent Bill, and according to the literature, he was a slave who fought for the Confederate army at the side his master. When I question my tour guide about the conspicuous absence of African Americans from the exhibit, especially given that they have long outnumbered whites in the town, she directs me to a darkened corner at the far end of the room where a small plaque reads "Black History." The black history exhibit consists of one glass display case about the size of an Igloo ice cooler. Most of the notable African Americans featured are black men from the community who had become professional athletes, such as Quincy Troupe who played on the All-Star team with Jackie Robinson, and Bill Robinson who played on the 1979 Pittsburgh Pirates World Series team. Susie W. Dasher, a respected educator in the community who helped raise teaching standards at black schools before segregation, is the lone African American woman featured in the exhibit. The black community's lack of representation here is striking.

As I'm leaving, I ask Mrs. Lord—who is eloquent, educated, and based on her stylish hairdo and smart pantsuit, from a moneyed antebellum family—what she thinks of the Redneck Games and the notoriety it has brought to Dublin. She rolls her eyes with exaggerated disapproval. "There's so much more to our town than those silly Games." She clears her throat, then offers, "But it's a way for those people to preserve their heritage, I guess. They're hard-working people and good folks. *Those* are the qualities that makes a town what it is."

It's dusk, and I've made my way across town to the County Farm Bureau for the *Redneck Rampage* wrestling event. I get in line with about three hundred diehard fans, mostly families with young children. Rowdy Thigpen, a friendly fireplug of a man, introduces me to his wife Deborah and their ten-year-old son Aaron, who is the 2002 and 2004 Redneck Games armpit serenade champion. When I ask him the secret to his armpit-twanging success, he replies in that ever-polite, Southern manner, "I just practice real hard, sir."

As we enter the square cinderblock building that resembles a grade school gymnasium, Rowdy explains that the venue is normally used for hog auctions and castrating sheep. At the center of the room is a tattered ring where strips of duct tape conceal rips in the Nixon-era canvas. Although it is after 8 PM, the temperature outside still registers in the low-90's and the humidity is stifling. Inside the poorly ventilated room, where the Farm Bureau apparently does not foot the bill for air conditioning, it is easily fifteen degrees hotter. The room stinks of body odor, stale hog urine, and of all things, Cool Ranch Dressing.

The low-budget event has the aura of a high school production, and the acting makes Hulk Hogan look like Olivier in *Othello*. In most cases, these wrestlers have regular jobs outside of the ring to pay the bills. By day, they might work at the mill or pour concrete for the county. But at night, when that bell rings, these blue-collar men become superstars with names like Loco Motive, Sugar Daddy Osborne, and Velvet Jones, who is the only black wrestler on the card and dresses like a pimp from the 1970s. For a few moments, they are showered with the adulation and recognition that escapes their daily lives. It's like karaoke, but with groin smashing.

One of the early matches features a wrestler named Oko Nono, a clownish villain purported to be a Japanese samurai from Nagasaki but is played to the hilt by a pale Southern white man. He wears a latex mask that is supposed to be in the Kabuki tradition, but instead recalls the Gimp from *Pulp Fiction*. He strikes faux karate poses and speaks in a horrendous Japanese accent, shouting anti-American slurs as if it's Iwo Jima circa 1942: "Stupid American! Shut you mouth! I *keel* you!" It is a blatantly offensive Japanese caricature, falling somewhere between Mickey Rooney's buck-toothed Mr. Yunioshi in *Breakfast at Tiffany's* and Gedde Watanabe's Long Duk Dong in *Sixteen Candles*. And the crowd eats it up. *Hey sexy girlfriend!*

The highlight of the evening is the steel cage match, where a bevy of wrestlers including Redneck Games founder "Mad" Mac Davis enter the cage and proceed to pummel each other with an assortment of chairs, garbage cans, and random pieces of lumber.

The crowd is whipped into a Budweiser-induced, orgiastic frenzy. One woman, 60-ish, with brassy stained teeth and an impressive mullet that's bleached white and feathered at the sides, unleashes a torrent of screams at a 500-pound spandex-clad wrestler called the Professor: "Get that sum bitch! Stomp his throat! Stomp it good!" Of course, professional wrestling matches are scripted and the blows are staged. Yet this crowd believes what they are watching is real because they *want* to believe it, the way one might believe in Santa Claus, leprechauns, or the musical talent of Mark McGrath. There is something beautifully simplistic and hopeful about a group of people giving themselves over to a common ideal, and I find myself cheering right alongside the frothing masses.

The next morning, I arrive at East Dublin's Buckeye Park for the 10th annual Summer Redneck Games. The grounds are situated along the shore of the Oconee River and surrounded by dense swampland. The area is a breeding ground for mosquitoes, West Nile Virus, and wild carnivorous hogs, and locals tell me that the murky waters are teeming with alligators. In other words, it is an ideal location for a large gathering of inebriated adults and their half-naked children. The crowd, which will swell to nearly 7,000 (down from previous years because of expected thundershowers), streams in on foot, by car, and by boat, with beer coolers and barbecue grills in tow. On the north side of the park is a large stage where most of the competitive events will take place. To the south, there are numerous food and merchandise vendors.

The first people I meet at the Games are Sue and Michelle (who asked me not to use their last names) from New York City, illustrating the far-reaching popularity of the redneck phenomenon. When I ask why they traveled nearly a thousand miles for this event, Sue says laughing, "We're here for the butt crack contest." She composes herself, adding, "And we're not looking for dates. We want to make that very clear."

Then Michelle, who I'd pegged as the quiet one, blurts out, "I want to suck face with the winner of the bobbin' for pigs' feet competition. That takes some serious lung power!"

Sue adds, "We graduated from Yeshiva, so we're nice Jewish girls. But don't tell anybody because there's a lot of rebel flags around here."

At noon, the crowd converges on the stage to witness the ceremonial lighting of the barbecue grill, signifying the start of the Games. A man named L-Bow, wearing tattered sun-bleached overalls, barefoot, and missing all his teeth, carries the official redneck torch—a flaming Budweiser can on a stick—through the crowd where he is greeted like a celebrity. He's been the official Redneck Games mascot for ten years, earning the name L-Bow when a "Yankee" told him, "Boy, you so ugly, I can't tell your ass from your elbow." He leaps onto the stage, flames up the beer-can torch, and lights the enormous grill in mock Olympic fashion. The crowd roars, and the Games are under way.

Each year, the Redneck Games has a special celebrity guest. Last year (2004) it was Miss Belgium 1998, because Miss Slovenia was unavailable, and this year it's Steve Schirripa, who plays Bobby "Bacala" Baccalieri on *The Sopranos*. This might seem like an odd choice—an Italian from Brooklyn—but he's a good sport and participates in all the events, nearly winning the redneck horseshoe competition that involves tossing toilet seats onto a plunger.

"Don't tell me I'm no redneck," he yells to the crowd. And that's part of this event's appeal: anyone from anywhere can be a redneck, regardless of social or economic status.

"People love rednecks, because it's a natural way of life," says Tracy Giddens of Cochran, Georgia. "You don't have to comb your hair or dress a certain way. You can be retarded or deformed, and still be a cool redneck."

Kliff Hanger, an African American pro wrestler known as "The Black Redneck" who drapes himself in the Confederate flag, adds, "People are ready for something that feels authentic. Most Americans are working class poor and they don't have disposable income. They do back-breaking jobs and their entire paychecks go to feeding their kids and paying for health insurance. And the redneck lifestyle is something they can relate to. It's accessible to everyone."

Sue, who made the trip from New York, adds, "We've got rednecks in Manhattan too, you know. But we call them alcoholics."

The competitive events at the Redneck Games are almost an afterthought, and though a few hundred people gather to watch bobbin' for pigs' feet champion Melvin Davis defend his title, most are simply content to be eating, drinking, and mingling with their brethren. The event that draws the biggest crowd is the mud pit belly flop, where a parade of fantastically obese men and women hurl themselves into a ditch filled with stinking orange muck. Afterwards, I hit the concourse in search of lunch, because nothing whets an appetite like the sight of mud-caked cellulite and sweaty, jiggling man-boobs. The food vendors are hawking every kind of charred meat imaginable, including Polish, Italian and possum sausages, deep-fried pork rinds, cheese steaks, and alligator kabobs. Unfortunately, I am doing a colon cleanse that prohibits me from eating meat, and I soon realize that I've stumbled upon Dante's 8th level of Vegetarian Hell. I settle for a bag of hot boiled peanuts and a deep-fried Twinkie, nutritious snacks that go down well in 110-degree heat.

Additionally, there are only eight Porta Potties for the thousands in attendance, and the lines stretch back to the river. Many people venture into the swamp to relieve themselves. I consider this option, until a young boy emerges from the bog with several enormous leeches attached to his leg. His mother, who is simultaneously smoking *and* chewing tobacco, takes the lit cigarette from her mouth and proceeds to burn the engorged parasites off, one-by-one. "Quit squirming," she tells the boy, squirting a bit of tobacco juice as she speaks. "This one's dug in *real* good."

I expected the Redneck Games to be a drunken, bawdy affair, but it's remarkably family-friendly and wholesome. At one point, a belligerent man who repeatedly yells, "Fuck!" within earshot of a group of children gets hauled away by security.

Many families set up large, colorfully decorated tents to provide refuge from the sweltering heat. Paul Schneider from Tampa, who won the mud pit belly flop contest, his girlfriend Lucy, and their baby Nevaeh ("heaven" spelled backwards) invite me into their double-wide tent for beer and barbecue with the entire extended family. They are kind, funny, and generous, handing me one Budweiser after another from an oversized cooler. David Green, the elder statesmen of the clan, offers a frightening demonstration of his award-winning hog call. Though the deafening, high-pitched squeal conjures images of Ned Beatty and the hillbilly-rape scene in *Deliverance*, I am more concerned that it will attract bloodthirsty razorbacks from the swamp. Their cousin James Estes, a proud redneck from Wrightsville, Georgia, asks me if I've ever "met the Lord." When I say no, he hands me an enormous jug of Lord Calvert's Canadian Whiskey and invites me to join him for a shot. I am goaded into doing whiskey shots with each family member as my indoctrination into the fun-loving clan.

The Redneck Games is essentially a large county fair, with a decidedly Confederate twist. And when I say Confederate, I mean white. In fact, it is difficult to find a single black person at the Redneck Games, which is disconcerting when you consider that Dublin is more than fifty percent African American. One look around, however, and it's easy to understand the conspicuous lack of diversity: the merchandise booths offer a wide variety of racially charged products. If you've ever wondered where you could purchase a rebel flag Speedo or a 16-inch hunting knife engraved with the words, "White is Right," this is the place. One booth sells bumper stickers with slogans like, "If I'd known this is how it would turn out, I would've picked my own cotton." It is these types of racist overtures that cast a pall on a seemingly good-natured event.

"It may seem like harmless fun, but an event like the Redneck Games has insidious undertones," says Dr. Susan Glisson, a professor at the Center for the Study of Southern Culture and Director of the William Winter Institute for Racial Reconciliation. "To promote an event that consciously or subconsciously excludes half of the community is inherently racist."

The line between rednecks and racism is blurred even

further by the Confederate stars-and-bars symbol that is synonymous with this culture. The Redneck Games is a vast sea of Confederate flags, proudly displayed on people's hats, t-shirts, bikinis, beer cozies, and even baby diapers. But the history of the symbol itself is not so innocent. "After the 1890's, the children of Confederate soldiers began to create this cult-like, mythical image of the South to assuage their anger that their fathers had been defeated, and they used the Confederate flag to embody those ideals," says Dr. Glisson. But the majority of Southerners will tell you that the rebel flag is a symbol of their history and nothing more.

"The Confederate flag is about heritage," says *Redneck World* magazine founder Frank Fraser. "There are many great great grandfathers from the South who died on those Civil War battlefields. The flag is a way of remembering them."

Ben "Cooter" Jones adds, "The Confederate flag issue is a manifestation of the liberal elite. Did you know that the Confederate symbol is the Christian cross of St. Andrew? It represents the independent spirit of the South and its heritage. It's not about slavery or hatred. Ninety-nine percent of the displays of the rebel flag are benign."

"What about the one-percent who use the flag as a symbol of their bigotry?" I ask him.

"You can't expect us to lower our flags because of a few bad apples," he says. "I mean, the Ku Klux Klan wears white sheets, so should we stop putting sheets on our beds?"

"The problem with the heritage-not-hate argument for the Confederate flag," says Dr. Glisson, "is that Southern blacks and whites have a shared, interdependent history.

And if we're not willing to include the interracial nature of our Southern heritage into the conception of who we are, racism will continue to exist."

Dr. Glisson adds, "Robert E. Lee said to 'furl the flag' when he died because he didn't want it displayed at his funeral. And the Confederate symbol did not appear on the Georgia state flag until 1956, as a direct response to the landmark 1954 *Brown vs. Education* decision that led to desegregation of public schools. It was a reminder to black people that even though they were gaining more Constitutional rights, it was the white people who were really in charge."

After searching the park for the better part of two hours, I locate the only two African Americans in the throng. Both are friendly women working at a Pizza Hut booth, and one of them, a 55-year-old grandmother named Marsha, speaks to me with a clarity I have yet to witness since my arrival in these parts. "Here in Dublin, things are polite between whites and blacks," she says. "But nothing really authentic—it's all on the surface. If you're a black person in this town, you have your place and don't you cross that line." She pauses to serve a slice of pepperoni pizza, and continues. "Things go on here you wouldn't believe. There are rich white people in this town who make black workers enter their homes through the back door, like it was the 1920s. *Through the back door*." She wipes her hands on her apron, scanning the white crowd.

"I'm old enough to remember when blacks weren't allowed inside the same restaurants as whites. And this still exists today for a lot of black people."

David (not his real name), a dark-skinned man from India and one of the few non-white business owners in

Dublin, reiterated this point when I met him for dinner last night. "There's only one bar in this town, and black folks know not to go in it," he told me. "Everything is controlled here. Everybody knows where you can go and where you can't. There are invisible walls all over this city."

"I'll tell you one thing you *won't* find here in Dublin: a black man holding a white woman's hand walking in the street," he said. "You will never see that here."

I asked David if he's had any difficult experiences as a non-white business owner in a racially divided town.

"I was at a city council meeting where they were voting to build a public pool in Dublin. It gets so hot here in the summer, and there's not a lot for kids to do when school is out. A public pool would be great for the community. But they voted it down, even though we had the money to build it. After the meeting, I asked a prominent council member why he voted against it, and he said, 'Because we don't want our kids swimming in the same water as those little colored babies.' And my heart just sank."

Back at the pizza stand, I ask Marsha if she feels nervous or uncomfortable about being one of the only black people at the Redneck Games. She stands up tall and says in a loud, clear voice, "This is a public park, and my tax dollars pay for it. So I have a right to be here. My spirit is very strong. And when you're standing with the truth, nothing can hurt you."

Later, I ask Freddie Baugus, president of the East Dublin Lion's Club, the main sponsor of the Redneck Games, what efforts, if any, are being made to increase diversity at the event. He tells me in a half-hearted, lazy molasses drawl that the Games are open to everyone and that all races of people attend. When I tell him that I counted only two African Americans out of more than 7,000 attendees, he deflects the issue. "*Look,* this is about good people getting together to have a good time. And all the proceeds from the gate charges and t-shirt sales go to charity."

"What about the proceeds from the racist bumper stickers and the 'white power' hunting knives?" I ask. "Does that money go to charity too?"

"I think we're finished here," Baugus says as he turns away in a huff.

By mid-afternoon, the sky darkens as ominous black clouds roll in, unleashing a deluge of wind and rain. Thunder crackles and lightning streaks the salmon sky. People scatter for cover, many returning to their cars and heading home early. The organizers cancel the remaining events—the armpit serenade, hubcap hurl, and the butt-crack contest—to the dismay of hopeful participants. I huddle under the Pizza Hut booth for shelter, chatting with Marsha.

"You know, I volunteered to be here because I thought it was important," she says. "I believe that by standing tall and proud, I am breaking down the racial barrier. And I will be here again next year and the year after, and I will tell more black people to come. You are going to see a variety of people here next year, and black people will be participating."

We share a smile, basking in this moment of optimism. But as we're exchanging contact information, two shirtless teenagers pass in front of us, wrestling over a half-empty beer bottle. One says to the other, "Gross, dude. Don't nigger-lip the thing." And I am suddenly jolted back to a world where African Americans aren't welcome at the only bar in town, and black laborers are forced to enter white homes through the back door. I want to chase down the teens and make them choke on their thoughtless, hateful words. But instead, I do nothing, pretending not to hear the remark. The truth is, aside from my dietary considerations and my aversion to handguns, I may not be so different from these rednecks after all. I live in San Francisco, one of the most ethnically and culturally diverse cities in the world, but I don't count a single black person among my friends. In fact, I don't really know any black people at all. Though I'm not consciously part of the race problem in America, I'm certainly not part of the solution. I wish Marsha luck with her crusade, and then I turn and walk out into the fine, steady drizzle, where you can't tell me from anyone else in the crowd.

All the Young Dudes

I'm waiting in line to buy a White Russian cocktail from a beverage cart at a non-descript bowling alley in southern California. In front of me, a heavy-set Latino man in a hand-stitched marmot costume is volleying movie quotes with a small woman dressed as a severed human toe. The exchange goes something like this:

> Woman: *Nice marmot.*
> Man: *You want a toe? I can get you a toe.*
> Woman: *That, and a pair of testicles.*

If you're a fan of cult films, or if you've smoked weed in a college dorm room at some point in the last two decades, then you'll recognize this bit of dialogue from the 1998 Coen brothers film *The Big Lebowski*. And this place, a bowling alley in an obscure suburb between Los Angeles and Long Beach, is home to tonight's Lebowski Fest. Described as a "chaotic celebration of the human spirit" by the LA times, the Lebowski Fest is a goofy two-day event that features a screening of the film, trivia contests, plenty of White Russian cocktails, a Creedence Clearwater

Revival cover band, costume contests, and of course lots of bowling. But mostly, the Lebowski Fest is a place where fans, known as Achievers, can come to celebrate the film and get a little weird with likeminded people.

The first Fest was launched in 2002 by Lebowski devotees Will Russell and Scott Shuffitt in Louisville, Kentucky and drew about 150 people. Today, the event travels to multiple cities each year drawing tens of thousands of fans. In 2007, Russell and Shuffitt took the event to London and Scotland, and the Lebowski Fest has landed on *Spin* magazine's list of "19 Summer Events You Can't Miss," *Rolling Stone's* "Hot List" and was voted one of the "Best Summer Road trips" by *Maxim* and *FHM*. In addition to the Fests, *The Big Lebowski* has inspired several books, including the best-selling *I'm a Lebowski, You're a Lebowski*, and a Lebowski-themed shop recently opened in New York's tony Greenwich Village where the employees all wear bathrobes and pajamas. This summer in San Francisco, a re-imagined Shakespeare play called *Much Ado About Lebowski* premiered, and at the time of this writing *The Big Lebowski* has more than 2 million Facebook fans. The movie even spawned its own religion called Dudeism, based on the Zen-like attitude of the Dude, Lebowski's underachieving antihero played by Jeff Bridges. And perhaps most baffling, there have been literally hundreds of doctoral dissertations, academic papers, and scholarly critiques written about the Lebowski phenomenon. In other words, this thing is big. Which raises an interesting question: how has this offbeat little film—a box-office flop and critical punching bag upon its 1998 theatrical release—garnered such a rabid following and become so thoroughly entrenched in the cultural zeitgeist?

When *The Big Lebowski* hit theaters in March of 1998, two years after *Fargo's* successful Oscar run, the United States was experiencing a period of unprecedented economic prosperity. This might be why Americans weren't particularly receptive to the seemingly radical, leftist social critiques so prevalent in the Coen brothers' acid-trippy, Raymond Chandler-esque bowling farce. But the cultural landscape has shifted dramatically in the decade-plus since *The Big Lebowski's* release. We've lived through the terror attacks of 9/11, two bloody wars in Iraq and Afghanistan, a devastating economic recession, and the comedy of Dane Cook. In his paper "The Big Lebowski as Carnivalesque Social Critique," Paul Martin describes the United States as a place where the mainstream media tends to legitimize official government spin and where political dissent is unpopular—or worse—unpatriotic. This narrow, oppressive climate, according to Martin, has created a void in popular critical discourse. "With this void begging to be filled by those left voiceless and powerless," says Martin, "*The Big Lebowski* has become even more relevant today." In other words, the radical, leftist social critiques of *The Big Lebowski* and its not-so-subtle statements about class warfare, Saddam Hussein, big business, and mass consumerism are just what Americans want (and maybe need) at this point in our history. In this sense, the Dude really is the man for his time.

While there may indeed be a socio-historic element to *The Big Lebowski* phenomenon, I think this is only one part of the equation. To begin to understand this film's cultural relevance, we first need to turn our attention to the fans. In the parlance of our times, these people are fucking crazy. Most Achievers can recite every line of dialogue in the movie, they claim to hate the fucking Eagles, and they make their own costumes for the Fests that they attend. Many come dressed as their favorite characters: you'll see plenty of Dudes, Walters, nihilists, and Jesuses at the events. But some fans take a more conceptual approach to their costumes, dressing as the Folger's coffee can that holds Donny's cremated ashes, the 69-cent check that the Dude writes for his half and half, or the severed human toe. To the Achievers, any bit of minutia related to the film is sacred. It could be a prop from the movie set, like the stuffed marmot the Coen brothers loaned the Fest back in 2004. Or it could be an extra from the film who had no speaking lines, like Jesus's bowling partner Liam or the gum-chewing checkout girl at Ralph's.

The Big Lebowski's fans are passionate, bordering on obsessive. But why are they so drawn to this particular film? Every generation has a quotable college stoner comedy. For me, it was *Animal House*, *Caddyshack* and *Fletch*. For you, it might be a Cheech & Chong movie, *Bill & Ted's Excellent Adventure* or *Office Space*. But they don't have Fletch Fests, and people don't dress up like Judge Smails or Carl Spackler, though I did once play Spaulding in a re-enactment of the candy bar scene from *Caddyshack* in my cousin's pool. The point is that these other highly-quotable, generation-defining comedies didn't have the same cultural impact as Lebowski. Some think it's because *The Big Lebowski* is the first major cult comedy of the internet age. And there may be some truth to that. But if you want my opinion, it all goes back to the Dude.

Achievers love the Dude. To them, he's the grinning Buddha Zen master and the relaxed slacker hero all rolled into one lumpy, disheveled, oat soda-drinking body. But the key word here is *hero*. James Hoosier, who played Jesus's bowling partner Liam in the movie, offers the following insight: "If I want to go out to the grocery store in my pajama bottoms, then I should be able to do that. But you know what? I always end up putting on pants anyway. That's why people love this movie: because the Dude does the things we want to but can't."

When we first meet the Dude—or his Dudeness, or Duder, or El Duderino if you're not into the whole brevity thing—he's in a supermarket writing a post-dated 69-cent check for a pint of half and half. He's wearing Bermuda shorts, sunglasses, and a ratty bathrobe. According to the character description in the Coen brothers' script, "His rumpled look and relaxed manner suggest a man in whom casualness runs deep." *Casual* is probably the most polite way to describe the Dude, since he exhibits all the telltale signs of a slacker hippie burnout: He's lazy. He's perpetually unemployed. He's habitually behind on his rent. He seems to subsist solely on White Russian cocktails, coffee, and breath mints lifted from a funeral parlor. And his only interests are bowling, listening to Creedence (or whale sounds), smoking weed, and taking bubble baths. By society's standards, the Dude is a loser. And this is where things get interesting.

On the surface, the Dude seems to embody the failure of the New Left, those activists, educators and agitators in the 1960s and 1970s who fought for social and political reforms in America. These idealistic youths tried to launch a much-ballyhooed counterculture revolution but it never really got off the ground. Hunter Thompson described the failure of the New Left and the downfall of the Love Generation thusly:

"No doubt they all got what was coming to them. All those pathetically eager acid freaks who thought they could buy Peace and Understanding for three bucks a hit. A generation of permanent cripples, failed seekers, who never understood the essential old-mystic fallacy of the Acid Culture: the desperate assumption that somebody— or at least some *force*—is tending that light at the end of the tunnel."

But what if Hunter Thompson is wrong on this one? Perhaps someone *is* tending that light at the end of the tunnel, and perhaps that someone shops at Ralph's in his bathrobe and has an intense fear of marmots. Is it conceivable, then, that the Dude *is not* the symbolic failure of the New Left after all, but rather a warrior who has remained faithful to his cause, a beacon of hope for the New Left that carries the dream from the 1960s into tomorrow, inspiring a new generation of revolutionaries (or stoned college sophomores) along the way? Think about it. The Dude has a history as an activist and spent his college years "occupying various administration buildings, smoking thai-stick, breaking into the ROTC, and bowling." He was a member of the radical Seattle Seven group and helped draft the original version of the Port Huron Statement. In her essay "The Dude and the New Left," Stacy Thompson describes the Port Huron Statement as a lazy version of the *Communist Manifesto*. The 1962 document argues that, "work should be educative, not stultifying; creative, not mechanical; self-directed, not manipulated, encouraging independence, a respect for others, a sense of dignity, and a willingness to accept social responsibility." Thompson suggests that the Dude is not lazy, but that he simply refuses to work in a stultifying, non-creative job. Essentially, by refusing to work, the Dude is enacting the tenets of the Port Huron Statement. As a result, he is the embodiment of those ideals, *today*. This means that the light at the end of the tunnel is indeed being tended. It means that the will of a single Creedence-loving man is keeping the dream of the New Left alive. Because as Walter tells the Dude, "If you will it, it is no dream."

While the Port Huron Statement only briefly touches on the concept of labor, I think our changing attitudes towards the American work ethic is the accelerant that fuels the Lebowski phenomenon today. In his book *Doing Nothing: A History of Loafers, Loungers, Slackers and Bums in America*, Tom Lutz asserts that the American work ethic, really the Protestant work ethic, is a relatively recent development. "Before the Industrial Revolution," says Lutz, "The slacker as an identity, as a kind of person, did not exist." He writes that the classical communities—the Greeks, Romans, and Middle Eastern civilizations—all considered work to be a curse, unless it served the higher mind. "Antipathy toward labor," Lutz writes, "has been the norm since the beginning of time." He traces this attitude to the "Book of Genesis" in the Old Testament, when God expels Adam and Eve from Paradise and damns them to a life of labor. "The necessity to work for survival," Lutz adds, "is the original curse, the punishment for the original sin." In other words, nobody fucks with the Jesus. It wasn't until the Protestant Reformation that our modern notion of a personal work ethic began to take shape. Even then, writers, artists and thinkers railed against having to work for a living. In 1706, the philosopher John Locke said, "Labour for labour's sake is against nature." In 1758, Samuel Johnson suggested that "idling is not a sin, but in fact the truest desire of all." Even Nietzsche voiced his opinion in *Thus Spoke Zarathustra*:

"One still works, for work is a form of entertainment. But one is careful that lest the entertainment be too harrowing. One no longer becomes rich or poor: both require too much exertion."

Fucking Nietzsche. It figures that a German philosopher who died of syphilis-related insanity would write the most Dude-like line of the 19th century. But the crazy old man gets right to the nut of it: being rich (achieving) requires too much effort, and being poor, well that's just a pain in the ass.

All across America, people, especially the younger generations, are questioning the way we think about work and the role that consumerism plays in our lives. If you're truly lucky, you actually enjoy your profession, or at least you don't hate it. But most people simply toil away in unsatisfying, creatively void jobs to pay their mortgage and put food on the table. But they also do it to buy big screen TVs, ridiculously impractical SUVs, and the newest iPhone or iPad that's on every must-have gadget list. They've unwittingly joined the dehumanizing world of consumption and competition, because that's the American way: we work, and then we buy. Because everyone's got to feed the monkey. But the Dude, he doesn't toil away in a job that he hates. And he doesn't have a big screen TV. And he certainly doesn't feed the monkey. And he seems content with his life. He seems content abiding. If all great art is simply a reflection of society, perhaps the Dude represents a new America, where less really is more, and where living a simple, decent life is at the heart of the new American dream.

Back at the Lebowski Fest, after several White Russians and an awkward conversation with a drunken, touchy-feely nihilist, I decide to pack up my things and head home. I say goodnight to the guy in the marmot suit and a young woman dressed as a cassette tape of the Eagles' *Hotel California*. As I exit the bowling alley, I come across several Dudes and a Maude outside smoking cigarettes on the sidewalk. I ask one of the Dudes, a twenty-something lawyer from Beverly Hills, why he thinks *The Big Lebowski* has captured the imagination of so many people:

"It's because of the Dude. He's the prince of under-achievers and I think we all aspire to do nothing. And he does nothing better than anyone else has ever done it. And it's not just about him doing nothing: it's about everyone in America doing nothing. It's the ideal of doing nothing, and not doing it phenomenally."

It's the ideal of doing nothing, and not doing it phenomenally. It won't fit on a bumper sticker, but hey, at least it's an ethos. And this idea, as radical as it may seem, offers a certain amount of comfort during these difficult times. Like the Stranger says, "It's good knowin' he's out there, the Dude, takin' her easy for all us sinners."

The Highwayman

There aren't many famous bus drivers in the world, and even if you include fictional film and TV characters, you can probably count them on one hand: Ralph Kramden on *The Honeymooners*, Otto Mann from *The Simpsons*, Sandra Bullock in *Speed*, and James F. Blake, who ordered Rosa Parks off an Alabama bus in 1955 for not surrendering her seat to a white man. And of course there's Hoot Borden, the greatest rock and roll bus driver of all time. Though he's not widely known to the general public, Hoot has been a legend in the music industry for more than fifty years.

On this unseasonably warm November afternoon, Hoot is in the front lounge of his spotless 1998 Prevost coach, dispensing tasty nuggets of country wisdom and spinning colorful yarns from a lifetime on the road. He leans back, legs outstretched in front of him, and says in his trademark Southern drawl, "You know, it ain't fair the way Britney gets hammered in the press. You reporters always trying to make a story where there ain't one." He coughs a bit of phlegm into a napkin and adds, "People forget she's just a kid from Louisiana. She's country folk.

In the South, everyone drives around with their baby on their lap. She's just doing what her momma taught her." For the record, Hoot Borden is 70 years old, and while it may seem odd for a crusty septuagenarian to pontificate on the media's treatment of Britney Spears, it's even more shocking when he comes out swinging in defense of the troubled pop star. But when you get to know Hoot, and you understand his loyalty to the artists he's hauled over the years, his reaction makes perfect sense: He's protecting Britney, just like any grandfather would. Then he leans toward me, almost conspiratorially, and in a low throaty voice, says, "I'll tell you what, though. I didn't like her husband one bit." When I press him for a reason—and there are many reasons to dislike Kevin Federline—Hoot replies candidly, "Because of the way he wore his hat. That crooked cap pissed me off." And then, as if speaking directly to Federline, Hoot growls, *"You little son of a bitch. I'll show you how to wear a damn hat."*

Hoot Borden has been part of the American music landscape since 1950, and his name is the stuff of legend. "Old Hooter's driven more miles backing out of his driveway than most people do in a lifetime," says Timmer Ground of Music City Coach, Borden's longtime employer. "He's an old road dog, and the last of a dying breed." Over the last half century, and he's never missed a week of work, Hoot has witnessed the birth of rock and roll and the rise of the music touring industry. His contemporaries, many of whom he considers personal friends, include such heavyweights as Johnny Cash, Ernest Tubb, Bill Monroe, and Willie Nelson—all members of the Country Music Hall of Fame, the Rock and Roll Hall of Fame, or both. And though he spent his early days on the country circuit, he's hauled a wide range of artists from Megadeth and Cher to Patti LaBelle and Poison. In the last year alone, he's driven for Bob Dylan, Rob Thomas, and Jack White. But Hoot Borden is more than a chauffeur who shuttles cranky superstars from one gig to another: he's a symbol of a forgotten era, when a business deal was sealed with a handshake, people took pride in their work, and a man's word was more important than his net worth. When I catch up with Hoot at the Wells Fargo Center for the Arts in Santa Rosa, California, he's driving a crew bus for iconic singer Anne Murray. He greets me with a warm smile and a handshake and invites me onboard. When we spoke on the phone a few days earlier, I'd offered to meet him at his hotel, since most drivers sleep in the afternoon so they can drive at night. "I'm more comfortable on the bus, if you don't mind," said Hoot. "This is my home. This is where I belong."

Hoot Borden was born into an Oklahoma farming family, but his passion was always music. In 1950 at the age of 14, he dropped out of school and left the family farm to become a professional drummer. "I was pretty good, too," says Hoot. "In those days, a recording session paid $42.30. And that was good money back then." Hoot's knowledge of heavy machinery from his farming days ensured that he got plenty of work: he could play drums for a honky-tonk band *and* keep the tour bus running. "Most musicians was so poor, they bought their buses off the scrap heap. So you weren't trying to make it to the end of a tour; you was just trying to make it to the next town."

He eventually landed on the Nevada Circuit, playing for groups like Tex Williams & His Western Caravan, The Starlighters, and Orville Couch, who had five number one hits for Capitol Records. But his life changed forever when he quit drumming in 1959 to take a full-time job driving country music pioneer Ernest Tubb and his band The Texas Troubadours. "I played my very last show in Duncan, Arizona at a cotton gin that had been turned into a dance hall. And I been driving these buses ever since."

Hoot would spend the next 24 years hauling Ernest Tubb and his band, playing every honky-tonk beer joint from Amarillo to Battle Mountain. This is the point in the story when Hoot's adventures begin to sound like something out of *Forrest Gump*. His travels would introduce him to all the Nashville legends, including an unknown singer named Elvis Presley, who couldn't get booked on the Grand Ole Opry until Ernest Tubb gave him a spot in his show. "I remember the first time I saw Elvis perform," recalls Hoot. "I thought, *that long-haired son-of-a-bitch*. And then I saw how the crowd reacted to him. And I knew he was gonna be something special." Hoot slides his calloused hands into the pockets of his crisp denim jeans, and adds, "Elvis was an enormous gentleman, right up until the day he died. My son and Lisa Marie Presley are great friends—he's even got a key to Graceland." Over the years, Hoot would find himself in the company of four U.S. Presidents, with a standing invitation to Lyndon Johnson's family barbecues at the 37th President's Texas ranch. In perhaps his most Gump-like episode, Hoot crossed paths with controversial Governor George Wallace, who had fought against segregation at the University of Alabama in 1963. "We didn't really get into the whole race issue," says Hoot. "But in the deep dark of night, I do remember the Governor saying, 'I didn't really want to keep those people out of the schools. It was the people who put me in office who wanted it.'" Coincidentally, this is the same night in history when the terms "pass the buck" and "cover your ass" entered into the American lexicon.

Hoot was also a first-hand witness to many of the technological innovations that would become standard in the music industry today. "I watched Shot Jackson and Buddy Emmons build the first Sho-Bud steel guitar in an auditorium in Witchita, Kansas," says Hoot. "Heck, I remember when Leo Fender built the first echo chamber. It was a little box that sat up on top of your amp, and you'd hit it and it would go *waa waa waa*."

Ernest Tubb's band, The Texas Troubadours, spawned some of the most influential country musicians of the modern era, including Cal Smith, Billy Byrd, Tommy "Butterball" Paige, and a skinny young man with an awkward singing voice named Hugh Nelson, better known to his millions of fans as Willie. "In the early days, Hugh (Willie) would fill in with the Troubadours and play bass guitar. He didn't look nuthin' like the Willie Nelson everybody knows today—he looked like a banker. He wore a snappy suit with a skinny tie, and he had a buzz cut." Hoot chuckles to himself, and continues. "Willie had a tough time in the beginning. He was writing all these brilliant songs—he wrote *Crazy* for Patsy Cline—but the world wasn't ready for him as a performer. Back in '61, Willie was so broke he sold the song *Hello Walls* to Faron Young for $50 just so he could eat." Hoot runs a hand through his whitish, close-cropped hair, adding, "He didn't become the Willie Nelson everybody knows until he quit Nashville and moved to Austin, sometime around 1970. That's when the outlaw movement was in its raw beginnings, with the long hair and the rebellion. He and Waylon (Jennings) kickstarted that whole scene. And the rest is history."

Hoot's personal life is just as colorful as his professional life, maybe even more so. Here's a list of random Hooter facts: he's been married five times, and he has three grown children. His sons are both bus drivers: one of them hauls Larry the Cable Guy, and the other pals around with Lisa Marie Presley and has a key to Graceland. His daughter is on a professional roller derby team out of Houston called the Burlesque Brawlers, skating under the name Ashley Juggs. The number on her uniform is 38D. Hoot swears he's never had a drink of liquor in his life, and he lives on a street with a funny name (Tater Peeler Road). He also spent many years as a deputy for the Sumner County Sheriff's Department in Hendersonville, Tennessee. He was a real officer with a uniform and a license to carry a gun, which he still does. And in between tours, he'd come home and help rustle up bad guys in the greater Nashville area.

One of Anne Murray's sound engineers climbs onto the bus and tells Hoot that dinner is ready in the backstage catering room. Hoot nods and asks me if I'll join them. Never one to turn down a free meal, I accept his offer and follow him into the building. As we move through the buffet line, various band and crewmembers greet Hoot with the warmth and respect generally reserved for the patriarch of a loving family. Everyone calls him Pops or Granddaddy Hoot, and he seems to relish every moment. They save him a seat at the head of the table, and then gather around like children pining for a bedtime story. Hoot sops a piece of white bread in some gravy on his plate, and launches into the following tale:

"When I was with Ernest Tubb back in the 1960s, we'd

always play this old beer joint in Austin, Texas called the Wagon Wheel. They had the best chicken-fried steak anywhere. And every time we'd play there, this little Mexican kid would come banging on the bus door. So we'd let him on, and Billie Byrd would sit there teaching him chords on the guitar. That kid didn't know what notes he was playing, but he could play the Hell out of that thing. Yes sir, that little kid could play guitar. His name was Stevie Ray Vaughan."

Hoot, who also witnessed the evolving cultural landscape through the turbulent 1960s and swinging 1970s, didn't always embrace the changes. "I was a typical, hardheaded Tennessee boy, and I resented the free-spirited nature of the hippie scene—the Haight Ashbury and the Grateful Dead and all that," says Hoot. "In Nashville, Wanda Jackson couldn't go on the Grand Ole Opry until she put a shawl over her shoulders because she had a strapless dress on. But out there in San Francisco, those hippies could walk around completely nekkid, smokin' their dope and doing whatever they wanted. Talk about two different worlds."

After driving Ernest Tubb and the Troubadours on the honky-tonk circuit for 24 years, Hoot's own world was about to turn upside down. On September 6th, 1984, Ernest Tubb died in a Nashville hospital at the age of 70, and Hoot Borden was without a job for the first time in a quarter century. With a wife and kids to support and the country music scene struggling—it would be another five years before artists like Garth Brooks and Trisha Yearwood reinvigorate the genre—Hoot made the big leap to rock and roll. His first tour was with Bruce Hornsby and the Range, followed by stints with Foreigner, Journey, and

Jefferson Starship. The differences between the Nashville honky-tonk circuit and the world of 80's arena rock were staggering. "In country music, everybody had one tour bus, and they stowed the music gear in the bays underneath. There were no trucks in those days," says Hoot. "But on a rock tour, there might be thirty or forty buses and trucks. It's like the damn carnival comin' to town." He laughs and says, "I didn't even know they had concerts in arenas. I thought they was just for basketball and the circus." But it wasn't just the size of the venues that was different: it was the entire rock and roll touring culture. "With Ernest Tubb, we didn't have tour managers or runners or even road crew," says Hoot. "We'd set up our own instruments and I'd sell the t-shirts. The band would do the show, and then we'd load the bus, swallow a handful of pills and drive 800 miles to the next town. It was like that every night." I ask Hoot about the technical differences between the over-the-top stadium concerts of the 80's and the old beer joint shows held in dusty saloons. "There were no pyrotechnics on the honky-tonk circuit," says Hoot. "If you wanted fancy lights, we'd run an extension cord from the bus to the stage and plug in a lamp. That was our light show," Hoot says laughing. "Much later, I toured with Kenny Rogers and he had all the laser lights and effects. One time I disconnected the hose from the laser machine and was using it to wash my bus. Almost burned down the whole building."

It didn't take long for Hoot to adapt to the world of rock and roll touring, and he hauled some of the biggest names of the 1980s, including Poison, Billy Joel, and Michael Jackson. "I drove Michael's family on the Victory tour, all his aunts and uncles," says Hoot. "Michael and his brothers, the Jackson 5, those boys could *really* sing. They'd stay up all night working on their dance steps. Nice boys, all of them. I drove on several Janet Jackson tours too. That's one talented family." Hoot adds, "Most singers nowadays are making millions of dollars and they got no talent at all. If you're gonna sit there and tell me Tim McGraw can sing, you're full of shit. Tim McGraw can't carry a tune with a bucket."

I arrange to meet with Hoot the next morning at his hotel in a quiet suburb of San Jose in Northern California. It's a day off from the Anne Murray tour, and when I arrive, he's out in the parking lot changing the oil in his bus. He waves me over, yelling, "Come here, I want to show you something." I follow him around to the rear of the coach where he lifts an enormous panel, revealing a shiny and spotless engine. I run my finger along the top of the big diesel motor and not surprisingly it is completely clean, without a trace of grease or grime. "She's a beauty, huh?" says Hoot with a wide grin. Then he adds the following kicker: "Not bad for having half a million miles on her." This attention to detail, however, is what makes Hoot a great driver and has contributed to his longevity in the business. "He's in love with his equipment, and he's in love with his job," says Joe Jackson, tour manager for Anne Murray and Bryan Adams. "And he never places himself first. It's always about the bus or the artist or the crew. Everybody loves old Hooter."

Perhaps the greatest testament to Hoot's staying power in the music industry is his relationship with the people he hauls, whether it's a temperamental pop star or a grungy road crew. Regardless of their position, social status, reputation, or background, Hoot treats his passengers with dignity and respect. In 1988, Hoot drove the much-maligned and oft-troubled Bobby Brown at the height of the bad boy singer's success. "I have nothing bad to say about Bobby Brown. I hauled him and six bodyguards, and we had a fine bus. We cooked food every night and had a good old time," says Hoot. "You can take a guy with all kinds of troubles, and you can teach him your way of life and he'll think the world of you." In one of his most fantastic stories, Hoot recalls the night of a St. Louis concert when a rival of Brown's fired a rocket launcher at the bus, exploding part of the rear panel. "It was a real rocket, like the ones they're using Afghanistan, and it blew up the back of my bus. One of the crew guys wrapped the smoldering shell in a blanket and took it home for a souvenir."

Hoot has also worked with difficult road crews, and he uses his unique brand of country psychology to manage unwieldy situations. The ZZ Top road crew was legendary for their foul behavior and bus drivers kept quitting in the middle of their tours. One fed-up driver unloaded the crew's belongings at a hotel in the middle of the night and left them stranded. Another driver dropped their personal effects at a truck stop and went home. So the band's management called Hoot for the impossible job. "Now these crew guys had been with ZZ Top since Day One," says Hoot. "Their production manager was being sued by the city of Houston because his front lawn was infested with rats. That's the kind of degenerates we were dealing with. These guys were animals. They could totally destroy a bus with puke and piss and God knows what." Hoot knew he had to take control of the situation from the outset, so he put an old Roy Rogers movie on the bus TV, and got out the loaded pistol Ernest Tubb had given him. "And I was sittin' right here when they first got on the bus, cleaning this gun so they could all see it. One of the crew guys asked me what we were doing, and I said, *We're watching Roy Rogers and cleaning this fucking gun in case I need to use it.* And I never had a single problem with them after that." Hoot developed a great relationship with the ZZ Top crew, dubbing them The Filthy McNasty Boys, a name they still proudly use today. "I got the swag guy to make up some ball caps and t-shirts, and I had giant letters put on the side of the bus that said *Hooter and the Filthy McNasty Boys,*" he says. "After two weeks, the crew started cleaning their own bus, and they'd make you take your shoes off before you came on board. Because it was *their* bus."

Hoot continues talking as he wipes down the kitchen counter in the bus. "Being a roadie is the greatest job in the world, and I'll tell you why," he says with a mischievous grin. "When you're at home and a tour hires you, you catch a cab to the airport and you're reimbursed for the fare. When you get to the airport, a plane ticket is waiting for you, and if you have bags to check they'll pay for those too. When your flight lands, a $500,000 tour bus is gonna pick you up and take you to your room at the Hilton, which is paid for. Then the road manager is gonna give you $40 a day per diem, which you ain't gonna spend—you're gonna pool it with the other crew guys and buy drugs with it, mostly. You get three meals a day when there's a show, and after the show they're gonna have hot pizzas waiting for you on the bus. And when you take a smoke break, Jesus Christ you smoke dope. And you don't have to be in the band to get girls, you just need one of these," says Hoot, holding up his all-access tour laminate. "If you're a roadie, you live like a damn king."

These days when he tours, Hoot prefers to drive the road crew instead of the artist. Perhaps it's because he's tired of hauling cranky divas, but more likely it's because he enjoys the blue-collar sensibility of most roadies. "I love my little crew guys," says Hoot. "They always say, *Pop, you've got to meet my lady. She's the most perfect thing.* So his lady comes out, and she's about six foot tall, weighs about 88 pounds. Got on sandals, with about 15 pounds of steel in her tongue and her nose. Tattoos all down her body. But that's *their* lady. That's their pride and joy, so you've got to treat them with respect. And that's really the secret to this business: keep a good bus, don't have a wreck, and treat people with respect."

Hoot believes in taking care of the people who ride on his bus. He often cooks meals for them on long rides and days off—his specialty is Texas chili. But he's quick to credit others for their generous spirit as well. "Lord, I've seen Patti LaBelle clear out a kitchen in an auditorium more than once. *'My people not gonna eat that shit,'* she'd say to the caterers. And she'd be back there cooking the whole meal for the crew and band herself. *'My babies got to have something good to eat,'* she'd be hollerin'. And that's what's so sad about the entertainment business today—there's nobody doing that. No one takes care of their people like that. Nobody except little Kenny Chesney. That guy's a real gentleman and he does it the right way. He's got the best tour going now."

Hoot Borden has touched many people's lives over his fifty-odd years in the music business, and their affection for him becomes tangible when you walk through the long corridor of his bus to the back lounge. The walls are lined with custom-made plaques given to him by the artists and crews he's hauled over the years, including Megadeth, Billy Joel, and yes, ZZ Top's Filthy McNasty Boys. He puts his arm on my shoulder and walks me through each one, reading me the personal inscriptions and explaining the stories behind the stories. "And this one's from the Elton John crew. They called me *the warden*, and they were all assigned prison numbers. Nice boys, yes they were." And that's when it occurs to me: this isn't just a tour bus. This is a man's home, and I'm standing in his living room. The people represented on these walls are not merely a byproduct of Hoot's career, they are his children and his grandchildren, a sprawling lineage from a lifetime of labor and love. Singer-songwriter Anna Nalick, who rode with Hoot last summer, says, "He's very protective of me. And every night before I go onstage, he always says, *I love you, Baby Girl. Now go out there and sing your tits off!* Only Hoot could get away with that, because that's *his* way, and I love him for it."

When I mention to Hoot that my grandmother is a big Anne Murray fan, he arranges for my entire family to see the show that night for free. "We got to keep Grandma happy," he tells me with a grin. I stick around after the show, talking with Hoot until the road crew is finished loading the trucks. "It's really been a great ride," he tells me. "I got to see this country being built, driving across it for 51 years. I got to see Hugh Nelson become Willie Nelson. I watched Paul Bigsby build them steel guitars. I watched Tommy Morel invent guitar pickups—all the things we take for granted today. And I got to see all those things come about. Yes sir, it's been one hell of a ride."

When the last of the roadies have boarded the bus, I thank Hoot for his time and head back to my car. The bus door closes and the big diesel engine rumbles to life. I watch as the bus pulls away from the curb and turns onto the street, its taillights burning holes in the night. Now get out there ol' Hooter, and drive your tits off.

You Can Still Rock in America

It's a balmy November evening and I'm sitting in a cruise ship karaoke lounge, fixated on the small stage where a shirtless fat man in a turquoise Mexican wrestling mask is singing, or rather grunting, a classic Mötley Crüe tune from 1983. Just before the Nacho Libre look-alike hits the chorus, he screams to the audience, "Y'all know the words. Sing it, motherfuckers!" The boisterous crowd rises to its feet, fists pumping the air, chanting in boozy unison:

Shout – Shout – Shout – Shout at the devil!

While there's no denying the allure of a chubby, half-naked man in fetishistic headgear performing karaoke for a drunken mob, it should be noted that this is not typical cruise ship fare. Today, most cruise lines cater to middle-American families and aging retirees, offering wholesome entertainment and a theme park sensibility. But the tattooed miscreants gathered in this lounge are not your ordinary cruisers. They are shadow people, existing on the fringes of society. They are the deviants your mother warned you about. They are the bastards, the rebels, the misfits, and the damned. Curiously, they're also tax attorneys, dental hygienists, and kindergarten teachers. And now these denizens of darkness, these orgiastic Satan worshippers and part-time Lamaze instructors, have gathered on this 93,000 ton party boat for Shiprocked, a Bahamas-bound cruise celebrating all things Rock. And when I say Rock, I don't mean the brooding melancholy of Pearl Jam or the electronic science fiction of Radiohead. I don't mean the esoteric blues of The White Stripes, and I certainly don't mean the bullshit studio formula of Seether or Finger Eleven. I'm talking about *rock and roll*, the kind that wears spandex and ladies' mascara while sucker-punching you in the balls; the kind that inspires the trashing of hotel rooms, grotesque inebriation, and a never-ending rotation of groupies sucking cock in the back lounge of a tour bus. I'm talking about 80's arena rock, with monster guitar riffs, sing-along choruses, and three-alarm pyro that'll singe the hair right off your junk. "This music is about pussy, parties, and paychecks," says Stephen Pearcy, lead singer of Ratt. "It's catchy and fun, and there's a stigma that gives it an element of danger. And some of us really like danger. I mean, I'll kill everybody."

Held on the gloriously tacky MSC *Poesia*, Shiprocked features a three-day itinerary packed with rock-related activities, including live concert performances by hair metal icons Cinderella, Tesla, Ratt, Slaughter, Skid Row, and Vince Neil of Mötley Crüe. Though it might be tempting to write off this event as a sad bit of nostalgia or an exercise in hipster irony, I assure you these diehard fans are serious about the music. "This isn't a vacation, it's a lifestyle," says Sherri, a wild-eyed woman wearing leather motorcycle chaps and a faded Guns 'N Roses t-shirt. "I quit my job two summers ago, and I've been following Mötley Crüe ever since. All my credit cards have been shut off and I'm about to get evicted from my place." She sips her frozen margarita adding, "I've basically given up my old life, and it's all good. I just want to rock out with my box out."

The MSC *Poesia* is a full-service cruise ship with every amenity for the discerning traveler, including spas, casinos, sushi bars, and a dinosaur-themed play area for those who want to get in touch with their inner Fred Flintstone. On this voyage, some 1200 metal heads registered for the Shiprocked event, giving them exclusive access to all the concerts and activities. This means that the other 1500 passengers on the ship, mostly families with children and tour groups of the elderly, have unknowingly been booked onto this floating Sodom and Gomorrah—a fact that does not go unnoticed by the wary travelers. "They took over the whole goddamn boat," I heard a crotchety senior tell his wife in the gift shop. "Did you see all the long hair and tattoos? They're goddamn hooligans."

Of course, not all the Shiprockers are hooligans, but they *are* a hard-partying bunch. For many of them, the blowout started several days before the *Poesia* even left port with pre-cruise gatherings at various Ft. Lauderdale watering holes. By the time these diehard fans actually boarded the ship, many were twisted three ways from Sunday. This was particularly evident during the mandatory safety drill where a pretty blonde crewmember gave evacuation instructions to the passengers. As she demonstrated the proper way to secure her life vest, a shoeless, slurring man in a frayed Trixter t-shirt screamed, "I've been drunk for fourteen hours. How am I supposed to remember this shit?" Another man, obviously intoxicated, repeatedly shouted to the woman, "Do you like seamen? Do you like seamen in your mouth?" His comments, thankfully out of earshot of the young woman, were vulgar, infantile, and delightfully profane. I am clearly among my people.

After the safety demonstration, I see the Trixter t-shirt guy at the casino bar and ask him why he was compelled to come on this cruise. "Because you can do anything on this boat and get away with it," he says. "You can get drunk and fall down. You can fuck in public. You can break shit. And nobody says a thing! I mean, what are they gonna do? Throw you overboard? Leave you in the Bahamas?"

When I told my family and friends that I was going on a heavy metal cruise with Cinderella, Tesla, and the lead singer of Mötley Crüe, I was greeted with a certain amount of bemusement. Most seemed to think that these former chart-topping rockers were either dead, working at Home Depot, or playing canasta with the dudes from Foghat at the retirement home of forgotten rock stars. The truth, however, is that nearly all 80's rock bands are touring in some capacity today. Many of these bands like Skid Row, Slaughter, LA Guns, and Warrant subsist at the club level, playing to a few hundred fans a night at beer-soaked dives with colorful names like The Crazy Donkey in Farmingdale, New York, Jerry's Bait Shop in Lenexa, Kansas, and G.B. Leighton's Pickle Park in Fridley, Minnesota. Though the stage may not be as grand as it once was for these middle-aged rockers, they can still make a living playing their music. But not all 80's rock bands are relegated to the biker bar circuit. The heavy hitters of the acid wash era—bands like Guns 'N Roses, Mötley Crüe, Aerosmith, the Scorpions, and Def Leppard—are selling out arenas in a tough economic climate when few artists have that kind of draw. In fact, the highest-grossing concert tour of 2010 belonged to New Jersey rockers Bon Jovi, not Lady Gaga, Taylor Swift, U2, or Justin Bieber.

But it's no longer just about touring: 80's rock has gone mainstream. The *Guitar Hero* and *Rock Band* video game franchises have boosted these artists' catalog sales and introduced their music to a new generation of fans. The wildly successful Broadway musical *Rock of Ages*, set on Hollywood's Sunset Strip in 1987 and featuring music by Night Ranger, Quiet Riot, and Whitesnake, was nominated for five Tony Awards and is now becoming a major motion picture starring Tom Cruise. Bret Michaels of Poison became a household name on VH1's *Rock of Love* and Donald Trump's *Celebrity Apprentice*. Vince Neil recently appeared on ABC's *Skating with the Stars*. And now, Steven Tyler of Aerosmith is a judge on *American Idol*, one of the most-watched shows on television. "For many of these artists, the marketing opportunities and potential revenue streams are greater than ever before," says Jeff Albright, president of the Albright Entertainment Group and publicist for several 80's rock bands. "With the combination of television, radio, video games, and internet, you can now be seen and heard 24-7. And more places to be seen and heard means more places to be sold."

On my way to dinner, I meet a fellow Shiprocker who looks exactly like Vince Neil in every way, except that he's noticeably smaller than the Mötley Crüe front man. Known to everyone on the cruise as 'mini-Vince,' this rock star wannabe meticulously molded his tiny body into a frighteningly realistic Vince Neil clone. He has the same perfectly-mussed sandy blonde hair and scraggly goatee, and he mastered the singer's loping swagger. He even reproduced every detail of Vince Neil's extensive tattoos on his own arms and torso, including Vince's most personal tattoos about his family and loved ones. As we're chatting, several people stop and ask him to sign autographs, which he gladly does.

I've got a few hours to kill before Cinderella takes the stage on this second night of the cruise, so I'm doing what any responsible journalist would do: I'm drinking Red Bull and Xanax daiquiris by the pool and sunning myself like a monitor lizard. All around me, attractive women in thong bikinis seductively oil themselves, splayed on chaise lounges like bronzed, silicone goddesses. Perhaps it's the brain fog from all the benzo and rum, but I suddenly feel as though I've wandered onto the set of a late-night Cinemax movie. I half-expect to find Frank Stallone and Shannon Tweed entwined in the Jacuzzi.

As I make my way across the sundeck to the bar for another round of drinks, I see Tesla lead singer Jeff Keith in shorts and flip flops carrying an enormous plate of hardboiled eggs back to his table. As he meanders through the crowd, people smile and pat him on the back, saying things like, "Dude, you fucking rock!" and "I want you to put a baby in me!" He is friendly and gracious, stopping to chat with everyone who crosses his path. And the fans are ecstatic. "I've never been backstage at a concert. I've never seen any rock stars, like, walking around eating eggs," says Myles, 39, from New Orleans. "But here, you might bump into Vince Neil in the buffet line, or see Tom Kiefer (Cinderella) at the bar." And this is exactly why celebrity theme cruises are so popular today: fans want up-close and personal interactions with their music idols. It's about access and inclusiveness. Because at some point, we've all been on the wrong side of the velvet rope at a trendy nightclub, denied entry because we weren't cool enough, or pretty enough, or willing to grease the steroid-engorged palm of a beefy, power-tripping door-man. An event like Shiprocked is your passport through the velvet rope to the VIP lounge on the other side. "Back in the day when I would go to concerts, I was usually in the nosebleed section because those were the only seats I could afford," says Nancy, 42, from Virginia Beach. "But now that I'm older and I have money, I can see these people up close. I can touch them. I can hang out with them. It's the ultimate experience."

But the lure of these events goes beyond access: it's also about fantasy and wish fulfillment. "Before I even got my first kiss, I was making out with the rock star posters on my bedroom wall," says Angelina Leigh, an actress and fetish model who has appeared in *Playboy*, *Hustler*, and *Juggs* magazine. "And now I get to party with those guys. Last year on Shiprocked, I hung out with Skid Row. And it was so cool, because I totally wanted to marry them when I was a kid, you know?"

It's ten o'clock and time to rock. More than a thousand rabid fans are packed into the Carlos Felice Theater wait-ing to be assaulted by the sonic donkey punch of Cinder-ella's delta blues metal. When the band takes the stage and kicks into "Somebody Save Me," the room becomes a rau-cous sea of split-fingered devil horns, a turbulent ocean of synchronized heads banging in unison like some futur-istic heavy metal hive mind. As they launch into "Gypsy Road," the electricity from the stage jolts through my body, shooting sparks up my spinal chord to my brain stem, cre-ating an aurora borealis of sound inside my frontal lobe. And that's the appeal of 80's rock: it exists for the flesh, not the intellect. It is the soundtrack of the id. Songs like "Girls, Girls, Girls," "Talk Dirty to Me," and "Cherry Pie" are testosterone-driven operettas about loose girls, fast cars, drinking whiskey, and raising hell. It's not supposed to make you think, it's supposed to make you feel. And if done properly, it'll make you feel like fighting or fucking. "I don't wanna go to a concert and hear about how shitty things are. I just wanna have fun tonight," says Vince Neil of Mötley Crüe. "That's what eighties music was all about: get drunk, get laid, have fun."

As Cinderella downshifts into the epic ballad "Don't Know What You've Got (Till It's Gone)," I start chatting with Karen and her husband who are sitting next to me. Karen is in her late 30's, sharp-dressed and stunning, with a hint of mischief lurking behind her green eyes. And she's completely hammered. "I'm a good girl, but when I drink tequila I get really bad. And when I'm bad, I start craving pussy," she says, causing me to snorf an entire Jäger Bomb out my nose. Then she leans in close like she's about to reveal a secret, her hot Jose Cuervo breath dripping with sex. "There's *nothing* like the taste of good pussy," she says. "It's way better than dick." At which point, she grabs the busty woman next to her and they start making out. Karen's husband looks over, completely disinterested. He shrugs his shoulders and continues watching the concert.

On the way back to my stateroom, I notice that my neighbors, two *Jersey Shore* wannabes with ripped abs and Oompa Loompa spray tans, have hung a sign on their cabin door that says "Teezin 'N Pleezin" in large block print, with the cryptic phrase "Squirters Welcome!!" scrawled beneath it. The poster is dotted with several red lipstick imprints, presumably belonging to Buffy, Stacy, and Lila, who dutifully signed their names at the bottom like some kind of twisted Declaration of Independence:

We hold these truths to be self-evident, that all bros are created equal, that they are endowed like wildebeests and have certain unalienable rights, that among these are a lifetime Gold's Gym membership and an unlimited Dave & Buster's Power Card, the freedom to tap hot random ass, and the pursuit of motherfucking rock and roll.

Later, I'm awakened by a cacophony of bleats and squeals echoing from the room next door. I'm not sure what kind of deranged sexual activity is going on over there, but it sounds like someone is slaughtering a goat.

It's the last full day of the cruise. We're docked in the Bahaman port city of Nassau and I'm at Señor Frogs, drinking a 64-ounce frozen daiquiri served in a three-foot tall cup shaped like a saxophone. Some two hundred fellow Shiprockers are here, grooving their way through another round of heavy metal karaoke. The mysterious fat man in the turquoise Mexican wrestling mask has returned to the stage, this time grunting his way through Bon Jovi's "You Give Love a Bad Name." Better yet, he's wearing a half-shirt that says, "Where's the Queef?" *Stay classy, Bahamas.*

A guy with a long, Billy Ray Cyrus mullet sees me jotting notes in my notebook. He staggers up to me and asks if I'm "a writer or some shit like that." I tell him that I am, and that I'm writing a story about this cruise and the revival of 80's rock and roll.

"The bands are still rockin'," he says enthusiastically. "And they're still putting out good music, you know what

I'm sayin'? Ratt's new record is the fucking tits! And there's some new metal bands that are pretty good too. You ever heard of a band called Snake Skin Prison?"

I tell him no.

"What about Nunwhore? Acid Witch? How about Shitstorm?"

This time I just shake my head.

"What the hell you listen to, then? Some kind of Lionel Richie bullshit?"

"Yes," I tell him. "I'm easy like a motherfucking Sunday morning."

He laughs, then he grabs me by the shoulders and screams, "Fuck it, brother—let's drink!"

While I'm waiting in line at the bar to get another giant saxophone daiquiri, I meet two guys from Indiana, one of whom is wearing an actual cowbell around his neck.

"What's the deal with the cowbell?" I ask him.

"Last year we went to Rocklahoma to see Vince Neil and during 'Live Wire,' his drummer didn't have a cowbell. And that's a song that *depends* on the cowbell," he says. "So when we saw Vince again in Nashville, we brought our own cowbell!"

"So at the concert, you played along with the band using your own cowbell?" I ask.

"Fuck yeah, buddy. Now we bring it everywhere. Because if you want to rock the fuck out of a party, wear a cowbell. People *love* the cowbell."

Moments later, the lead singer of a Mötley Crüe tribute band takes the stage and launches into a blistering karaoke version of "Live Wire." The cowbell guy promptly removes a drumstick from his back pocket and begins playing along in perfect time, even doing Tommy Lee's signature stick twirl. And the crowd goes completely bananas. Maybe it's the liquor, maybe it's the sheer goofiness of a guy beating on a cowbell around his neck, but I feel connected to the people in that room, connected to something familiar from my past. "This is the music we listened to when we were kids. And now we've got money to spend, and we can still blow it out with the best of 'em. We are ferocious rockers," says James, an investment banker from New York. "This music helps us get away from our humdrum corporate lives and makes us feel like we're nineteen again. It helps us get back to our roots." The waitress brings over a bucket of a beer. He hands me a frosty Corona, adding, "We have no responsibilities here. No schedules. No alarm clocks. No kids. Total freedom. And if I walk away from Shiprocked with anything less than a two-thousand dollar bar tab, I'm gonna be pissed."

As I'm leaving to go back to the ship, I see the Billy Ray Cyrus mullet-dude staggering out the door. Though he seems to have come on this trip alone, he's having the time of his life. We talk some more, and I ask him if he wants to share a cab back to the dock. "This music just brings people together," he says in the taxi. "This is where I feel like I'm at home, know what I'm sayin'? Everywhere else, I feel like I'm just sort of existing—just goin' through the motions of daily life. But when I come out here, everybody's sayin' hi to me, everybody's really cool and respectful. 'Cuz the rest of the world, they don't always treat people so good. But here—I can just be myself and rock the fuck out."

As we're walking down the long dock to board the MSC *Poesia*, we see mini-Vince with his luggage being escorted off the ship by Bahaman police. Apparently, in a drunken rage after arguing with his girlfriend, he trashed his cabin and threw the flat-screen TV over his balcony and into sea. And now, the cruise line is filing criminal charges against him and leaving him behind in the Bahamas. Now *that's* fucking rock and roll.

There will always be people who think 80's rock is a joke. And the genre doesn't do itself any favors. After all, it can be hard to take a guy seriously who's wearing a steel codpiece and platform moon boots. And songs with ridiculous, raunchy titles like "Lick it Up," "Slide it In," and "I Hate Every Bone in Your Body But Mine," don't exactly exude artistic credibility. Frank Sinatra even famously said, "Rock and roll smells phony and false. It is sung, played and written by cretinous goons... it manages to be the martial music of every side-burned delinquent on the face of the earth." But fans of the genre are unfazed by its lack of critical recognition. "It's *real* music, because it's just four guys beating the shit out of themselves every night, for us. You gotta love that," says Craig, 38, from Vancouver. "And it's not about focus groups or marketing or brand awareness or any of that business school bullshit. It's just fucking rock and roll, and you don't see that any more. All the new artists are just prepackaged products. They're the Chicken McNuggets of the music industry. I mean, what the fuck is a Justin Bieber, anyway?"

Many critics are quick to dismiss the 80's rock revival as an exercise in nostalgia. And they might just be right. Nostalgia—from the Greek *nostos* meaning "return home," and *algos*, meaning "longing"—is a longing for a home that no longer exists. "At first glance, nostalgia is a longing for place, but actually it is a yearning for a different time—the time of our youth," writes Harvard Professor

Svetlana Boym in her book *The Future of Nostalgia.* "It is an affective yearning for a community with a collective memory, a longing for continuity in a fragmented world." I don't disagree with Professor Boym's reading, but I do reject the negative connotations often associated with the term. Because deep down, don't we all yearn for a community with a collective memory? Don't we all long for continuity in this increasingly fragmented world? Without these things, we have no sense of history, no sense of place. Without them we are lost. And if banging my head to Steelheart's "Down 'N Dirty" with 300 other cretinous goons in some greasy Wisconsin biker bar is the only way I can go home again, then bring on the spandex and the Aqua Net, because I'll rock that shit like it's 1987.

As I'm disembarking the MSC *Poesia* back in Fort Lauderdale, I see a table set up where people are pre-registering for next year's Shiprocked event, the line snaking around the corner and out of sight. I start chatting with a sunburned, hungover-looking woman named Tiffany from Tarpon Springs, Florida who is waiting to register. "This is my second Shiprocked, and before that I went on Vince Neil's Mötley Cruise," she tells me. "And I'll keep going every year." I ask her what it is about these bands that keeps bringing her back. "You can't put an expiration date on good music, because it lives forever. It's ageless. The Beatles wrote songs that will live forever, so did Led Zeppelin and the Rolling Stones. And now people are realizing that Mötley Crüe and Guns 'N Roses and Slaughter did too," she says. "Maybe subconsciously I'm regressing, or trying to relive some piece of my past, but I honestly think it's the best music in the world. I'll be seventy-five years old and still listening to my Slaughter records. My grandchildren will be saying, "What are you listening to, grandma? Turn down that noise."

Girl From the North Country

It's mid-March in Woody Creek, the small Rocky Mountain community just outside of Aspen. The air up here is thin and crisp, and the drifts of winter snow are melting into spring. I've come here to meet Anita Thompson, wife of the late, legendary outlaw writer Hunter S. Thompson, and I'm about to have the first of several *holy shit* moments that will rock me throughout the evening. Anita, a pretty 35 year-old blonde, holds up a carton of orange juice and a bottle of vodka, and says with a warm smile, "How 'bout a screwdriver?"

For the record, I do not usually booze with my interview subjects, not while I'm playing serious journalist. But on this particular occasion, I feel morally obligated to have a drink or three. I am, after all, standing in the kitchen of the man who wrote *Fear & Loathing in Las Vegas*, the man who was attacked by giant bats on a lonely desert road paved with mescaline and shattered visions of the American Dream.

"Sounds good," I say. "Better make it a double."

Though it's been two years since Hunter Thompson ended his brilliant, chaotic life in this very room, his presence remains vibrant and palpable. Anita keeps the house—called Owl Farm—exactly as he left it, from the hand-written notes plastering the refrigerator and walls (including an ominous one that says *Never call 911 – This Means You*), to the tall lampshade adorned with Mardi Gras beads, political campaign buttons, and all-access rock and roll tour laminates. In fact, the entire house is filled with bizarre objects from a lifetime of Gonzo adventures. In the living room, you'll find an oversized Che Guevara banner, boxing gloves from the epic 1971 Ali-Frazier bout, an authentic Native American battle shield, and the razor-toothed jaws of a man-eating shark.

And then of course, there are the peacocks.

On a whim some years back, Hunter purchased several of the gangly creatures from a classified ad in the local paper, and now they roam the grounds like refugees from a forgotten Dr. Seuss book. If you listen closely, you can almost hear Hunter muttering, *"We need birds. Large, exotic birds."*

Amidst the strange universe inhabited by Hunter Thompson and his merry band of co-conspirators, legendary for their pharmaceutical excess, antiauthoritarian values, and deviant behavior, Anita was clearly a stabilizing force. Though they were married 22 months before his death in 2005, their relationship would span eight years and have a profound impact on the final chapter of Hunter's life. As with many great love stories, their meeting was a fortuitous blend of timing and happenstance.

In 1992, Anita Thompson, then Anita Bejmuk, left college during her sophomore year to work for the Sierra Club, a renowned environmental group in Northern California. "At the time, I was very political, and very angry," recalls Anita. "I was the angry vegan." Eventually, she fled the tense world of nonprofit fundraising and headed for the ski slopes, landing a job at a snowboard rental shop on Aspen Mountain. These were carefree times for Anita, spending her days on the slopes and her nights mingling with Aspen's social elite. One evening in 1997, she told her friend Don Dixon that she wanted to learn about football, hoping to better understand this male bonding experience. "I know just the person to teach you," said Dixon. "His name is Hunter Thompson." Driving back through Woody Creek, Dixon called to arrange the meeting.

"I'll never forget the first time I heard Hunter's voice," Anita says fondly. "I could hear him through Don's cell phone—he had such a *powerful* voice. And I remember exactly where we were on the road. I remember the railroad tracks. I remember the meadow. It was a beautiful voice." She takes a sip of her drink, adding, "I could tell there was something very special about this man, so I really wanted to meet him."

When football season rolled around, Anita, just 25, was invited to Owl Farm and given a crash course on the gridiron basics. "Hunter taught me the rules by betting, incessantly, on every play," Anita says, laughing. "Game time was a big deal at Owl Farm. Everybody here took it seriously, and a lot of money was constantly changing hands. But it was always festive, with smoke in the air and drinks flowing."

Over the next two years, Anita would become part of Hunter's exclusive inner circle, meeting regularly at Owl Farm for sporting events and other social occasions. By the spring of 1999, though, Anita was planning to leave Aspen and return to college. Upon hearing the news, Hunter threw a curveball that would change their lives forever.

"Wait," Hunter pleaded. "I have an urgent situation." He asked Anita to stay and help him work on his second book of letters, called *Fear and Loathing in America*. For Anita, the decision was an easy one. She would become Hunter's de facto assistant on the project, reading letters to him, photocopying, researching, and digging through some 800 boxes of unpublished archived material. "The hours he worked were just odd," says Anita. "He'd start between 9 PM and midnight and work straight through, sometimes until dawn. And I still had my job at the snowboard shop. Hunter would drive me to work at eight in the morning after we'd been up all night researching the book."

Anita and Hunter had been platonic friends for the better part of two years, but that was about to change. "Once I started working with him one-on-one, it was impossible *not* to get together," says Anita. "By the time I quit the snowboarding shop, we were definitely an item."

Over the years, Hunter had many romantic liaisons with star-struck women, including several of his former assistants. And many of Hunter's friends, at least initially, wondered if Anita wasn't just another notch on the Gonzo belt.

"At first, you really didn't know her significance in this whole thing," says Ralph Steadman, the English artist whose brilliantly twisted illustrations accompanied much of Hunter's work. "Was Anita part of it, or was she just another piece of totty?"

But Anita was more than a pretty conquest. And unlike many of the women who pursued Hunter in the past, she wasn't a literary groupie, a gold digger, or a fame junkie out to fuck a superstar. "Sure, I'd heard of Hunter Thompson," Anita says, "But I hadn't read *Vegas* or *Hell's Angels* or any of his work. I had no preconceptions about him, except that he knew a lot about football."

"Anita wasn't enthralled by his legend," confirms Steadman. "She just met the guy she thought was really interesting. It was quite a lovely relationship."

Anita was 27 when she moved in with Hunter, and her parents were unhappy because she'd once again postponed her college plans. "That's when my mom started reading up on Hunter, and she came across all the drug rumors," recalls Anita. "And being a traditional Polish woman, she was terribly worried." In a classic bit of melodrama that plays like a scene from *Dirty Dancing*, Anita's mother forced her to choose between her family and her new lover. She chose Hunter, and it caused a terrible rift within the Bejmuk clan.

Her family was also concerned with the age disparity. There were 34 years between them, and at 61, Hunter was older than Anita's mother. For Anita, this was never an issue. "The age thing was all blurred with Hunter," says Anita. "He was very childlike—not childish, but childlike—in so many ways. Sometimes, I was definitely the more responsible one in our relationship."

Life with the legendary writer could be challenging, and no one knew this better than his longtime friend Ralph Steadman. "Living with Hunter is a bit like having a gorilla in your house," says Steadman, laughing. "And he lived out there in that old farm—it was like entering a gorilla's cage. He needed someone who would understand the gorilla." Fortunately, Anita understood the gorilla all too well, and her relationship with Hunter thrived—both romantically and creatively.

Anita and Hunter certainly loved each other and were even trying to have children, but theirs was a relationship based on work, and Anita quickly assumed a more active role in the creative process. Her most significant contribution, however, was that she motivated Hunter to write. He'd been in a creative slump for over a decade and hadn't produced any work of real importance since *The Curse of Lono* in 1983.

"Hunter wanted to write again," says Steadman. "Because you can actually burn out, you know. And he burned out more times than once. Anita gave him a great deal of hope. A lot of relationships he'd been indulging in were not creative relationships. But I think with Anita, there was a genuine sense of getting back on track."

It's important to note that Hunter had been married once before for seventeen years to a woman named Sandra Dawn. She's the mother of his son Juan, and is believed to have been the source of Hunter's strength in the early part of his career. They divorced in 1979, and many see a correlation between her departure and his diminished creative output in the subsequent years. Nearly 20 years would pass before Anita came into his life, re-igniting the spark that had dimmed.

With Anita's unflagging love and support, Hunter began to turn out the kind of biting, insightful and politically vitriolic work that had made him famous. It was a true return to form, and in those last years he published the books *Kingdom of Fear, Proud Highway, Fear and Loathing in America,* and his "lost" novel *The Rum Diary.* He also wrote a weekly column for ESPN, and contributed to high-profile magazines such as *Playboy* and *Rolling Stone*.

When I ask Anita how she inspired Hunter to write again, how she effectively became his muse, she laughs and says, "It's really a question of motivation. What do you need to do to get the writing done?" She takes a sip of her drink and says, "Here's a typical scenario: it would be midnight with a deadline looming, and he still hadn't written anything. So I'd say, *Come on Hunter—let's write.* And he loved having someone encouraging him."

At this point, Anita asks if she can refresh my drink, so I follow her back into the kitchen. She continues talking as she mixes another round of screwdrivers. "Hunter wrote about me after I helped him on the first book, and I was very proud to appear in his work. Very proud." She hands me the tall cocktail glass and adds, "I wanted to make him proud too, and I did that by motivating him to write. I wanted him to be successful on my watch."

When assisting Hunter with his writing, Anita learned to accommodate his unique creative process. He worked in the kitchen, always late at night, and always on a typewriter. "He wrote on an IBM Selectric. He had six of them," recalls Anita. "Sometimes he'd say, *the typewriter's broken* or *goddammit, this one has the wrong font.* I've gone through three typewriters in one night with him."

Music was a key component of the writing process. "When Hunter liked something, he'd play it over and over. I loved it too, especially when we were hooked on the same song," says Anita. "We must've listened to Gordon Lightfoot's "Sundown" 25 times a night. Same with Dolly Parton's "Silver Dagger." And Dylan's "A Hard

Rain's A-Gonna Fall." I think we had to buy a second "Hard Rain" CD because we wore out the first one."

Any conversation about Hunter must eventually turn to the topic of drugs. Though his predilection for narcotics, both legal and illegal, has been covered ad nauseam, it's important to note their place in his creative process. He referred to certain drugs as his "tools"—particularly marijuana, alcohol, and cocaine—and often used them to facilitate his writing, the way an athlete might dope before a competition. "If your goal for that evening is to write three pages or finish an article, then you could use some pot or some coke to help you get the pages," says Anita. "It was all about getting the pages."

"Hunter's first book was *Hell's Angels*, and it came out when he was 29," she offers, by way of illustration. "He always thought that if he didn't have a book published by the time he turned 30, the gig was up. He even went to barber school just in case the writing thing didn't pan out. Can you imagine Hunter as a barber? So he finally got a contract with a publisher, and he'd written half of *Hell's Angels* and it was fantastic. So he checked himself into a hotel room by himself, and stayed up for four days on Wild Turkey and Dexedrine. He finished the book on time, and it was brilliant. So he used the Wild Turkey and Dexedrine as a tool."

Anita pauses to check on a rustling noise coming from the back porch—it's just the peacocks settling into their pen for the night. She continues her thought, saying, "Hunter could consume more than any human I've ever met, but you would rarely see him drunk. He handled his substances differently than other people for some reason, which may have been a curse, and may have been a bless-ing—I'm not sure."

The sky is dimming as the sun prepares to set on Owl Farm. Anita and I are trudging through calf-deep snow at the edge of the property, angling for the best view of the valley at twilight. The house sits on acres of pristine, untamed land and stretches back to the mountains behind it. In the distance, I can see the leveled mound where Hunter's cremated ashes were shot from a giant cannon as Norman Greenbaum's "Spirit in the Sky" ripped a hole in the night. As we push a bit further, we come across the fresh remains of a bloodied deer sprawled helplessly in the snow. "The wolves are all around," says Anita. "They killed this one today." It's easy to see why Hunter loved this place—the raw natural beauty of it all, and the limit-less realm of savage possibilities. The only thing he may have loved more in his final days was Anita.

"Once you move into Hunter's life, you quickly become a part of it," says Ralph Steadman. "You become a satellite, and you revolve around Hunter. And that's not demean-ing in any way. I think Anita filled an enormous space in his life. She became extremely important to him."

Hunter's health had begun to deteriorate in the last few years of his life, and this may have hastened his desire to get married. A lifetime of substance abuse had taken its toll on his body, and the chronic back pain, which had troubled him for years, was becoming unbearable. He was scheduled for surgery to replace a portion of his spine and wanted to exchange vows before undergoing the risky operation. "He was worried that if something happened to him during the surgery, if he died on the operating table, that I wouldn't be protected," says Anita. "He said they would eat me alive, although he never specified who *they* were. So that's one reason why the marriage certificate, the legal piece of paper, was so important to Hunter. He wanted me to have some kind of legal leverage."

Hunter would ask Anita to marry him several times in the months leading up to his surgery, until she finally said yes. "He wrote me the most beautiful letter you've ever read. It was like something from a fairytale, and it came with a traditional ring," recalls Anita. "So I said yes, I'd love to be your wife."

They were married on April 24, 2003. "We went down to the courthouse in Aspen with a small group of friends," says Anita. "We stopped by the Woody Creek Tavern on the way back—we didn't even get out of the car. Hunter drove his Jeep up into the tables on the patio, right up to the front door."

Hunter described the nuptials with typical flair in his ESPN column:

"It was done in fine style and secrecy in order to avoid the craziness and drunken violence that local lawmen feared would inevitably have followed the ceremony... Our honeymoon was even simpler. We drank heavily for a few hours and accepted fine gifts from strangers, then we drove erratically back out to the Owl Farm and prepared for our own, very private celebration by building a huge fire, icing down a magnum of Crystal Champagne, and turning on the Lakers game until we passed out and crawled to the bedroom."

Hunter survived the back surgery, but his health continued to deteriorate. He had serious complications from a previous hip replacement operation, and in December 2003 he shattered his leg bone while in Hawaii. "There was a lot of care involved with his health issues, especially in the last year," says Anita. "It could be so tiring at times, for everyone, especially Hunter. At the end, I think he was just exhausted. We all were." As the pain increased, his moods began to wildly fluctuate. "The last few months before he died were not easy," says Anita. "He had these awful drops in his personality, and he could be very cruel."

The night before his death, Hunter was more affectionate and loving than he'd been in months. On February 20, 2005, Hunter shot and killed himself in the Owl Farm kitchen. His son Juan, who was visiting, found Hunter's body slumped over in his writing chair. Anita was not home at the time. "I was at the gym," she says. "We were actually on the phone when he did it. He told me that he loved me, and then I heard the gunshot. It was like he wanted me to be there with him when he went.

"Buddhists believe in planning every detail of your death: where you'll be, what you'll be wearing, who you'll be with. So that way, your death is this beautiful experience. It wasn't out of cruelty that we were on the phone when he did it. It was part of his plan."

I ask Anita, who is now visibly choking back tears, if she wants to take a break, but she shakes her head and continues. "At that moment, there was a lot of tumult and chaos and pain and love and beauty all swirled into this kitchen. But he was very peaceful."

In the two years since his death, Anita has worked tirelessly to preserve Hunter's literary legacy for future generations and to save his beloved Owl Farm. Unfortunately, he left very little money and a mountain of debt. "He'd mortgaged Owl Farm off to so many people," says Ralph Steadman. "And pretty soon they'll all come collecting. And it's not just the house—he sold the rights to *Fear and Loathing in Las Vegas* more times than he's had hot dinners."

"People want to tear down this place and build condos," says Anita. "So we're hoping to sell Hunter's archives to a university. That would allow us to support Owl Farm for many years to come. Eventually, I'd like to turn this place into a retreat for writers. Hunter would've loved that."

There have been other hurdles as well. Since the days immediately following Hunter's death, the Thompson family has been battling Anita for control of Owl Farm and its valuable land. "She was in danger of being marginalized by the armies of lawyers with guns and money," says Steadman, one of Anita's staunchest supporters. "They are trying to diminish her role in this, and that's terribly unfair. Anita was anything but a wife for hire. She was absolutely the personification of a young wife who was devoted to Hunter Thompson."

Though Anita refused to recriminate anyone from the Thompson family, their actions have made one thing abundantly clear: *the wolves are all around.*

Despite this adversity, Anita has soldiered on. In the fall of 2006, she enrolled at Columbia University in New York to finish her degree—she's on Spring Break when this interview takes place. She's also doing her best to keep the Thompson literary tradition alive. Her first book called *The Gonzo Way*, a collection of the wisdom she gleaned from Hunter, is due out next month. She's also helping to edit Hunter's third book of letters, and is hoping to release his long-in-the-works novel *Polo is My Life.*

It's just after midnight, and the vodka bottle is empty, which means it's time to wrap things up. Anita continues talking as I pack my things. "People should know that Hunter was the ultimate student of life. It wasn't about the mescaline and the uppers, downers, or the saltshaker full of cocaine. It was about learning as much as he could." She hands me my jacket, adding, "That's why he admired excellence in any field. It didn't matter if you were a lawyer, an actor, a cowboy, or a garbage man—you just had to be excellent at what you do. It's like Hunter said: 'At the top of the mountain, we are all snow leopards.'"

As I'm driving away from Owl Farm, down the twisting road into blackness, I push *The Freewheelin' Bob Dylan* CD into the player and turn up the volume. Though Hunter was fond of "A Hard Rain's A-Gonna Fall" on this record, I skip ahead to "Girl From the North Country" because it seems like a fitting coda to the evening:

> *So if you're travelin' in the North Country fair*
> *Where the winds hit heavy on the borderline*
> *Remember me to one who lives there*
> *She once was a true love of mine*

As I round the narrow bend heading into the gully, something leaps from the underbrush and darts across the road in front of my car, something that looks like a giant wild cat. Though it's probably the vodka playing tricks on me, I choose to take this as a sign that one day, with enough hard work and determination, I too may join the snow leopards atop the mountain. Then my vision sharpens into focus, and I see that the creature is actually an enormous grizzled skunk, waddling across the street into the ravine. So I continue down into the valley, down, down into the darkness.

Afterword

Hello again, friend.

I hope you enjoyed Oddities. If you take away just one thing from this experience, I hope it's this: be kind to each other, because we're all just trying to find our place in this complicated world. The truth is, we all have amazing stories to tell. We just need someone to listen.

Here is a picture of my three-legged cat Queso:

Acknowledgements

This book is the culmination of a lifelong journey, and I want to thank everyone who helped me along the way: my lovely and patient wife Brett who never stopped believing in me even when I didn't believe in myself; my incredibly supportive family; the brilliant and creative Chris Tokunaga; Ronnie Campagna, my high school journalism teacher whose early encouragement is the reason this book exists; the incomparable Sia Michel and Tracey Pepper, who gave me my first writing gig for a national magazine; the legendary, exceedingly generous Ralph Steadman; all the brave and gracious people in these pages who invited me into their lives and allowed me to tell their stories, especially Red Stuart, Connie Hamzy, Hoot Borden, Kumori, and Anita Thompson; all the bands and all the dirty rock and roll roadies I've had the privilege of working with over the last 25 years; and the late David Rakoff, whose writing continues to amaze and inspire me. And finally, a special thank you to my mom, that fabulous gypsy fairy earth goddess whose love, support, and sacrifice made everything in my life possible.

About the Author

RODGER CAMBRIA has written for *Details, Spin, Marie Claire, Penthouse, Modern Drunkard, Blurt, Dairy Goat Journal, Tacoma Weekly, No Cover, Harp,* and *Poultry World*. He's spent more than 25 years traversing the globe as a rock and roll roadie, and he's seen Lionel Richie and Meat Loaf in their underpants. He currently lives in a yurt behind a burned-out Shoney's with his wife and their fourteen cats.

Made in the USA
Coppell, TX
16 November 2019